WHAT NEXT IN THE LAW

Not 'forgetting those things which are behind,
and reaching forth unto these things which are before,
I press toward the mark . . .'

Philippians III: 13, 14
Authorised Version (slightly amended)

WHAT NEXT IN THE LAW

by the Rt Hon
LORD DENNING
Master of the Rolls

London
BUTTERWORTHS
1982

United Kingdom	Butterworth & Co (Publishers) Ltd, 88 Kingsway, LONDON WC2B 6AB and 4 Hill Street, EDINBURGH EH2 3JZ
Australia	Butterworths Pty Ltd, SYDNEY, MELBOURNE, BRISBANE, ADELAIDE, PERTH, CANBERRA and HOBART
Canada	Butterworths Canada Ltd, TORONTO and VANCOUVER
Ireland	Butterworth (Ireland) Ltd, DUBLIN
Malaysia	Malayan Law Journal Sdn Bhd, KUALA LUMPUR
New Zealand	Butterworths of New Zealand Ltd, WELLINGTON and AUCKLAND
Singapore	Butterworth & Co (Asia) Pte Ltd, SINGAPORE
USA	Butterworths Legal Publishers, ST PAUL, Minnesota, SEATTLE, Washington, BOSTON, Massachusetts, AUSTIN, Texas and D & S Publishers, CLEARWATER, Florida

ISBN Hardcover 0 406 17601 9
Softcover 0 406 17602 7

Printed in Great Britain by Mackays of Chatham PLC, Chatham, Kent

Preface

After *The Family Story*, being still active, I thought of writing another book. But what should it be about? Seeing that, at my age, I shall not see as much done as I would like, I decided to look into the future and to set down some things – in the hope that they perhaps may be done by those who come after. Not in any visionary sense. Not the idealism of Tennyson who looked to the time

> 'Till the war-drum throbb'd no longer,
>   and the battle-flags were furl'd
> In the Parliament of man, the Federation
>   of the world.
>
> There the common sense of most shall
>   hold a fretful realm in awe,
> And the kindly earth shall slumber, lapt
>   in universal law.'[1]

I decided to reach forth to the reform of the law in the several branches where it is most in need of reform – and where there is, or should be – a reasonable prospect of it being achieved.

Soon I found that there had been others already engaged on the same task. There have been Royal Commissions, Departmental Committees and Blue Books – all recommending reforms. But each turned down by the Government for one reason or another –

1 *Locksley Hall.*

v

or for no reason – just for lack of parliamentary time. Sometimes there has been a debate in Parliament. Sometimes not.

So I thought: Some spur is needed so as to get things done. Then I added, with undue presumption: My book shall be the spur. I will try to make it interesting – not only to lawyers – but also to others who may be concerned. Perhaps then something may be done. After all, everyone should be concerned – seeing that the law affects the lives of all of us at some time or other.

Here it is. You will find many descriptions of law cases in times past. Some of them are of importance in the history of our country. Some of them are of importance in establishing legal principles. Some of them are fascinating in themselves. Time after time you will find that current events turn up in the courts of law. So they fit in with my theme. The experience of the past points the way to the future. Some of you will be familiar with the cases already. If so, do pass them by: and turn to those you have not met before.

I start by telling you of a few men who did much in their time to reform the law. We can learn from their examples as well as by our own exertions.

I then take you to several topics and go into details of proposals. I hope you will forgive the occasional lapse into intricacies. Legal argument abounds with them. You cannot avoid them. Skip them if you please – until you have a case which depends on them.

Finally, I leave the special topics and speak generally. I take you to the Richard Dimbleby Lecture which I gave on the *Misuse of Power*. Many saw it on television: but will not have read it. So I set it out to remind you of it – because it deals with somewhat the same theme. In it, too, I have tried to show that the most important function of the law is to restrain the abuse of power by any of the holders of it – no matter whether they be the Government, the newspapers, the television, the trade unions, the multi-national companies, or anyone else.

There it is in outline. Most of it is controversial – I have deliberately made it so. It is to set you thinking, talking and

writing about what I have said. None of it is a final view. It is
done without hearing argument. It is done without consulting
others. As always, I am ready to change my mind. So agree or
disagree. But do please help to get things going.

Denning.

February 1982

Contents

Contents

Contents

Contents

Part seven

A Bill of Rights

Contents

Table of cases

Part one

Some great reformers

Introduction

Most of us like to read the stories of the lives of great men. Whenever one of our statesmen retires, he writes his memoirs. Politicians do also. The newspapers take them up. They are keen to discover whether the memoirs disclose confidential matters. They also like to see if there are any exciting personal reminiscences.

In this Part I tell of some great reformers of the law. You will see that each of them relied on the power of exposition – by writing or by speaking. By expounding the law, you pave the way for reforming it. You must needs point out its deficiencies – and so pave the way for remedying them. You will see, too, that style plays a great part – the style of writing – the style of oratory – the style of giving judgment. So in some I give examples of their style. You will see also that, on occasion, when they sought to make the law more just or more equitable, they came under criticism by some of their contemporaries: both Sir Edward Coke (known by his contemporaries as Lord Coke) and Lord Mansfield did so. So your reformer must be sensitive to criticism but not so as to discourage him overmuch. Else nothing will get done.

It is not, of course, possible for me to go through many, so I have only taken five, spread over the centuries.

1 Henry Bracton c 1200—1268

My first great name in the law is Henry Bracton. He was a Devon man and is remembered in the cathedral at Exeter. He lived long long ago – over 700 years ago – and was a judge of the King's Bench. He was also an ecclesiastic as most judges were then. The red robe which the judges still wear was originally a cassock.

Bracton was the first to make the law into a science.

1 'From precedent to precedent'

Bracton kept a notebook. He made notes of 2,000 cases from the old plea rolls in the thirteenth century. These were rolls of parchment on which were written the pleadings in the cases tried by the judges. They were all in Latin. Bracton wrote in Latin. He used his notebook as the basis of a treatise on the *Laws and Customs of England*. In this treatise he gave references to previous cases, just as we do now. By using decided cases in this way he started the English system of precedent. In his notebook he says:

> '*Si tamen similia evenerint, per simile judicentur, cum bona sit occasio a similibus procedere ad similia.*' (If however similar things happen to take place, they should be adjudged in a similar way: for it is good to proceed from precedent to precedent.)

Tennyson took up that phrase when he wrote of England that it is a land where

'A man may speak the thing he will,
A land of settled government,
A land of just and old renown,
Where Freedom slowly broadens down
From precedent to precedent.'

2 'The King is under no man'

The other legacy of Bracton (which has remained firm throughout our history) is that which he learnt from the troubled days of King John. Bracton was only a boy when the Great Charter was sealed in 1215. He served as a judge in the years of King Henry III when it was paramount in men's minds. In his treatise he wrote:

'*Quod Rex non debet esse sub homine, sed sub Deo et Lege.*' (That the King should not be under man, but under God and the law.)

Those words were quoted time and time again when the Stuart Kings claimed to rule over us by divine right. When James I once declared:

'Then I am to be under the law. It is treason to affirm it',

Sir Edward Coke replied:

'Thus wrote Bracton, "The King is under no man, but under God and the law." '

And when Charles I was on trial for his life, the Lord President of the specially constituted High Court of Justice was John Bradshaw. With him were 150 Commissioners. He was a Serjeant-at-Law of some eminence. He was treated with all the forms of judicial state, decorated with a scarlet robe, a sword and mace were borne before him. If you should read the report in the *State Trials* you will see that John Bradshaw repeatedly quoted Bracton:

'The King is under no man, but under God and the law.'

The King refused to plead. He denied that the court was competent to try him. Like the Nazi war criminals at Nuremburg.

He disputed with John Bradshaw. All very unseemly. He was sentenced to death. John Bradshaw was the first to sign the death warrant.

Charles only redeemed himself by his demeanour when he walked out of the window of the Banqueting House at Whitehall and mounted the scaffold. As Andrew Marvell said of 'the Royal actor':

> 'He nothing common did or mean
> Upon that memorable scene:
> But with his keener eye
> The axe's edge did try. . . .
> But bowed his comely head,
> Down as upon a bed.'

2 Sir Edward Coke 1552—1634

The next great reformer is Edward Coke from Norfolk. He was a strange mixture. As Attorney-General he was cruel and unjust. As Chief Justice he was wise and just. But his fame rests on his writings on law. Sir William Holdsworth gives him this high praise:

> 'What Shakespeare has been to literature, what Bacon has been to philosophy, what the translators of the authorised version of the Bible have been to religion, Coke has been to the public and private law of England.'

1 The trial of Sir Walter Ralegh

Many nowadays do not know of Coke's disgraceful conduct when he was Attorney-General. It came to a head when he prosecuted Sir Walter Ralegh. Let me remind you of Sir Walter Ralegh. He was a poet, a writer and a courtier. It was he who threw his cloak across the muddy ground for Her Majesty Queen Elizabeth I to walk upon. After the death of Queen Elizabeth it was alleged that Sir Walter had conspired to kill the new King (James I), to raise rebellion and set Arabella Stuart on the throne. There was plague in London – so the trial was held in the Great Hall of Winchester Castle – where I myself have often appeared. At a critical point in the case Coke, it is said, shook his fist at Ralegh. His voice filled the Hall. He held a paper in his hand.

Coke: Thou art the most vile and execrable traitor that ever lived!
Ralegh: You speak indiscreetly, uncivilly and barbarously.

8

Coke: Thou art an odious fellow! Thy name is hateful to all the realm of England for thy pride.

Ralegh: It will go near to prove a measuring cast between you and me, Mr Attorney.

Coke: Well, I will now lay you open for the greatest traitor that ever was. . . .

Coke then held up the paper. It was a letter which had been faked. It was afterwards shown to be a fake. But it had its effect. Sir Walter Ralegh was found guilty. He was sentenced to death. The sentence was respited: and he was sent to the Tower. Seventeen years later he was executed.

2 'Yes, Yes, Yes' – 'No' said Coke

Yet when Coke became Chief Justice of the King's Bench he showed great courage. He stood up against the pretensions of the King. The crux came in the *Commendam case* (*John Colt and Glover v Bishop of Coventry and Lichfield*)[1] where two gentlemen had a case against the Bishop of Coventry and Lichfield. It was about the right to present a clergyman to the living of a church at Clifton Camvill. The King sent a message to the judges saying that they must not proceed further with the case until he had been consulted. Coke resolutely refused. He said:

'Obedience to His Majesty's command to stay proceedings would have been a delay of justice, contrary to the law, and contrary to oaths of the judges.'

The question was put to all twelve judges:

'When the King believes his interest is concerned and requires the judges to attend him for their advice, ought they not to stay proceedings till His Majesty has consulted them?'

All the judges save Coke said:

'Yes, Yes, Yes.'

But Coke said:

1 (1617) Hob 140.

9

'When that happens, I will do that which it shall be fit for a judge to do.'

Afterwards the King dismissed him from his office as a judge, but there is no doubt that the attitude which he took up was fully approved by the people of England.

By those words Coke was saying: 'I will not do what the King asks. A judge ought not to delay a case at the request of the King.'

3 Revise those *Reports*

This disobedience offended the King greatly. It was followed by another piece of disobedience. The King took objection to many of the decisions reported by Coke. He told him to revise his *Reports* in these words:

'. . . that during the vacation, while he hath time to live privately, and dispose himself at home, he take into consideration and review his book of reports wherein, as his Majesty is informed, be many extravagant and exorbitant opinions set down and published for positive and good law.'

There were 500 cases in his *Reports*. Coke revised them and admitted only to five small, wholly trivial mistakes of fact or of Latin translation.

4 Coke is dismissed

Coke had an enemy in the King's Bench. No other than Francis Bacon. Bacon drew up a list of decisions of Coke which were considered objectionable. The King used them as ground for dismissing Coke. He did it by the writ of *supersedeas*:

'For certain causes now moving us, we will that you shall be no longer our Chief Justice to hold pleas before us, and we command you that you no longer interfere in that office, and by virtue of this presence, we at once remove and exonerate you from the same.'

Taking the scroll in his hand, Coke read it, then bowed his head and wept.

5 He is active in Parliament

After his dismissal Coke became a Member of Parliament and took an important part in public affairs. He advocated the liberty of the subject with an energy which was surprising in a man of his age for he was seventy-six when he succeeded in carrying the famous Petition of Right in 1628. He overcame by his arguments and perseverance all the objections and impediments raised against it. I will tell you more of this later.

On retiring from Parliament he went back to his seat at Stoke Poges and occupied the remaining years of his life in writing.

6 Coke's *Reports*

Coke's fame rests on his work as a law reporter and commentator. His *Reports* cover forty years of court cases. They were issued from 1600 to 1616. They are written in Norman-French, with the pleadings in Latin. He reports the cases and judgments. Then he adds many notes of his own – which have come to be regarded as having as much authority as the decisions themselves. He wrote prefaces in English for the students. He uses words with which I would like to associate myself:

'There is no jewel in the world comparable to learning: no learning so excellent both for Prince and subject, as knowledge of laws; and no knowledge of any laws (I speak of human) so necessary for all estates and for all causes, concerning goods, lands or life, as the common laws of England.'

Then he recommends a simple style such as I myself would advise:

'To speak effectually, plainly, and shortly, it becometh the gravity of this profession. Truth takes small delight with varnish of words and garnish of flowers.'

7 Coke's *Institutes*

During his retirement Coke wrote his *Institutes*. He took the title from the Latin: *instituo* – I instruct, I arrange and make order.

'I have termed them *Institutes* (he wrote) because my desire is, that they should institute and instruct the studious, and guide him in a ready way to the knowledge of the national laws of England.'

Mr Justice Stephen said of them:

'The *Institutes* have had a greater influence on the law of England than any work written between the days of Bracton and those of Blackstone.'

So I leave Sir Edward Coke.[1] He took over old mediaeval law and remodelled it. He expounded it in words which have had a permanent influence. As Francis Bacon said:

'To give every man his due, had it not been for Sir Edward Coke's *Reports* . . . the law by this time had been almost like a ship without ballast.'

1 I would like to express my gratitude to Catherine Drinker Bowen for much information about Sir Edward Coke from her book, *The Lion and the Throne*.

3 Sir William Blackstone 1723—1780

Now I would come to William Blackstone whose family came from Wiltshire. He was the greatest exponent of the common law that we have ever had. But, strangely enough, when I was at Oxford I was told nothing about him. I was compelled to read the *Institutes of the Emperor Justinian* in their original Latin – without the aid of an English translation. Justinian's *Institutes* were written in AD 535 as an introduction for students to the Roman law. Blackstone's *Commentaries* were published in AD 1765 as an introduction for students to the common law.

1 'Render each man his due'

Justinian's opening sentences have come down the centuries. They express the moral and philosophical basis of jurisprudence for all time.

'*Iustitia est constans et perpetua voluntas ius suum cuique tribuens.*'

To which my effort at translation is: Justice is the constant and perpetual purpose of rendering each man his due.

'*Iuris prudentia est divinarum atque humanarum rerum notitia, iusti atque iniusti scientia.*'

Jurisprudence is the knowledge of things divine as well as human – the science of the just as well as the unjust.

'*Iuris praecepta sunt haec: honeste vivere, alterum non laedere, suum cuique tribuere.*'

13

The precepts of the law are these: to live honestly, not to injure your neighbour, to render each man his due.

(In my own college, Magdalen at Oxford, when the loving cup goes round, each says the words, '*Ius suum cuique*' (Render each man his due).)

You may recall something of the same precepts in the Bible in *Micah* 6:8:

> 'He hath shewed thee, O man, what is good; and what doth the Lord require of thee, but to do justly, and to love mercy, and to walk humbly with thy God?'

William Blackstone was an exhibitioner of Pembroke College, Oxford. He was called to the Bar by the Middle Temple. He was no good as a practising barrister. He got little work. But he was once junior in a case to Mr William Murray, then Solicitor-General, afterwards to become the great Lord Mansfield of whom I will tell you soon. The turning-point in Blackstone's life was when he was elected a fellow of All Souls' College (the college that turned me down). He began to give lectures on law to students. Then the post of Regius Professor of Civil Law became vacant.

2 The Duke was 'the most curiously ridiculous being'

I should tell you a little about these Regius Professorships. They were founded by Henry VIII in 1546 out of the moneys he got by his compulsory acquisition of the monasteries. The professorship was of the civil law as opposed to the common law. So it was the old Roman law. The appointment was in the hands of the Prime Minister. It became vacant at the time when the Prime Minister was the Duke of Newcastle. He has been described as 'the most curiously ridiculous being who ever took a leading part in public affairs'. Fortunately, William Pitt the Elder was Secretary of State and directed the war with France. The Duke made the appointments. He was very rich and with his money bought and sold the 'rotten boroughs'. Trevelyan describes him as 'the greatest boroughmonger England ever produced'. Every appointment he made was on political grounds. The man must be ready to help the Whigs.

William Murray (still Solicitor-General) recommended Blackstone for the Regius Professorship. The Duke of Newcastle was ready to give it to him if Blackstone would become his party tool. The Duke said to Blackstone:

'Sir, I can rely on your friend Mr Murray's judgment as to your giving law-lectures in a good style, so as to benefit the students; and I dare say I may safely rely upon you, whenever anything in the political hemisphere is agitated in that University, you will, sir, exert yourself in our behalf.'

Blackstone answered this intimating that he would not take part in the political sphere, and left the room.

3 Mr Viner leaves money

Blackstone's answer did not please the Duke. So he appointed a man called Jenner. He knew no law. Certainly nothing about the civil law. But Blackstone's time was to come. He was still giving lectures at Oxford. Then there died a Mr Viner. He was a very learned lawyer who had compiled twenty-four volumes of *An Abridgment of Law and Equity*. The dullest stuff imaginable. But he left a large sum of money to the University to promote the study of the law. In 1756 Blackstone was appointed the first Vinerian Professor of Law.

4 Blackstone's *Commentaries*

To this we owe his immortal *Commentaries on the Laws of England. In four books.* They were the product of his lectures over a period of twelve years. The work was at once acclaimed as a classic by lawyers and by men of letters. It has remained a classic ever since. I have an early edition in my library. I refer to it constantly when I want to know what the law was in his day. I am always amazed at the breadth of his knowledge, the research which he did, the style of his prose, and his statement of principles. It is the greatest law-book that we have ever had.

Edward Gibbon read it three times and made a copious extract of it. When Lord Mansfield was asked what books he would recommend for a son about to read law, he replied:

'My good Lord, till of late I could never with any satisfaction to myself answer such a question; but since the publication of Mr Blackstone's *Commentaries* I can never be at a loss. *There* your son will find analytical reasoning, diffused in a pleasing and perspicuous style. *There* he may inhale imperceptibly the first principles on which our excellent laws are founded.'

As an example of his style I would give the passage in which, describing the way of going in for law at the Inns of Court, he advocates learning it at the university. Today, as a result of Lord Justice Ormrod's Report, all law students should first have a university degree. These are Blackstone's words:

'For I think it past dispute that those gentlemen, who resort to the inns of court with a view to pursue the profession, will find it expedient (whenever it is practicable) to lay the previous foundations of this, as well as every other science, in one of our learned universities. We may appeal to the experience of every sensible lawyer, whether any thing can be more hazardous or discouraging than the usual entrance on the study of the law. A raw and unexperienced youth, in the most dangerous season of life, is transplanted on a sudden into the midst of allurements to pleasure, without any restraint or check but what his own prudence can suggest; with no public direction in what course to pursue his enquiries; no private assistance to remove the distresses and difficulties, which will always embarrass a beginner. In this situation he is expected to sequester himself from the world, and by a tedious lonely process to extract the theory of law from a mass of undigested learning; or else by an assiduous attendance on the courts to pick up theory and practice together, sufficient to qualify him for the ordinary run of business. How little therefore is it to be wondered at, that we hear of so frequent miscarriages; that so many gentlemen of bright imaginations grow weary of so unpromising a search, and addict themselves wholly to amusements, or other less innocent pursuits; and that so many persons of moderate capacity confuse themselves at first setting out, and continue ever dark and puzzled during the remainder of their lives!'

5 Jeremy Bentham writes from Whitchurch

But Jeremy Bentham opposed Blackstone most bitterly. He went to Oxford to hear the lectures. He said:[1]

'I attended with two collegiates of my acquaintance. They both took notes: which I attempted to do, but could not continue it, as my thoughts were occupied in reflecting on what I heard. I immediately detected his fallacy respecting natural rights; I thought his notions very frivolous and illogical. . . . Blackstone was a formal, precise and affected lecturer – just what you would expect from the character of his writings: cold, reserved, and wary – exhibiting a frigid pride.'

He made a critical attack on Blackstone's *Commentaries* in a book called *Fragment on Government*. He started it, I am sorry to say, when he was staying at my little town of Whitchurch in Hampshire – one of the few bad things to come out of it.

6 'Eureka!'

But there, I never thought anything of Jeremy Bentham. He was the most pretentious person that ever lived. Like Archimedes in his bath, he cried 'Eureka!' (I have found it) in 1768 when he discovered the phrase 'the greatest happiness of the greatest number'. He regarded that – the philosophy of utilitarianism – as the solution for all legal problems as well as social ones. It solves nothing. He started many books but finished none of them. He sought to perpetuate himself for ever. If you go to University College, London, you will see him in a glass case, mummified, with his actual clothes on, dressed as he was in life – to the horror of visitors who come to the lectures of the Bentham Club.

1 Everett *The Education of Jeremy Bentham* (1931) p. 37.

7 A squib is thrown

But I must return to Blackstone. His fame was so great that he was made a judge of the Court of Common Pleas. But, like many learned men, he was not a great judge. He was too technical. He was one of four judges in an important case of those days called *Scott v Shepherd*.[1] Every student used to know about it. It was known as the *Squib* case.

It was the fair day at Milborne Port near Bridgwater. Shepherd threw a lighted squib, made of gunpowder, from the street into the market-house. It fell upon the stall of Yates who sold gingerbread. Willis, who was close by, took it up and threw it across the market-house. It fell upon the stall of Ryal who also sold gingerbread. Ryal took it up and threw it across the market-house. It hit Scott in the face. It exploded and put out one of Scott's eyes. Scott sued Shepherd for damages for trespass. Three out of four judges awarded damages against Shepherd. Blackstone alone dissented. He had a technical point about the difference in ancient learning between an action of trespass and an action on the case. He said that the settled distinction was that, where the injury is *immediate*, an action of *trespass* will lie; but where it is only *consequential*, it must be an action on the *case*.

8 Too fat

He was not long on the Bench. He had studied too long and too much. He took no exercise. He hated it. He ate too much. He got fatter and fatter. He died at the age of fifty-seven.

1 (1773) 2 Wm Bl 892.

18

4 William Murray, afterwards Earl of Mansfield 1705—1793

1 He came from Scotland

William Murray was a Scotsman. Make no mistake about it. He was born in 1705, two years before the Act of Union in 1707. He was of high lineage, the fourth son of Lord Stormont. He was born at Scone, the site of the ancient abbey where the Kings of Scotland had been crowned. His family were Jacobites to the core. They supported the Old Pretender in the rebellion of 1715, and also his son, the Young Pretender, in the rebellion of 1745. William himself remained in Scotland until he was fourteen. He must have imbibed the family's Jacobite sympathies. Throughout his life, many in England suspected him of being a Jacobite. But he managed to live it down.

Scotsmen now dominate us in most things. We no longer resent it. But people did in the time of William Murray. He became in time more English than the English. When he was fourteen he was sent to England and never saw Scotland again. He rode his own pony down. It took him six weeks. He went to Westminster School, then to Christ Church, Oxford (where he was exposed to the two great perils, 'Port' and 'Prejudice', but avoided them); thence to Lincoln's Inn where he was called to the Bar. His elegance and eloquence soon gained him a practice. His most distinguished client was Sarah, Duchess of Marlborough, the wife of the great Duke. An amusing story is told about one occasion when she went to his chambers and found him out, as he was dining with Alexander Pope. His clerk, next morning, said to him:

'I could not make out, sir, who she was for she would not tell me her name, but she swore so dreadfully that she must be a lady of quality.'

2 Englishmen dislike Scotsmen

When he was thirty-three he married the daughter of an English earl: and a few years later he was made Solicitor-General. Before long it was rumoured that he was to be made a judge. Thereupon in 1746 there appeared in the *Broadbottom Journal* one of the most abusive tirades ever made by Englishmen against Scotsmen, complaining that they come and take up positions in England:

'They have pounced upon us, like swarms of locusts, into every quarter and every scene of life. The Army abounds with them, Divinity is not without them: and even the Law, which used to be pretty clear of them, begins to abound with their dissonant notes, and ragged Quality. Physic has them plentifully likewise. And when there is anything to be got, you may be sure to find a number of Scotchmen conven'd, like Hounds over a Carrion: or flies in the shambles.'

The *Broadbottom Journal* was plainly directed at William Murray: and he answered it himself in a pamphlet called *The Thistle* but to which he did not append his name:

'I will point out to you a short way to get rid of the Scots and your fears at once. The remedy is at hand and in your own power. It is to repeal the Act of Union of 1707. Let the Scots have their own Parliaments again; let them enjoy the pageantry of their ancient royalty, restore them to their independency; and I dare assure you they will no longer sneak into your Bar, nor pulpits, nor be convened like hounds over your carrion, nor like flies over your shambles.'

3 But English *women* do not

You will remember that William Murray was married to an English woman and he was careful not to include the ladies in his rebuke. English women, he said, looked favourably on Scotsmen.

'It is peculiarly remarkable (he said) that the Prejudice to the *Scotch* . . . in England, is confined to the Males only; the *English Fair* being too discerning and generous to indulge a native, interested, unjust *Prejudice* to all who are not born among themselves. But this is not the only Instance of the Superiority of the *English Fair* over *English Men*. The first are as open, frank, generous, gay, vacant (sic), sprightly, polite, compassionate and humane, as the latter are dark, sullen, niggardly but to indulge their own Passions, dull, stupid, vain, prejudiced, cruel and merciless.'

4 Any prejudice overcome

Despite the *Broadbottom Journal* the English certainly overcame their prejudice against Scotsmen in general and William Murray in particular. It was to their great advantage. In 1756 he was made Lord Chief Justice of the Court of King's Bench and created a peer by the title of Lord Mansfield: and for the next thirty-two years he held that high office with the greatest distinction. He attained such ascendancy over his colleagues that they hardly ever dared differ from him and his decisions were only reversed on two occasions. He laid down principles of law which have since been carried over more than half the world. He took special interest in students. He had places kept for them in his court. They all worshipped him. Bentham said:

'Days and weeks together have I made my morning pilgrimage to the chief seat of the living idol, with a devotion no less ardent and longing, and somewhat less irrational, than if it had been a dead one.'

5 His contributions to English law

Whence did Lord Mansfield derive his principles of law? Not from the crabbed and uncouth compositions of our law-books.

Those often filled him with disgust and sometimes with despair. He derived his principles, as a good Scotsman would, from the Roman civil law and from the writers who built upon it in the Scottish, Dutch and French legal systems. He grounded himself thoroughly in ancient and modern history. Law, he said, was founded upon ethics. And he always strongly recommended the philosophical works of Cicero. He had read widely and mingled much in literary society. In Dr Johnson's phrase he was 'not a mere lawyer; he drank champagne with the wits'.

You may ask, however, what were the contributions which Lord Mansfield made to our law? They are so many that I hardly know where to begin, but perhaps the greatest is the way in which he was not content with isolated instances after our fashion but sought to generalise the principles of the law and to state them for the guidance of the future. This is, after all, the way in which it is done in the Roman law and in the Scottish law which follows it. State the principle and apply it to the facts. And Lord Mansfield excelled in doing this with the great body of commercial law. Before his time all the evidence in mercantile cases was thrown together. The cases were left generally to a jury and they produced no established principles. Lord Mansfield set to work to find out the general principles. In order to get help from the business community, he used to have a body of special jurymen who served in nearly every commercial case which he tried at Guildhall. They were so well known that they were called 'Lord Mansfield's jurymen'. One of them, Mr Edward Vaux, always wore a cocked hat and had almost as much authority as the Lord Chief Justice himself. Lord Mansfield used to talk freely with them in court and had them to dine with him. From them he learned the usages of trade and in return he took great pains in explaining to them the principles of jurisprudence by which they were to be guided. He laid down the principles of the law of insurance and of bills of exchange and cheques and other commercial subjects in such a satisfactory manner that they have spread throughout the commercial communities of the world. He was described by a great judge, Mr Justice Buller, as 'the founder of the commercial law of this country'.[1]

1 *Lickbarrow v Mason* (1787) 2 Term Rep 63.

6 Infusing equity

The next great achievement of Lord Mansfield was to infuse the principles of equity and good conscience into the rigid formulae of our law. He was, however, subject to many criticisms for the extent to which he borrowed. He was censured for bringing too much of Roman law into our jurisprudence: and he was charged with overstepping the boundary between equity and law. Junius, the anonymous writer, said this about him:

'Instead of those certain positive rules by which the judgments of a court of law should invariably be determined, you have fondly introduced your own unsettled notions of equity and substantial justice.'[1]

And Lord Redesdale said of him:

'Lord Mansfield had in his mind prejudices derived from his familiarity with the Scots law, where law and equity are administered in the same courts, and where the distinction between them which subsists with us is not known. . . . Lord Mansfield seems to have considered that it manifested liberality of sentiment to endeavour to give the courts of law the powers which are vested in equity.'[2]

Yet time has shown that these criticisms were not merited. English law in his time needed an infusion of the principles of equity.

7 His views on religious toleration

The greatest tragedy that befell Lord Mansfield was in the Gordon Riots of 1780.

One of the subjects on which he had always shown his enlightened views was that of religious toleration. He would have subscribed to the principle of freedom of religion as we know it today. But he was in advance of his time. On one occasion the City of London elected a man as sheriff. They knew he was a

1 *Letters of Junius* 14 November 1770.
2 *French v Woolston* 1 Sch & Lef 152.

dissenter and would not serve. They imposed a fine on him for not serving. Lord Mansfield held that the fine was invalid. It was a piece of persecution. He said:

'Temporal punishment ought not to be inflicted for mere opinions with respect to particular modes of worship.'

The City was so upset that many regarded Lord Mansfield as 'little better than an infidel'.

On another occasion a Roman Catholic priest had said mass contrary to the law of the land. He was tried before Lord Mansfield and a jury. He was undoubtedly guilty as the law then stood. But Lord Mansfield summed up for an acquittal. His final words to the jury were:

'Take notice, if you bring him in *guilty* the punishment is very severe; a dreadful punishment indeed! Nothing less than perpetual imprisonment!'

The jury found a verdict of 'Not Guilty': but many zealous Protestants were scandalised. Rumours were spread abroad that the Lord Chief Justice was not only a Jacobite but a Papist, and some even asserted that he was a Jesuit in disguise.

8 His library goes up in flames

Lord George Gordon then led the cry of 'No Popery' and stirred up the people to violence. The great object of vengeance was Lord Mansfield. The mob marched on his house in Bloomsbury Square. The magistrates wished him to call in the soldiers to defend him. But he refused. The multitude came on, carrying torches and combustibles. They began to batter his front door. He then escaped with his wife through the back door. They burnt his house and all that was in it. His precious library went up in flames. Everyone was sorry for him. William Cowper, the poet, wrote:

> 'O'er Murray's loss the Muses wept:
> They felt the rude alarm;
> Yet bless'd the guardian care that kept

His sacred head from harm. . . .
The lawless herd, with fury blind,
Have done him cruel wrong.'

9 He presides at the trial of Gordon

The insurrection was quelled. Lord George Gordon was tried for high treason. Lord Mansfield presided at the trial with a jury. Nowadays we should have considered it undesirable, lest he be thought to be prejudiced against Gordon. But Lord Mansfield tried the case with perfect propriety. Erskine defended Gordon. The defence was that Gordon himself had no hand in the violence. It was 'the lawless herd, with fury blind' who did it. The jury acquitted Gordon. It was the best thing that could happen.

10 'The great Lord Mansfield'

I am afraid I have taken up too much of your time in telling you of Lord Mansfield. His influence on the law was immense. He extricated it from pedantry, technicalities and narrow-mindedness. He brought into it broad principles of justice and of equity. Not by means of any writings. He wrote no law-books or any other books. He was eloquent. He made speeches. He gave judgments. He was fortunate in having as the reporter in the court – Burrow. But I fancy that he corrected the transcripts just as we do. His principal legacy to posterity is his contribution to commercial law. He was the founder of commercial law, not only of England but of the world. He was known to his contemporaries as 'the great Lord Mansfield'. So also to all of us who follow him.

5 Lord Brougham 1778—1868

1 A skit on him

Henry Brougham is not in the same class as the others. Yet he made a great speech on Law Reform: and was the leading spirit in the great Reform Bill of 1832. That is why I include him. He dabbled in science, he dabbled in politics, he dabbled in literature, he dabbled in everything. It was said of him that 'If he only knew a little of law, he would know a little of everything'.

I cannot forbear from quoting T L Peacock's skit on him as *The Learned Friend*:

' "God bless my soul, sir!" exclaimed the Reverend Doctor Folliott, bursting, one fine May morning, into the breakfast-room at Crotchet Castle, "I am out of all patience with this march of mind. Here has my house been nearly burned down, by my cook taking it into her head to study hydrostatics, in a sixpenny-tract, published by the Steam Intellect Society, and written by a learned friend who is for doing all the world's business as well as his own, and is equally well qualified to handle every branch of human knowledge. I have a great abomination of this learned friend; as author, lawyer, and politician, he is *triformis*, like Hecate: and in every one of his three forms he is *bifrons*, like Janus; the true Mr Facing-both-ways of Vanity Fair. My cook must read his rubbish in bed; and as might naturally be expected, she dropped suddenly fast asleep, overturned the candle, and set the curtains in a blaze. Luckily, the footman went into the room at the moment, in time to tear down the curtains and throw them into the chimney, and a pitcher of water on her nightcap extinguished

her wick: she is a greasy subject, and would have burned like a
short mould." '

2 His defence of Queen Caroline

So far as law is concerned, Henry Brougham gained fame in the
public eye by his defence of Queen Caroline. A Bill was laid
before the House of Lords charging her with adultery committed
abroad with an Italian. Brougham made his name famous by
getting her acquitted. His oratory was ornate in the extreme.
This is the sort of thing which went down well with the House of
Lords in those days. It would not do so today. At any rate not
before the Law Lords.

'Such, my Lords, is the case now before you! Such is the evidence in support of this measure – evidence, inadequate to
prove a debt – impotent to deprive of a civil right – ridiculous
to convict of the lowest offence – scandalous if brought forward to support a charge of the highest nature which the law
knows – monstrous to ruin the honour, to blast the name, of an
English Queen! What shall I say, then, if this is the proof by
which an act of judicial legislation, a Parliamentary sentence,
an *ex post facto* law, is sought to be passed against this defence-
less woman? My Lords, I pray you to pause. I do earnestly
beseech you to take heed! . . . You have said, my Lords, you
have willed – the Church and the King have willed – that the
Queen should be deprived of its solemn service. She has
instead of that solemnity the heartfelt prayers of the people.
She wants no prayers of mine. But I do here pour forth my
humble supplications at the throne of mercy, that that mercy
may be poured down upon the people in a larger measure
than the merits of their rulers may deserve, and that your hearts
may be turned to justice!'

3 His speech on Law Reform

Next, I come to his celebrated speech on Law Reform. It was in
1828 when he was in the House of Commons. It lasted about six

hours. He refreshed himself with oranges – and, I would guess, with port. He must have been well briefed beforehand. He discussed every field of jurisprudence and every kind of court. From the criminal to the ecclesiastical. From the House of Lords to the Court of Pie Powder. He pointed out defects and suggested remedies. He was at his most eloquent in his eulogy of law reform. He asked for the help of the House

'in the best and greatest work which the hands of the lawgiver can undertake. The course is clear before us; the race is glorious to run. You have the power of sending your name down through all times.'

Then he drew a parallel with Napoleon, the greatest warrior of the age, whose Code is the foundation of most European law. Napoleon, Brougham said,

'could pronounce his memorable boast, "I shall go down to posterity with the Code in my hand!" You have vanquished him in the field; strive now to rival him in the sacred arts of peace! Outstrip him as a lawgiver, whom in arms you overcame!'

Then Brougham finished with a peroration which has often been repeated:

'It was the boast of Augustus . . . that he found Rome of brick, and left it of marble. . . . But how much nobler will be the Sovereign's boast when he shall have it to say that he found law dear, and left it cheap; found it a sealed book – left it a living letter; found it the patrimony of the rich – left it the inheritance of the poor; found it the two-edged sword of craft and oppression – left it the staff of honesty and the shield of innocence!'

That speech ushered in one of the most important eras of law reform in our history. Royal commissions were held. Acts of Parliament were passed. Much was done to fit the law to suit the days of the Industrial Revolution.

4 The great Reform Bill

Soon afterwards Henry Brougham devoted himself to the reform of Parliament. He was, as I have said, the leading figure in promoting the great Reform Bill. In the new Government in 1830 he was made Lord Chancellor. One of the objects of the Bill was to do away with the 'rotten boroughs' (which were in the pocket of the landed nobility who nominated the members) and to substitute a democratically elected House of Commons. Many of the peers were against the Bill (because they had a vested interest in maintaining the 'rotten boroughs'). Lord Brougham, as Lord Chancellor, made a great speech in support of the Bill. It was considered his *chef-d'oeuvre*. *The Times* described it as 'overpowering, matchless, and immortal'.

5 The effects of the mulled port

The speech took four hours. Towards the conclusion he drank copiously of mulled port. They kept filling his glass. Then, in his final sentence, he sank dramatically on to his knees in front of the whole packed House:

> 'Therefore I pray and I exhort you not to reject this measure. By all you hold most dear – by all the ties that bind every one of us to our common order and our common country, I solemnly adjure you – I warn you – I implore you – yea, on my bended knees (he kneels), I supplicate you – reject not this bill!'

Then there is this delightful comment by Lord Campbell in his *Lives of the Lord Chancellors*:

> 'He continued for some time as if in prayer; but his friends, alarmed for him lest he should be suffering from the effects of the mulled port, picked him up and placed him safely on the woolsack.'

The ridiculous ending ruined the effect of the speech. The House rejected the Bill by forty-one votes. There was nearly a revolution in the country. But eventually the peers had to give in. The

Reform Bill was passed in 1832. Trevelyan's comment on it is that:

'The people, as a whole, had wrenched the modern Magna Carta from the governing class.'

6 'A magnificent oddity'

That is why I have included Lord Brougham. Of all men, he was the one most instrumental in getting this modern Magna Carta on to the statute book. With it, he reached his highest point of greatness. Lord Campbell says that for a brief span he enjoyed a greater supremacy and popularity than any of his predecessors, Cardinal Wolsey alone excepted. But it only lasted a few months. In the next Government he was dropped.

But he made one other valuable contribution. It was due to him that in 1833 there was created a Judicial Committee of the Privy Council. It heard appeals from all over the British Empire (as it used to be). It had immense influence on the constitutions of Canada and Australia. It used to hear many appeals from India. Much of its jurisdiction has now gone. But in its day it was a great world-wide tribunal.

This is Trevelyan's epitaph on Lord Brougham:

'If his wisdom and reliability as a colleague in office had been on a level with his activity and genius as a free lance in opposition, he would have been the leading statesman of the new era; but he declined, instead, into its most magnificent oddity.'

A magnificent oddity! Leave him there.

Part two

Trial by jury

1 Its glories

1 Panegyrics

I have always been a firm believer in trial by jury. Somehow it is ingrained in me. As it is in most Englishmen. Not that we were taught it in school. The duties of citizenship were not taught in schools in my day. Nor are they taught enough today. I suppose I got to know something of it when my father was summoned to serve on a jury. He was a householder and so qualified. It is such service which gives to ordinary folk their most useful lesson in citizenship. It is a lesson which has been handed down from one generation to another during the last 800 years. The people of England, by sitting as jurors, have taken an active part, indeed a decisive part, in the administration of justice. They have always had the last word on the guilt or innocence of their fellow-men. This participation in justice has, I believe, done more than anything else to establish the English habit of obedience to law which a great historian has described as 'the strongest of all the forces making for the nation's peaceful continuity and progress'.

Panegyrics have been written extolling the virtues of trial by jury. Over 200 years ago when Sir William Blackstone gave his lectures in Oxford he said in 1758:[1]

> 'Trial by jury ever has been, and I trust ever will be, looked upon as the glory of the English law. . . . it is the most transcendent privilege which any subject can enjoy, or wish for, that he cannot be affected either in his property, his liberty, or his person, but by the unanimous consent of twelve of his neighbours and equals.'

1 *Commentaries* III, 379.

This was followed by the encomium:[1]

'So that the liberties of England cannot but subsist, so long as this *palladium* remains sacred and inviolate.'

2 Embodied in the USA Constitution

Blackstone's lectures, afterwards published in his *Commentaries*, became the bible of the settlers in the American colonies. When the British Parliament unwisely sought to tax them in the Stamp Act 1765 the colonists declared: 'No taxation without representation'. In their first Congress in 1765 (in opposition to, as they said, 'the Tyrannical Acts of the British Parliament') they included this in their Declaration of Rights:[2]

'That trial by jury is the inherent and invaluable right of every British subject in these colonies.'

On attaining independence, the American Colonies enshrined in their Constitution in 1791 these provisions:[3]

'*Art*. VI. In all criminal prosecutions the accused shall enjoy the right to a speedy and public trial, by an impartial jury of the State and district wherein the crime shall have been committed. . . .

Art. VII. In suits at common law, where the value in controversy shall exceed twenty dollars, the right of trial by jury shall be preserved. . . .'

This trial by jury, taken from England, is embodied for ever as part of the Constitution of the United States.

3 The lamp of freedom

To these great instruments I would add the praise by my friend Lord Devlin, one of the ablest judges with whom I have ever sat:[4]

1 *Commentaries* IV, 350.
2 *Journal of the First Congress of the American Colonies* (New York, 1845) pp. 27–29.
3 1 US *Statutes at Large* 21, The First Ten Amendments to the Constitution.
4 *Trial by Jury* (London, 1956) p. 164.

'So that trial by jury is more than an instrument of justice and more than one wheel of the constitution: it is the lamp that shows that freedom lives.'

You must not suppose from all this that trial by jury has remained unchanged. It has been altered beyond recognition. It has been whittled away. It no longer subsists in civil cases in England save for libel. It is still retained in criminal cases of any consequence, but it has defects which cause concern. I will later on suggest the path of reform. But meanwhile let me tell the fascinating story by reference to some *causes célèbres* in which the jury played the decisive part.

2 *Causes célèbres* 1367—1688

1 'I would rather die in prison'

In 1367 the judges of Assize went to Northampton. It is recorded in the *Year Books*. A merchant called Henry at Northampton had got all his cloths and merchandise in his cart ready to take to Stamford Fair. Another called Robert seized them, claiming that they belonged to him. Henry sued Robert in the form of action called trespass *vi et armis et contra pacem Domini Regis* (with force and arms and contrary to the King's peace). Robert pleaded 'Not Guilty' and put himself upon his country. The 'country' is the neighbourhood. The charge to the jury ran:

> 'To this charge he has pleaded "Not Guilty" and puts himself upon his country, which country you are.'

After the judge summed up, the jury were divided in opinion. They said they could not agree. The judge directed each to give his verdict separately. Eleven said 'Guilty'. One said 'Not Guilty'. Then there was this interchange:

> Judge: I will cast you into prison unless you agree with the others.
>
> Juror: I would rather die in prison than give a verdict against my conscience.

The judge then realised that he had made a mistake. He ought not to have threatened the juror. He had no power to cast a juryman into prison for not agreeing with the others. So he accepted the verdict of the eleven and found Robert guilty.

Thereupon Robert applied to the Court of King's Bench at Westminster. The court quashed the verdict. They said:

'The verdict of the eleven is no verdict: because no man is bound to give a verdict against his conscience.'

The court added that what the judge ought to have done was to 'carry the jurors round the circuit with him from town to town in a waggon until they were agreed'. That was the way to secure unanimity. The eleven would bring such pressure to bear on the one that he would stand out no longer. Or perhaps he might be so obstinate that they would give way to him.

So the principle was established which lasted for 600 years. The jury must be unanimous. It was only in 1967 that Parliament altered it. It allowed a verdict to be valid if it was given by a majority of ten to two. But that was when much had altered.

2 'Without meat, drink, fire or candle'

There was yet another way of securing unanimity. Once the case had started, the jury were not allowed to separate – for fear they would be 'got at' by one side or the other. And once they had retired to consider their verdict, they were kept without food, heat or light of any kind. In the time-hallowed formula: 'Without meat, drink, fire or candle'. As Blackstone puts it:[1]

'In order to avoid intemperance and causeless delay, they are to be kept without meat, drink, fire or candle, unless by permission of the judge, till they are all unanimously agreed. . . . If our juries eat or drink at all, or have any eatables about them, without consent of the court, and before verdict, it is fineable; and if they do so at his charge for whom they afterwards find, it will set aside the verdict.'

3 Pippins in their pockets

There is a charming – and true – story about this from the time of the first Elizabeth. Lord Devlin says that it reads like 'a cautionary tale from the Garden of Eden'.[2] To appreciate it you must

1 *Commentaries* III, 375.
2 *Trial by Jury* (London, 1956) p. 50.

realise that in Elizabethan days, many sorts of apples were called 'pippins'. To entertain you, I would quote from my treasured *Paradisi in Sole* (page 587) by John Parkinson in 1629 which was given to me by the Law Society on my eightieth birthday:

'The kindes or sorts of Apples

The Summer pippin is a very good apple first ripe, and therefore to bee first spent, because it will not abide so long as the other.

The French pippin is also a good fruit and yellow.

The Golding pippin is the greatest and best of all sorts of pippins.

The Russet pippin is as good an apple as most of the other sorts of pippins.

The spotted pippin is the most durable pippin of all the other sorts.

The ordinary yellow pippin is like the other, and as good; for indeed I know no sort of pippins but are excellent good well rellished fruites.'

Now this is the case taken from *The Complete Juryman* (1752) page 171:

'The Jury being withdrawn after Evidence, and remaining a long Time without concluding on their Verdict, the Officers, who attended them, seeing their Delay, searched them, and found that some had Figs and others had Pippins; which being moved to the Court, they were examined on Oath, and two of them confessed that they had eaten Figs before they were agreed on their Verdict, and three confessed that they had Pippins, but had not eat any of them; and that this was unknown to the Parties. Those who had eaten were each of them fined five Pounds, and those who had not eaten the Pippins, were each of them fined forty Shillings; but the Verdict was, upon great consideration, and Conference with the other Judges, held to be good.'

Another story of the same era shows that jurors took sweetmeats with them for sustenance. One John Mucklow was fined twenty shillings for being found with 'sugar-candy and liquorish'.

4 The trial of the Quakers

But the most celebrated case of all is that of the jurors in the trial of the Quakers, William Penn and William Mead. I have told it before but it is so appropriate to my present theme that I would repeat it here – to save you looking it up.

All that William Penn and William Mead had done was to preach in Gracechurch Street in the City of London on a Sunday afternoon in 1670. They were charged with causing an unlawful and tumultuous assembly there. The Recorder directed the jury to find the Quakers guilty, but they refused. The jury said Penn was 'guilty of preaching in Gracechurch Street', but not of an unlawful assembly. The Recorder refused to accept this verdict. He threatened them with all sorts of pains and punishments. He kept them 'all night without meat, drink, fire or other accommodation: they had not so much as a chamber-pot, though desired'. They still refused to find the Quakers guilty of an unlawful assembly. He kept them another night, and still they refused. He then commanded each to answer to his name and give his verdict separately. Each gave his verdict 'Not Guilty'. For this the Recorder fined them 40 marks apiece and cast them in prison until it was paid. One of them, Edward Bushell, thereupon brought his habeas corpus before the Court of King's Bench. It was there held that no judge had any right to imprison a juryman for finding against his direction in point of law; for the judge could never direct what the law was without knowing the facts, and of the facts the jury were the sole judges. The jury were thereupon set free. By their conduct they had established the right of a jury to give a general verdict of 'Not Guilty'; and once this is given, the accused man is free. The prosecution cannot appeal from their verdict. It is useless for them to say it was wrong in law. No one in the land – be he statesman or judge – can go behind their decision of 'Not Guilty'.

5 The infamous conduct of Judge Jeffreys

This power of the judges – given so as to secure unanimity – was on one sad occasion abused so as to secure the conviction of an innocent person – Dame Alice Lisle.

I was surprised to find how few, even in my county of Hampshire, had heard of Alice Lisle. Everyone has heard of Judge Jeffreys and the Bloody Assize. But they seem to be unaware of the way in which he browbeat the jury consisting, we are told, of the 'best quality of the county'. All that the little old lady had done was to let a man called Hicks – a nonconformist minister – have a night's lodging in her house near Fordingbridge. She did not know that he had been in the rebellion on the side of the Duke of Monmouth. He only stayed one night and left the next day. But she was charged with high treason. You may be interested in the way it was put to her:

> Clerk of Arraigns: How sayest thou, Alice Lisle, are thou Guilty of the high-treason contained in the indictment or Not Guilty?
> Lisle: Not Guilty.
> Clerk of Arraigns: Culprit, by whom wilt thou be tried?
> Lisle: By God and my country.
> Clerk of Arraigns: God send thee a good deliverance.

Now there was in law no case against her. And Jeffreys should have known it: because Hicks had not been tried, nor had he been convicted of treason. She took the legal objection herself that the principal traitor ought first to have been convicted

> 'because, peradventure, he might afterwards be acquitted as innocent after she had been condemned for harbouring him'.

But Jeffreys would have none of it. He summed up furiously against her. The jury retired. It is said by almost all the contemporary authorities that

> 'thrice did the Jury refuse to find a verdict of *Guilty*, and thrice did Lord Chief Justice Jeffreys send them back to reconsider their verdict'.

The jury remained long in consultation. He then sent a messenger to tell them that, if they did not instantly return, he would adjourn the court and lock them up all night. So they came back. But not to find Alice Lisle guilty. They said that they doubted whether the charge was made out. Then Jeffreys said:

Jeffreys: The circumstances and management of the thing is as full a proof as can be. I wonder what it is you doubt of.
Lisle: My Lord, I hope –
Jeffreys: You must not speak now.

So she was not allowed to speak any more. The jury laid their heads together for near a quarter of an hour. I am sorry to say that they gave in. They did not hold out as good men of Hampshire should have done. They found her guilty. Trial by jury had failed – because of an unjust judge. Jeffreys then pronounced sentence on her that she be burnt alive:

'That you be conveyed from hence to the place from whence you came, and from thence you are to be drawn on a hurdle to the place of execution, where your body is to be burnt alive till you be dead. And the Lord have mercy on your soul.'

Macaulay tells us that:[1]

'The clergy of Winchester Cathedral remonstrated with the Chief Justice. . . . The utmost that could be obtained was that her sentence should be commuted from burning to beheading. She was put to death on a scaffold in the market place of Winchester, and underwent her fate with serene courage.'

6 The King's Brewer and the Seven Bishops

But the rule that the jury were to be 'without meat, drink, fire or candle' proved to be of great consequence in the most important *State Trial* recorded in our annals. I refer of course to the trial of the Seven Bishops in 1688.

The King, James II, had claimed a power to dispense with the laws of England. The Bishops had presented a petition to the King. In it they said that he had no power to dispense with the statutes of the realm. On this account the Seven Bishops were charged with a seditious libel. The people of England were whole-heartedly behind the Bishops. The King tried to pack the jury with his own supporters. The foreman was Sir Roger

1 *History of England* vol I, p. 314.

Langley, a baronet of old and honourable family. One of the others was Michael Arnold. He was brewer to the King. He complained bitterly of the position in which he found himself:

> 'Whatever I do, I am sure to be half ruined. If I say Not Guilty, I shall brew no more for the King; and if I say Guilty, I shall brew no more for anybody else.'

The Chief Justice was Sir Robert Wright. He is described by Lord Campbell as 'the lowest wretch that had ever appeared on the bench in England'.[1] He was the nominee of Judge Jeffreys. He sat alongside Jeffreys on the Bloody Assize. He had expelled the fellows of my own college – Magdalen College, Oxford: for the purpose of turning it into a popish seminary. He said to one of the fellows who protested that it was contrary to law: 'Your Oxford law is no better than your Oxford divinity'. He was the subservient tool of the King. At the trial of the Seven Bishops, he directed the jury that the Seven Bishops were guilty. He gave them this totally wrong direction:

> 'The next consideration is, whether the Petition be a seditious libel, and this is a question of law on which I must direct you. Now, gentlemen, anything that shall disturb the government, or make mischief and a stir among the people, is certainly within the case "De Libellis Famosis", and I must, in short, give you my opinion, I do take it to be a libel.'

Seeing that I am here concerned with the behaviour of the jury, I have to tell you that strict watch was kept on the doors – by the solicitor for the Bishops. It was feared that the officers might furnish a courtly juryman with food and it would have enabled him to starve out the other eleven. Not even a candle to light a pipe was permitted to enter. All night they argued. At first nine were for acquitting and three for convicting. Two of the three soon gave way. But Arnold, the King's Brewer, was obstinate. He stood out. But then Thomas Austin, a country gentleman of great estate – and also, I may add, of great size in body – said to Arnold:

1 *Lives of the Chief Justices* vol II, p. 104.

'Look at me. I am the largest and strongest of the twelve; and before I find such a petition as this a libel, here I will stay till I am no bigger than a tobacco pipe.'

It was six in the morning before Arnold yielded. At ten the court again met. The clerk asked:

'Do you find the defendants, or any of them, guilty of the misdemeanour whereof they are impeached, or not guilty?'

Sir Roger Langley answered, 'Not Guilty'.

Thereupon the City went mad with joy. As the jury went out of the hall, all wanted to shake their hands. 'God bless you!' cried the people, 'you have saved us all today'.

They had saved the English Constitution. Their decision meant that the executive Government – the King – had no power to dispense with the laws of England. It was for Parliament alone to enact, amend or repeal the laws.

You will notice that the jurors must have told their friends what happened in the jury-room. Otherwise we should have known nothing of the King's Brewer. Similarly, in the recent case concerning Mr Jeremy Thorpe some of the jurors told *The New Statesman* of what had happened in the jury-room – and they published it. That must not happen again. In the Contempt of Court Act 1981 (section 8) it is prohibited. So we shall never again have a story like that of the King's Brewer.

3 *Causes célèbres* in crime since 1770

1 Erskine defies the judge

The jury played a decisive part in securing the freedom of the press. It was due largely to the speeches of Thomas Erskine, one of the greatest advocates of all time. Let me tell you how it came about.

In the years between 1770 and 1784 there was much criticism of the King and of the Government, and there was a strong demand for reform of the constitution. One of the reformers was Dr Shipley, the Dean of St Asaph, who had handed out to some of his friends a pamphlet advocating that every man over twenty-one should have the right to vote. The Government sought to put down these criticisms by charging the reformers with seditious libel. The Dean of St Asaph was charged at the Shropshire Assizes and Erskine was instructed to defend him. The judge was Mr Justice Buller who knew Erskine well. Indeed Erskine had been his pupil. Now it so happened that at that time the judges, including the great Lord Mansfield, had a wrong notion of the law of libel. They held that the question of libel or no libel was for the judge and not for the jury; and the only question for the jury was whether the pamphlet was published. This state of the law made it difficult for Erskine to defend the Dean, but he was so successful with the jury that, despite the judge's direction, they did not give a simple verdict of guilty. The foreman said: 'We find him guilty of publishing only'. The judge was not prepared to accept that verdict and said to the jury: 'You must explain that, one way or the other'. But Erskine then took the bold and unusual course of himself asking the jury: 'Is the word "only" to stand as part of the verdict?' The foreman said:

'Certainly'. This dialogue then took place between Erskine and the judge:

Erskine: I insist that the verdict shall be recorded.
Buller J: Then the verdict must be misunderstood; let me understand the jury.
Erskine: The jury do understand their verdict.
Buller J: Sir, I will not be interrupted.
Erskine: I stand here as an advocate for a brother citizen, and I desire that the word 'only' may be recorded.
Buller J: Sit down, Sir. Remember your duty, or I shall be obliged to proceed in another manner

(which was a broad hint that he would be obliged to commit him for contempt) but Erskine replied:

Erskine: Your Lordship may proceed in what manner he thinks fit: I know my duty as well as your Lordship knows yours. I shall not alter my conduct.

The judge gave in. He did not commit Erskine and eventually the verdict was entered in the form:

'Guilty of publishing, but whether a libel or not we do not find.'

Erskine then took the case before Lord Mansfield and the judges in London. He made a speech which Charles James Fox declared to be the finest piece of reasoning in the English language. In it he contended that the jury had the right to determine generally whether the publication was or was not a libel. But Lord Mansfield and the judges were against him on this point. They denied that the jury had any such right. So it looked as if Erskine's argument had not succeeded. True it had not succeeded with the judges. But it succeeded with the people at large. The whole country protested against the attitude of the judges. Charles James Fox introduced a Bill into the House of Commons which condemned as illegal the directions which the judges had been giving. It was declared and enacted by Parliament that the jury may give a general verdict of 'Guilty' or 'Not Guilty', and should not be required to find the defendants guilty merely on proof of publication of the paper. In this way there was established the freedom of the press in England: and the principal exponent was Thomas Erskine. 'If it were not for him', says Lord Campbell, 'the Star Chamber might have been re-established in England.'[1]

2 The golden age of trial by jury

As we move into the nineteenth century, we find that juries were treated in a more civilised manner. They were not starved or locked up so as to secure unanimity. They were not carried round the circuit in a waggon. If there was a disagreement – even if one only dissented – there was no verdict. There had to be a new trial. The judge would try to get them to agree but, if it was unsuccessful, the judge used no threats and no pressure. He ordered a new trial. If on a re-trial there was still a disagreement, the prosecution used to drop the case.

But still throughout the nineteenth century the jury played the predominant role in the decision of all cases. Not only in criminal cases, but also in civil cases. The jury were in the eye of the law all 'reasonable men'. They were all householders. They were all male, middle-class and middle-aged. Their verdicts did represent the views of right-minded people. The nineteenth century was the golden age of trial by jury.

But the judges sought to exercise more control over juries. They did it sometimes by holding that there was no case to go to the jury. They did it at other times by holding that the verdict was perverse and by ordering a new trial. They gave them directions on points of law – which the jury had to follow. And so forth. The trials of the nineteenth century became not so much 'trial by jury' as 'trial by judge and jury'. To illustrate this I will tell of some famous cases – now often forgotten – of the time.

3 When is a man insane?

Daniel M'Naghten's case is perhaps the most controversial of all cases in the criminal law – at any rate it was for at least 100 years

1 *Lives of the Lord Chancellors* vol VI, p. 602.

or so. At common law if a man killed or maimed another – when he was mad – he was to be found 'Not Guilty' of any crime. What then constitutes madness? Is it for the jury to say without any help from the judge? The answer is that the judge must direct the jury upon it. What ruling is the judge then to give? That was the question in *M'Naghten's case*.[1]

Daniel M'Naghten was charged with murder. The indictment said that on 20 January 1843 he got

'. . . a certain pistol of the value of 20 shillings, loaded and charged it with gunpowder and a leaden bullet. He held it in his right hand and shot Edward Drummond in the back . . . of which wound the said E Drummond languished until the 25th of April and then died.'

The prisoner pleaded 'Not Guilty'. Evidence was given that Daniel M'Naghten believed that he had a mission from God to kill Edward Drummond. Lord Chief Justice Tindal in his charge to the jury said:

'The question to be determined is, whether at the time the act in question was committed, the prisoner had or had not the use of his understanding, so as to know that he was doing a wrong or wicked act. If the jurors should be of opinion that the prisoner was not sensible, at the time he committed it, that he was violating the laws both of God and man, then he would be entitled to a verdict in his favour: but if, on the contrary, they were of opinion that when he committed the act he was in a sound state of mind, then their verdict must be against him.'

The jury gave their verdict of 'Not Guilty on the ground of insanity'.

That direction and that verdict came under much criticism in Parliament and outside. In consequence the judges were asked by the House of Lords to give their opinion. To this they gave the answer:

'The jurors ought to be told in all cases that every man is to be presumed to be sane, and to possess a sufficient degree of reason

1 (1843) 10 Cl & Fin 200.

to be responsible for his crimes, until the contrary be proved to their satisfaction; and that to establish a defence on the ground of insanity, it must be clearly proved that, at the time of the committing of the act, the party accused was labouring under such a defect of reason, from disease of the mind, as not to know the nature and quality of the act he was doing; or, if he did know it, that he did not know he was doing what was wrong.'

I have many times followed that direction. I have told the jury to ask themselves: Did he know what he was doing? Or, if he did know, did he know that it was wrong? It sounds all right but, like many other directions, it is so vague as to be of little use.

4 A shot at Queen Victoria

But the story does not end there. Queen Victoria did not like the verdict 'Not Guilty on the ground of insanity'. In 1883 a man shot at her and missed. He was acquitted on the ground of insanity. The Queen said:

'He must have been Guilty. I myself saw him fire off the pistol.'

So Parliament enacted that the verdict in future should be 'Guilty but insane'. I must say that I would agree with the Queen – although it is quite illogical. On such a verdict the judge always ordered the man to be kept in custody until Her Majesty's pleasure be known. That is, kept in Broadmoor.

5 The three sailors ate the cabin boy

I turn now to a case[1] where a judge took away from a jury their right of giving a general verdict of 'Not Guilty'. It is perhaps the most dramatic of all the *causes célèbres* of the nineteenth century.

The crew of an English yacht, *Mignonette* – three men and the cabin boy – were cast away in a storm 1,600 miles from the Cape

1 *R v Dudley and Stephens* (1884) 14 QBD 273.

of Good Hope and were compelled to put off in an open boat. No water. No food except two one-pound tins of turnips. After four days they caught a turtle. After twelve days they had nothing to eat. On the twentieth day the three men decided for the sake of their families to kill the boy. They said a prayer, killed him, and fed on his body and blood. Beyond doubt they would all have died if they had not killed the boy. As it was, four days later they were sighted by the barque *Montezuma*. They were picked up almost dead. The *Montezuma* took them and their boat to Falmouth. On landing there they immediately told the whole story to the Customs Officers. The men thought they would be able to return home the same night. But no. They were arrested and charged with murder. They were kept in prison and brought before the magistrates.

Counsel for the Treasury knew that his weakest case was against one of the three, Brooks, who had not actually agreed to participate in the murder. He asked the Falmouth Bench to discharge Brooks so that he might be called to give evidence, and the Bench complied. He asked for the other two, Dudley and Stephens, to be committed for trial for murder. Their counsel asked for them to be let out on bail. He quoted that great criminal judge, Mr Justice Stephen:[1]

'Homicide is also justifiable from the great universal principle of self-preservation, which prompts every man to save his own life preferably to that of another, where one of them must inevitably perish.'

The magistrates let them out on bail. The decision was received with applause in a crowded court. The men were the objects of intense public sympathy.

The two men were tried at the Assizes at Exeter. The judge was Mr Baron Huddleston. (The title 'Baron' was given to the judges of the Court of Exchequer. The judges were not peers and the title 'Baron' was equivalent to that of 'Justice'. The phrase 'Mr Baron . . .' was often used just as in other courts 'Mr Justice . . .'.) Mr Baron Huddleston took a course which had not been taken for nearly 100 years. He had formed a clear view that the men were

1 *Commentaries on the Laws of England* (1st edn, 1841) p. 101.

guilty of murder. He directed the jury that it was murder, and told them they would have to obey his direction. In this he was wrong. It is the right of every jury to give a general verdict of 'Guilty' or 'Not Guilty'. But he suggested to them that, instead of finding the men guilty of murder they could find a special verdict, that is, set out all the facts and ask the Court of Queen's Bench to say whether it was murder or not. That is what the jury did. Mr Baron Huddleston himself drew up a statement of the facts.

The case was argued before Lord Chief Justice Coleridge and four other judges, including Mr Baron Huddleston himself. They all held that the men were guilty of murder and sentenced them to death. Their finding was supported by all the eloquence at the command of Lord Coleridge. He excuses the finding in this passage (page 288):

> 'It must not be supposed that in refusing to admit temptation to be an excuse for crime it is forgotten how terrible the temptation was; how awful the suffering; how hard in such trials to keep the judgment straight and the conduct pure. We are often compelled to set up standards we cannot reach ourselves, and to lay down rules which we could not ourselves satisfy. But a man has no right to declare temptation to be an excuse, though he might himself have yielded to it, nor allow compassion for the criminal to change or weaken in any manner the legal definition of the crime. It is therefore our duty to declare that the prisoners' act in this case was wilful murder.'

None of that eloquence satisfies me that the judges were right. I think that Mr Baron Huddleston ought to have left the decision to the jury without directing them that the men were guilty of murder. He should have left it to them to say whether the men were to be excused by the extreme peril in which they were placed. I have no doubt that, left to give a general verdict, a Devon jury would have found the men 'Not Guilty'.

As it is, I am quite sure that the judges themselves would not have found them guilty except that they knew for a certainty that they would be reprieved. Lord Coleridge showed that by not wearing the black cap when he pronounced sentence of death.

The sentence was commuted by the Crown to six months' imprisonment.

6 Getting rid of the body

In my time at the Bar a murderer – in order to avoid being sentenced to death – often pleaded insanity. He would rather go to Broadmoor for life than be hanged. Such was John George Haigh. Keith Simpson tells the story in his autobiography, *Forty Years of Murder*.

In February 1949 Haigh murdered an old lady, Mrs Durand-Deacon, and put her fully-clothed body into a 40-gallon steel tank into which he pumped concentrated sulphuric acid. Three days later, judging decomposition to be complete and that everything in the tank was sludge, he poured it off. But Professor Keith Simpson found in the sludge – a gallstone – which does not dissolve in an acid. It was proved it came from the body of Mrs Durand-Deacon.

The trial took place at Lewes. The Attorney-General (Sir Hartley Shawcross) led for the Crown. Sir David Maxwell Fyfe (afterwards Lord Chancellor) led for the defence. The defence ran insanity. They relied on the M'Naghten Rules. They called Dr Yellowlees. He said that Haigh was paranoiac. But then in regard to the M'Naghten Rules, he was asked and gave these devastating answers – devastating, that is, to the defence:

> 'Would it be right to say at once', Maxwell Fyfe concluded his examination, 'that you are not prepared to express an opinion on whether he knew he was doing what was wrong?'
> 'That is so.'

In cross-examination the Attorney-General (Sir Hartley Shawcross) pressed for an opinion and finally got one.

> 'I will say "yes" to you if you say "punishable by law" instead of wrong', offered Yellowlees.
> 'Punishable by law and, therefore, wrong by the law of this country?'
> 'Yes, I think he knew that.'

The jury took only eighteen minutes. They found Haigh guilty of murder. He was sentenced to death and hanged in Wandsworth prison.

7 Diminished responsibility

Nowadays, however, the plea of insanity is rarely raised. It has been replaced by the doctrine of diminished responsibility. It had been in use in Scotland ever since 1867. It was brought to the notice of the Royal Commission on Capital Punishment. I remember how interested they were in it. It was introduced into England by the Homicide Act 1957. It says that a man shall not be convicted of murder if he was suffering from such abnormality of mind as substantially impaired his mental responsibility for his action. He is instead to be convicted of manslaughter on the ground of diminished responsibility.

4 Civil cases tried by jury

1 The train was too long for the platform

Now I would consider the juries in civil cases in the nineteenth century. Throughout that century the great majority of civil cases were all tried by juries. The reports are full of claims against railway companies for personal injuries. The issues of liability and of damages were left to the jury. The judges often interfered too much. They used to favour the railway companies. They often withdrew a case from the jury on the ground that there was no evidence to go to them: as in a much litigated case, *Bridges v LNER*.[1]

A train stopped at a station. It was too long for the platform. A passenger, thinking it was not going to pull up any further, jumped out on to a pile of rubbish. He was severely injured. One of the best of judges, Mr Justice Blackburn, thought there was no evidence to go to the jury. He directed a non-suit. The jury protested. They told the judge that they thought there was evidence and awarded £1,200. The case was carried to the House of Lords. The judges were summoned to advise the House. All the way up there was a divergence of opinion among them. Eventually the jury were upheld.

2 The condition on the excursion ticket

Even as late as 1929 there was another case where a train was too long for a platform and a lady was injured in getting out. The

1 (1874) LR 7 HL 213.

case is *Thompson v LMS*.[1] She had taken an excursion ticket which had a condition on the back saying 'See time-table'. If she had bought a time-table and looked at the small print on the back page she would have found a condition exempting the company from any liability. The jury found that the company were negligent: and that they had not taken reasonable steps to bring the condition to her notice. Nevertheless the Court of Appeal overruled the jury. They held that the company were exempted from liability by the condition. Another example of the judges interfering too much with the decision of juries.

3 The ship on the rocks

Commercial cases were regularly tried by juries. One of the first importance was *Jackson v Union Marine*.[2] A vessel called the *Spirit of the Dawn* was chartered to carry a cargo of iron rails. She was to go from Liverpool in ballast round to Newport in Monmouthshire. There she was to take on board a cargo of iron rails and carry them right round Cape Horn and up to San Francisco. She started from Liverpool but on the second day out she went aground on the rocks in Carnarvon Bay. She was got off but so badly damaged – and it would take so long to repair her – that the charterers at Newport chartered another vessel and sent the rails by her to San Francisco. The question was whether the charterers were in breach of their contract. The case was tried at the Liverpool Assizes by judge and jury. The jury found

'that the time necessary to get the ship off and repairing her so as to be a cargo-carrying ship was so long as to put an end in a commercial sense to the commercial speculation entered into by the ship-owners and the charterers'.

So the charterers were not liable. That finding by the jury (no doubt under the guidance of the judge) was the foundation of the law as to frustration – which has dominated the law of contract

1 [1930] 1 KB 41.
2 (1874) LR 10 CP 125.

ever since. No one would ever dream of such a case being tried by a jury nowadays.

4 The Russell baby

Divorce cases were also tried by jury. I remember well the controversy about the Russell baby. It was the talk of everyone when I was called to the Bar. John Russell was the heir to the Russell title and estates. He married his wife Christine in 1918. She gave birth to a son on 5 October 1921. He said he was not the father of it. He brought a petition for divorce on the grounds of her adultery. He charged her with adultery with two named men and with an unknown man. The case was tried with a special jury. They acquitted her in respect of the two named men but disagreed as to the unknown man. The husband then brought another petition charging her with adultery with another named man and also an unknown man. The jury found that she had not committed adultery with this other named man but that she had committed adultery with a man unknown. The judge thereupon granted a decree of divorce. Their decision was upheld by the Court of Appeal[1] but it was reversed by the House of Lords[2] – but only by a majority of three to two.

The crucial dates were these: The husband admitted that on 18 and 19 December 1920 he had slept in the same bed with his wife; but he said that on those occasions no marital intercourse of any kind had taken place. He said that the last time that marital intercourse had taken place was in August 1920. So everything depended on whether he was believed or not as to what took place in the marriage bed. If he did have marital intercourse with his wife on 18 and 19 December 1920 – then he might well be the father of the child born just under ten months later on 5 October 1921. If he did not, then he would not be the father, but some unknown man would be.

The jury believed the husband. They disbelieved the wife. They found that she had committed adultery. Six judges upheld the jury's findings. But three overruled them. And the three – in

1 *Russell v Russell* [1924] P 1.
2 *Ibid* [1924] AC 687.

the House of Lords – prevailed. They held that the husband's evidence was inadmissible. They went on the rule of law that had been stated by Lord Mansfield in 1777:

'It is a rule, founded on decency, morality and policy, that they shall not be permitted to say after marriage, that they have had no connection and therefore that the offspring is spurious.'

It was my task in 1947 to consider that rule when I was Chairman of the Committee on Procedure in Matrimonial Causes. We recommended that the rule should be altered

'so as to enable a party to give evidence tending to show that he or she did not have marital intercourse, notwithstanding that such evidence would tend to bastardise a child prima facie born in wedlock'.[1]

This was one of the few occasions on which Parliament acted quickly. Two years later by section 7 of the Law Reform (Miscellaneous) Provisions Act 1949 it was enacted that:

'Notwithstanding any rule of law, the evidence of a husband or wife shall be admissible in any proceedings to prove that marital intercourse did or did not take place between them during any period.'

That Act was not retrospective. If it had been in force in 1920 the baby would have been found to be illegitimate. But as it was not in force until 1949 the baby was legitimate, and the title and estates descended accordingly. I like to think that this was the right result. It still seems to me unseemly to allow a husband – who slept in the same bed with his wife for two nights – to say that he did not then have marital intercourse with her.

1 Cmnd 7024, para 69.

5 A glance backward

1 All reasonable men

I have given you all those cases so as to show you how trial by
jury dominated the administration of justice in England right up
to the end of the First World War. Everyone had confidence in it.
The jurors were not chosen at random from the whole population. They were chosen from a select band of the middle classes.
They were responsible heads of households – who came without
any pay – not so much even as their expenses. Never was any one
of them challenged. Each was educated and of good understanding. Each was a worthy representative of the 'reasonable
man' so well respected by the law.

2 High drama

Trial by jury had its moments of high drama. Especially in cases
of murder where the judge had no option but to pronounce
sentence of death if the man was found guilty. From the very
outset the court was tense. Counsel for the prosecution would
emphasise the solemnity of the charge. Each witness would give
his evidence slowly and quietly. Everyone would wait to see if
the accused would go into the witness-box or not. Everyone
listened with bated breath. Much depended on it – both on what
he said in examination – and in cross-examination. Then the
speeches by the leading advocates of the day. The Erskines, the
Marshall-Halls, the Norman Birketts all made their reputations
by their speeches in trials by jury. Then the summing-up by the
judge. The jury, who up till then had been looking to the

advocate, now turned in their seats to the judge. At once everyone in court realised that the time for decision was at hand. Always there was a feeling of mutual confidence between judge and jury. Never was it lost. The judge said to them:

'Now, gentlemen of the jury, it is for you to decide this case. It is my task to direct you upon the law. But the facts are for you. And the verdict is for you. If I let fall any views of my own, do not feel bound by them. Remember that, in the end, the decision is yours.'

After he finished his summing-up, the jury retired. The judge went out to his room. The onlookers waited, whispering to one another, wondering what the result would be. At last the word came round: 'The jury are agreed. They are coming back.' They file back into the jury-box. The judge comes back into court. Everyone waits expectantly. You could hear a pin drop. The foreman stands up. The clerk of the court asks them:

'Are you all agreed upon your verdict?'
Answer: 'We are.'
'Do you find the accused "Guilty" or "Not Guilty"?'
Answer: 'Guilty.'

In capital cases there was no need for more. The judge's clerk put the black cap on his head. The judge pronounced sentence of death, ending: 'May the Lord have mercy on your soul.' The chaplain said: 'Amen.'

In other cases, before sentence was passed, a police officer would come into the court to give the prisoner's record. Often enough he would give a list of previous convictions. The jury look at one another well satisfied. Their decision has been right.

6 Reforms in my time

1 No juries in civil cases

There have been so many reforms – good or bad – in my time that I hardly know where to begin.

The first is the virtual disappearance in civil cases of trial by jury. Up till the First World War there was a right of trial by jury – the overwhelming number of civil cases were tried by jury. During the war the judges were given a discretion whether to order a jury or not. This was continued after the war. But the courts still gave priority to trial by jury. The position was well stated by Lord Justice Atkin in the important case of *Ford v Blurton*:[1]

'Trial by jury, except in the very limited classes of cases assigned to the Chancery Court, is an essential principle of our law. It has been the bulwark of liberty, the shield of the poor from the oppression of the rich and powerful. Anyone who knows the history of our law knows that many of the liberties of the subject were originally established and are maintained by the verdicts of juries in *civil cases*. Many will think that at the present time the danger of attack by powerful private organisations or by encroachments of the executive is not diminishing. It is not without importance that the right now taken away is expressly established as part of the American constitution. . . . Hitherto, notwithstanding the far-reaching changes of the Judicature Acts, the right to trial by jury *has been substantially maintained*. . . .

I do not myself see any inconvenience in trying before a jury

1 (1922) 38 TLR 801 at 805.

59

contested facts, even though upon their ascertainment questions of law may emerge.'

That feeling was still prevalent in my early days at the Bar. Most personal injury cases were tried by a judge and jury. Leading counsel used to be paid 10 guineas for him and 2 guineas for his clerk. A '10 and 2 shout' it was called.

Over the years, however, parties have come to ask less and less for juries in civil cases. Eventually it was a decision of the Court of Appeal in 1965 which transformed everything. The case was *Ward v James*.[1] As Master of the Rolls I convened a full court of five judges. Both sides agreed to accept our decision and not to appeal to the House of Lords. It was a case where a warrant officer in the Army was badly injured in a road accident. He was left with both his arms and his legs paralysed. The damages would be very large. He wanted them to be assessed by a jury. We held that he had no right to a jury. The court in their discretion could refuse it. In the course of the judgment the court laid down guide-lines for the exercise of the discretion. These have been so interpreted that no one gets a trial by jury now in any civil case except in very rare cases in which by statute it is explicitly provided that the party has a right to trial by jury. The most important of these exceptions are in libel cases. I will tell you more of these later.

2 Majority verdicts

In 1967 the rule requiring unanimity was abrogated. Instead, a verdict of a majority of ten to two was to be accepted. I confess that I was against the change. I spoke against it in the House of Lords.[2] But the voting was seventy-four to eight in favour of majority verdicts.

The reasoning for the change was impressive. It was based on the new type of crime. This was highly organised by men who robbed banks and stole huge sums. If they were charged, one of their friends or associates would try to bribe or threaten one of the

1 [1966] 1 QB 273.
2 155 HL Official Report 6 June 1967.

jurors – or his wife or relative – and induce that juror to disagree. This was possible in any long case. Time after time this happened. A case would go on for three or four weeks. The evidence would be clear and convincing. But at the end there would be a disagreement of the jury. It was an affront to justice – and a great waste of time and money. To try and circumvent this, the police had to put a guard on the jurors and their relatives. Lord Stonham for the Home Office told the House of Lords that

> 'there are 82 police officers, plus a detective inspector and a detective sergeant, engaged in aiding the jury in one case'.

The Lord Chancellor told the House of a case where five men were charged with conspiring to break into a bank in London. During the first three days of the trial it was noticed that two of the jurors had been approached by associates of one of the accused. It was brought to the notice of the judge. He discharged the jury. A week later the second trial started. A few days later a man – well-known to the police as having a criminal record – approached one of the jurors and made a proposition to him which he was considering. The same evening three men approached a coloured juror and offered him £600 to bring in a verdict in favour of the accused. A few days later a man called at the house of another juror and offered him £100 to help the prisoners. Those jurors reported to the police. The trial went on. In the result four out of the five were acquitted.

In view of this menace to justice, the House overwhelmingly approved the introduction of majority verdicts. It may be possible to bribe or threaten one or two of the jurors, but it is not very likely to be successful in more.

So we now have majority verdicts of ten to two. It has proved very successful. Everyone has confidence in the verdict of a jury, even when it is non-unanimous but only by a majority – as in the recent case of the 'Yorkshire Ripper'.

3 No room for complacency

I must point out, however, that there is no room for complacency. The danger – that juries may be bribed or threatened – is still with us. In cases of big robberies the police have still to keep watch and guard over jurors to see that they are not corrupted by the associates of the prisoners. £1,000 to a juror may enable the robbers to get clear away with £1,000,000. All the more so when the jurors are drawn from all elements of the population.

Very recently a man was on trial for incitement to race hatred. The jurors were all white – seven men and five women. One of the jurors sent a note to the judge. It would appear that he or she had been threatened. The judge told them:

'If any of you feels the need for further protection from any kind of interference, it will be given to you.'

The jury remained in the court building and were later escorted to their homes under a police guard.

4 Anyone can be on a jury

Over all the centuries there were qualifications required of every man to serve on a jury. Originally he had to be a freeholder. In the nineteenth century he had to be a householder. He was, in the words of Lord Devlin, 'predominantly male, middle-aged and middle-class'. But then in 1965 a Committee was appointed under Lord Morris of Borth-y-Gest to reconsider the matter. On their recommendation[1] the qualification was simply that of being qualified to vote at an election of a Member of Parliament. Under the Juries Act 1974 every person is qualified to serve as a juror if he is registered on the voting list as an elector, and is not less than eighteen nor more than sixty-five, and has been resident in the country for more than five years. No crook or criminal is disqualified unless he has, in the last ten years, served a prison sentence of three months or more. But so long as there is no means of 'vetting' the list, it means that, if he keeps quiet about it, a man who has been convicted and served a sentence of imprisonment – long or short – is able to sit on a jury. Any convicted

1 Cmnd 2627.

criminal is entitled to be on the voting list. It includes criminals, crooks, rogues and vagabonds, and all sorts and conditions of men. No matter whether he can read or write. No matter whether he can hear or see. No matter whether he is learned or ignorant. He can be summoned to serve on a jury. Not only he, but she. Men and women, boys and girls, can all serve, so long as they are not less than eighteen nor more than sixty-five.

5 Jury vetting – rival philosophies

By making everyone qualified to sit on a jury, it led inevitably to the practice of 'jury vetting'. The prosecuting authorities naturally wanted to exclude criminals – who would presumably be biased in favour of their companions in crime. It would lead to the guilty being acquitted. So the practice grew up in some places of the prosecuting authorities searching through the criminal records – and checking them against the jury panel – and objecting to them. Was this 'jury vetting' lawful or not?

There are two rival philosophies. One philosophy says that the parties to a dispute ought to know whether the jurors are suitable to try the case. They ought to have access to the antecedents of the persons on the panel: so that they may be able to object to those who are unsuitable to sit in judgment. That philosophy prevails in the United States of America. So much so that the parties in that country can cross-examine the potential jurors before they are sworn: not only about their previous convictions, but also upon their occupations, their views on this matter or that which may arise in the course of the hearing – so as to see if they are prejudiced in any way.

That philosophy has never prevailed in England. Our philosophy is that the jury should be selected at random – from a panel of persons who are nominated at random. We believe that twelve persons selected at random are likely to be a cross-section of the people as a whole – and thus represent the views of the common man. Some may be moral. Others not. Some may be honest. Others not. Some may be bad drivers with many convictions for motoring offences. Others may not have a single thing against them. The parties must take them as they come. There are a few exceptions. Someone may be disqualified. Another may be banned because the prosecution has asked that he 'stand by for the Crown', that is, because the prosecution can ask that he does not serve as a juror. Yet another because the defence have exercised their right of 'peremptory' challenge (to which I will soon refer). But subject to these exceptions, the principle of English law is that jurors should be selected at random.

6 Jury vetting – now approved

In recent times, however, there has been a change. Some prosecuting authorities seem sometimes to have searched through the criminal records – and the records of Special Branch – checking to see if any of those on the jury panel have anything entered against their names; and then, if they think any one of them is unsuitable, to require him to 'stand by for the Crown'. This is called a 'jury check' or 'jury vetting'. In the House of Commons in 1980 the Attorney-General disclosed that

'the Northamptonshire police were checking all jury panels against Criminal Records Office records. This information was passed on to prosecuting counsel: see Hansard *Parliamentary Debates, Commons,* 25 February 1980, col 948.'

This sort of thing can be done without anyone outside the police force knowing anything about it.

7 Is it constitutional?

In *R v Sheffield Crown Court, ex parte Brownlow*,[1] I thought that it was unconstitutional. I said (page 900):

'To my mind it is unconstitutional for the police authorities to engage in "jury vetting". So long as a person is eligible for jury service, and is not disqualified, I cannot think it right that, behind his back, the police should go through his record so as

1 [1980] 1 WLR 892.

to enable him to be asked to "stand by for the Crown", or to be challenged by the defence. If this sort of thing is to be allowed, what comes of a man's right of privacy? He is bound to serve on a jury when summoned. Is he thereby liable to have his past record raked up against him – and presented on a plate to prosecuting and defending lawyers – who may use it to keep him out of the jury – and, who knows, it may become known to his neighbours and those about him?'

8 I stand corrected

My view was rebutted by Lord Justice Lawton in the more recent case of *R v Mason*.[1] On a trial for burglary, the Crown objected to four jurors: and asked them to 'stand by for the Crown' because they had previous convictions. The accused was found guilty and then complained of 'jury vetting'. The Court of Appeal held that it was perfectly lawful. Lord Justice Lawton said (page 625):

'The facts which have been revealed show that some scrutiny of jury panels is necessary if disqualified persons are to be excluded from juries. The police are the only authority able to do this. Since it is a criminal offence for a person to serve on a jury knowing that he is disqualified, for the police to scrutinise the list of potential jurors to see if any are disqualified is to do no more than to perform their usual function of preventing the commission of offences. In the course of looking at criminal records convictions are likely to be revealed which do not amount to disqualifications. We can see no reason why information about such convictions should not be passed on to prosecuting counsel. He may consider that a juror with a conviction for burglary would be unsuitable to sit on a jury trying a burglar; and if he does so he can exercise the Crown's rights. Many persons, but not burglars, would probably think that he should.

The practice of supplying prosecuting counsel with information about potential jurors' convictions has been followed

1 [1980] 3 WLR 617.

during the whole of our professional lives, and almost certainly
for generations before us. It is not unlawful, and has not until
recently been thought to be unsatisfactory.'

I stand corrected.

9 Right of challenge

The right of challenge goes back to time immemorial. It means
that the accused man can object to anyone who is called to be on
the jury. The clerk tells the accused of his right in these words:

'If therefore you object to them or any of them, you must
object to them as they come to the book to be sworn and
before they are sworn and you shall be heard.'

In olden days there used to be a large folio Bible on which each
member of the jury, as his name was called, placed his hand and
took the oath. Nowadays he is given a New Testament – unless
he is of another religion. For instance, if he is a Jew, he has the
Old Testament; if a Moslem, he has the Koran; and so forth.

There were – and are – two kinds of challenge. One is called a
'peremptory' challenge. This means that the accused can say 'I
object' without giving any reason: and the juror has to stand
down. The other is called challenge for 'cause'. This means that
the accused has to show good cause in order to justify his objection.

As usual we turn to Blackstone to know the reason for this
differentiation. Challenge for 'cause' is obvious. If the accused can
show that the juror may not be impartial, he can object. The
judge will rule whether the cause is sufficient or not. Lord
Devlin, in *Trial by Jury* (page 29), said it was obsolescent. I do not
think this is so. It still exists but it is rarely invoked because it is so
difficult to show good cause. If the cause given is because of
colour – white or black – or of sex – male or female – the objection will clearly be overruled.

10 'Peremptory' challenge

'Peremptory' challenge is more difficult to justify. Blackstone suggested that it is confined to capital cases where the accused may be sentenced to death if he is convicted. He should be able to object to a man if he does not like the look of him. It is

'. . . a provision full of that tenderness and humanity to prisoners, for which our English laws are justly famous. . . . As every one must be sensible, what sudden impressions and unaccountable prejudices we are apt to conceive upon the bare looks and gestures of another; and how necessary it is, that a prisoner (when put to defend his life) should have a good opinion of his jury, the want of which might totally disconcert him; the law wills not that he should be tried by any one man against whom he has conceived a prejudice, even without being able to assign a reason for such his dislike.'[1]

At common law the accused was allowed thirty-five 'peremptory' challenges. Under a statute of 1509 no person arraigned for felony was allowed more than twenty 'peremptory' challenges. This continued for centuries. There was a case in 1840 where a solicitor accused of perjury used up all his twenty 'peremptory' challenges.[2] Thenceforward 'peremptory' challenges seem to have fallen into disuse. Presumably there was no point in making them. All the jurors were respectable householders. All looked reliable. But when in 1919 by the Sex Disqualification Act women became qualified to be jurors, sometimes counsel for the accused would think that he would do better with an all-male jury – or an all-female jury – and would use the 'peremptory' challenges to secure this result. This was put to an end by section 35 of the Criminal Justice Act 1948 which said:

'A person arraigned on an indictment for any felony or misdemeanour may challenge not more than seven jurors without cause and any juror or jurors with cause.'

That meant he could only object to seven men or seven women.

1 *Commentaries* IV, 353.
2 *R v Geach* (1840) 9 C & P 499 at 502.

He could not get an all-male jury or an all-female jury. That continued until 1977 when 'three' was substituted for 'seven' by the Criminal Law Act of that year.

The biggest change was in extending the peremptory challenge to 'any felony or misdemeanour'. This meant that it was available in every case tried by a jury. Not only to murders, robberies and rapes, but also to conspiracies, riots and affrays. These are offences committed by groups. Each of the accused can use his three peremptory challenges. If six are accused, they have eighteen between them. If nine, twenty-seven. If twelve, thirty-six.

11 'Packing' the jury

It is now becoming apparent that the accused, by using the 'peremptory' challenge, may seek to 'pack' the jury-box with jurors who are sympathetic to his side, or at any rate to get enough so that more than two will disagree. There was a recent case about the disturbances at Bristol. The accused were encouraged by the judge to use their peremptory challenges so as to secure a representative jury. So the accused were fully justified to use them as they did. It is always desirable that a jury should reflect the community from which its members are drawn. The use for that purpose is quite proper. But it is not right to use it otherwise.

There was a case, a little while ago, when the Common Serjeant of London was trying five men charged with robbery with violence. It was so serious that during the trial there was a police guard to protect the jurors and also the judge himself. The defendants used their challenges so as to secure as many women on the jury as possible. There were eight women and four men. In the result three of the defendants were convicted. One was acquitted. There was a disagreement on the fifth. He was retried and was convicted.

Apart from that case, the right of 'peremptory' challenge has been used to secure for the defence a jury thought to be more sympathetic to the defence – such as long-haired youths – or women – according to the nature of the case. Sometimes it is used so as to object to any man who is dressed well or who looks intelligent or middle-class.

This prompts the reflection: What is the justification today of the right of the accused to 'peremptory' challenges? Should we any longer permit the accused to exclude a juror simply because of his looks?

7 Proposals for consideration

Such being the past and present, I turn to the future. These are the reforms which I suggest for consideration.

1 Abolish the 'peremptory' challenge

Simplest and shortest is to abolish the right to make 'peremptory' challenges. The origin of this right, as I have shown, was in the days when the death penalty was inflicted for many offences. Blackstone felt it was justified *in favorem vitae* (in favour of life). The accused man knew nothing of the man to whom he objected. He had no good cause to urge why he should not be on the jury. He could only go by the 'look of him'. That seems to me altogether an insufficient basis for giving the accused this right.

Now that the panel of jurors consists of everyone on the voting list, there is less reason than ever for continuing the 'peremptory' challenge. Because it can be, and is, abused. The jurors should be selected at random. But the 'peremptory' challenge enables the accused to 'pack' the jury with those whom he thinks will be sympathetic to his point of view. Just by what the jurors 'look like'! The accused will be the exponent of sex discrimination, race discrimination, class discrimination, dress discrimination, hair-cutting discrimination, youth discrimination – any other kind of discrimination which suits his book. That is all wrong.

Challenge for 'cause' is another matter. But it should exist only to the extent that it now exists in England. We should not copy the American model. Suffice it that the judge should himself tell the jurors in a proper case of any reason why any one of their number should not sit on the case. It is always done if the case is to take such a long time that it would be a hardship on the juror to have to sit on it; also if a juror cannot read or hear properly; also if he has read so much in the papers beforehand that he has formed a view already; and so forth.

2 The panel of jurors

In former times the panel of jurors was selected by the Sheriff out of those persons qualified to be jurors. I have already mentioned the jury at the trial of Alice Lisle where

> 'it being a case of great expectation and moment the Lord Chief Justice ordered the Sheriff to take care that a very substantial jury should be returned of the best quality in the county'

and I have told of how Lord Mansfield had his own special jurymen who served in nearly every commercial case.

In the days when I sat to try cases with a jury, the Sheriff's officer used in some way to exercise a discreet mode of selection. I remember a long case which I tried at the Old Bailey – a very complicated case about the 'black market' – where the jury was composed of bank clerks, insurance clerks, and other city persons. They followed the evidence very intelligently. They had the accounts before them and examined them.

3 Special jurors for fraud cases

To my mind, cases of fraud involving complicated accounts should not be tried by jurors on the ordinary panel. They should be tried by special jurors. These cases are quite unsuitable to be tried by a jury selected at random. Just think how random the selection is to be in the future. The people on the voting list all have numbers. Their numbers are to be put into a hat or into a computer. The lucky (or unlucky) numbers will constitute the panel of jurors.

Now think of what happens when a jury at the Old Bailey has to try a long fraud case or any case involving accounts and masses of figures; or a case with a mass of detail. On the law of averages, there may not be a single member of the jury who can comprehend it – or at any rate only one or two of them. It is altogether wrong that such a jury should try such a case. Each one of the jurors should be able to follow the evidence intelligently so as to be able to fulfil the oath as it was administered for centuries:

'I will well and truly try, and true deliverance make, between our Sovereign Lady the Queen and the prisoner at the bar whom I shall have in charge; and a true verdict give, according to the evidence. So help me God.'

The present form is not nearly so good but still the juror should be able to fulfil it:

'I will faithfully try the several issues joined between our Sovereign Lady the Queen and the prisoner at the bar, and a true verdict give according to the evidence.'

I ask the question: How can he give a true verdict – in a fraud or complicated case or any case – according to the evidence – unless he can follow and understand the evidence?

I should like to see revived a panel of special jurors for commercial frauds and like cases. I would suggest that the panel could be selected from names put forward by the business houses in the City of London – or wider still, in Greater London – by the trade unions – by the local authorities – and other reputable bodies. These bodies could be relied upon to nominate suitable persons who could follow accounts and figures and the evidence given in cases of this kind.

4 Alternatively, judge with assessors

As an alternative I would suggest that these fraud cases should be tried by a High Court Judge with two assessors. At present they are tried by Circuit Judges and a jury of nondescripts. Counsel for the accused do their best to confuse the issue. They say it is not fraud – just a mistake in accountancy. They breed such an atmosphere of complication and doubt that the jury are too bemused to find a verdict of guilty.

I would compare this with the Disciplinary Tribunals of the great professions. They have to deal with cases which involve much the same issues. A solicitor uses his client's money or converts it to his own use. A chartered accountant gives a certificate which he knows, or should know, is false or inaccurate – so as to support a bogus claim or excuse by his client. The penalty is as severe a sentence as a circuit court would impose. For a professional man to be struck off the roll is just as serious – more serious – than for a city man to be fined a large sum or sent to prison for six months. In such cases the Disciplinary Tribunals consist of two members of the profession and a lay member of good standing and intelligence. The professional tribunals are some of the best I have ever known. I see no reason why city frauds should not be tried by similar tribunals constituted of a High Court Judge and two assessors. One might be an accountant. The other a solicitor. They could proceed in much the same way as in the many countries (of the old Commonwealth) where there is trial by judge and assessors. The judge sums up to the assessors as if they were a jury. His summing-up to the assessors can be considered by the Court of Appeal just as a summing-up to a jury.

5 Let minor cases be tried by magistrates

Every person who is liable, on being found guilty, to be sent to prison for more than three months is entitled to be tried by jury. But there are many cases in which he can waive this right. He can agree to be dealt with summarily by the magistrates. I am sorry to say that, since the introduction of legal aid, some accused persons (who would otherwise have been dealt with summarily) elect for trial by jury. It costs them nothing. It gives them time – months and months – in which to prepare their defence – and for witnesses to forget what happened – and for the accused to dispose of any of his assets – and to make arrangements against the time when he is sentenced. The lawyers benefit too. Their fees are all the more if the case goes for trial than if it is tried summarily.

These minor cases – such as small thefts (like shop-lifting) and

73

small criminal damage (like breaking windows) should, I suggest, be tried by magistrates. In 1975 Lord Justice James and a good Committee so recommended[1] when the sum involved was less than £20. But it was rejected by the House of Lords.

Very recently there was a good illustration which shows the comment of a judge – and the reaction of bodies which seek to retain trial by jury.

A man had travelled on the London Underground and at the end of his journey put 20p into the ticket collector's box at Greenford and then walked away. Two inspectors happened to see him and asked him where he joined the train. He said that he had travelled from Perivale, one stop down the line, but it had been observed that he had come from a station much further away – Mile End – from which the correct fare was £1.05. He was charged with travelling with intent to avoid payment of his fare. His defence was that he had been stopped by the inspectors before he had a chance to pay his fare. He claimed trial by jury and the case was tried at the Old Bailey. He had legal aid. The case lasted two days and cost at least £4,000. The jury found him guilty and he was fined £50. That was no doubt the correct sentence for the offence but this is what Judge Abdela (a judge of much experience and ability) had to say:

> 'A case of this sort should never, never have found its way into a court of this standing and have to be dealt with by a jury who have to give up their time. It should have been dealt with elsewhere.
>
> Maybe the law will be changed at a future date so that persons involved in offences which concern small monetary matters only will be dealt with in courts of summary jurisdiction and nowhere else.'

In the special circumstances of the case, the judge marked his disapproval by ordering the accused himself to pay the legal aid costs of £500.

After that case *The Times* asked many people for their views about it. Two Members of Parliament disagreed entirely with the judge. One said:

1 Cmnd 6323.

'A basic right of the British citizen would be taken away if the right to a trial by jury is removed.'

This was followed shortly after by a case where a postman was charged with stealing a box of chocolates valued at £1.03. He claimed trial by jury. He told the court that he picked up the chocolates accidentally when collecting mail. The jury found him not guilty. The judge in that case considered it a vindication of the right of trial by jury.

Now my comment is this: A bench of magistrates would, I expect, have come to the same decision as the jury. When people cite cases like this, they assume (a) that the man was truly innocent and (b) that the magistrates would have wrongly found him guilty. Their whole argument fails if they assume that the man was truly guilty and was wrongly acquitted by the jury. I would repudiate the suggestion that magistrates would ever find an innocent man guilty. They give every man the benefit of the doubt just as much as any jury: and, if he should be wrongly convicted, he has always an appeal to the Crown Court.

6 The qualification to be a juror

It seems to me that there is need for a new assessment by Parliament of the merits of trial by jury. Many – myself included – have been brought up to have a profound belief in the jury system. It grew up in the ages when the English were a homogeneous race. Although in origin they were diverse – Saxon, Dane and Norman – yet by the time that trial by jury became enshrined in our constitution – an unwritten constitution – the English were one race. They shared the same standards of conduct, the same code of morals, and the same religious beliefs. Above all they adhered uniformly to the rule of law. Those who were qualified as jurors were freeholders and householders – who held passionately that no person should be deprived of life, liberty or property without due process of law.

The Committee presided over by Lord Morris of Borth-y-Gest made a complete assessment of the qualities required of jurors:

'It is necessary to have on a jury men and women who will bring common sense to their task of exercising judgment; who have knowledge of the ways of the world and of the ways of human beings; who have a sense of belonging to a community; who are actuated by a desire to see fair play; and above all who will strive to come to an honest conclusion in regard to the issues which are for them to decide. We think that in any healthy community there will be a high sense of duty, a fundamental respect for law and order, and a wish that principles of honesty and decency should prevail. A jury should represent a cross-section drawn at random from the community, and should be the means of bringing to bear on the issues that face them the corporate good sense of that community. This cannot be in the keeping of the few, but is something to which all men and women of good will must contribute.'[1]

Strangely enough, however, the Committee thought that all citizens would have those desirable qualifications. They said:[2]

'. . . Our view is that jury service should be regarded as a duty which is a counterpart of the privilege of being a citizen. From this view it follows that citizenship should be the basis from which the duty to serve arises. A convenient register of citizens (in the broad sense) is to be found in the register of those qualified to vote at parliamentary and local government elections.'

7 The ordinary man is no longer suitable

The underlying assumption is that all citizens are sufficiently qualified to serve on a jury. I do not agree. Nowadays virtually every member of the population is qualified to sit as a juror. No matter how illiterate or uneducated or unsuitable he may be. And where the chances, by sheer weight of numbers, are loaded heavily against the jurors being the sensible and responsible members of the community.

1 Cmnd 2627, para 53.
2 Cmnd 2627, para 60.

8 A new way of selecting jurors

To my mind this is what should happen: There should be a qualification for service as a juror so that a jury is composed of sensible and responsible members of the community. It should be representative of the best of them of whatever sex or colour, and of whatever age or occupation. Service as a juror should be regarded as a service to the community – as indeed it is. It should command the respect of the people generally – much as service as a magistrate does now. Those on the jury list should be selected in much the same way as magistrates are now. Sometimes people apply. Sometimes they are recommended by others. Always references are required. Interviews are held to assess suitability. In the make-up of the jurors' list, the magistrate could be of the greatest help. It should be part of their function to make up the jury list for their neighbourhood.

In this way I suggest that trial by jury can be retained as the great institution it always has been. Otherwise, I suggest it should be replaced by trial by judge and assessors.

It is sometimes suggested that instead of a jury of twelve, there should be seven. I do not agree. There is something convincing about a verdict of twelve which is not the same with seven.

Conclusion

I would like to see:

1 'Peremptory' challenges abolished.
2 Complicated cases of fraud or accounts tried by special jurors of the City of London; or alternatively by a judge with assessors.
3 Minor cases tried by magistrates in accordance with the recommendation of the Committee of Lord Justice James.*
4 Jurors no longer to be taken at random from the electoral register.
5 A new way of selecting jurors so that all should be fit to try the case. There should be a list of qualified persons: and the panel taken at random from that list.

*During this very time whilst these pages are in proof, the Justices' Clerks' Society have produced a most valuable paper. They propose that there should be a redistribution of criminal business – on the lines recommended by the James Committee – so that more cases are tried by magistrates' courts. They emphasise quite rightly that

'The magistrates' courts are the real courts of the people where not only the question of guilt or innocence is decided by fellow-members of the community but determination of the sentence as well – a unique feature.'

Part three

Legal aid

Introduction

I have often said that since the Second World War the greatest revolution in the law has been the system of legal aid. It means that in many cases the lawyers' fees and expenses are paid for by the state: and not by the party concerned. It is a subject of such importance that I venture to look at the law about costs – as it was – as it is – and as it should be.

1 Costs as they used to be

1 Don't go to law

In the old days before the Second World War, whenever there was litigation in the courts, each party had to pay his own lawyer his 'costs', that is, his fees and expenses – including the sum his lawyer had to pay out to counsel or experts or witnesses, which were called his 'disbursements' – and also the reward which his lawyer required for his own work – which was called his 'fees and profit costs'.

The general rule was this: If the plaintiff won the case, the court would order the defendant to pay the plaintiff's costs. So the defendant had to pay the plaintiff's costs as well as his own. If the plaintiff lost the case, the court would order him to pay the defendant's costs. So the plaintiff had to pay the defendant's costs as well as his own.

This was – for either party – so onerous a prospect that litigants would hesitate long before going to law – to make or resist a claim. No wise man would go to law unless he was pretty sure of winning – or the circumstances made it inevitable.

But the old system gave rise to such abuse that reform became imperative. You will find little in the old law reports about costs. But you will find much in the novels by Charles Dickens. I read many of them when I was very young – at a time when I understood nothing about costs. They did more for law reform than all the treatises of Jeremy Bentham. He, Charles Dickens, had seen costs operate at first hand. He wrote *Pickwick Papers* at the age of twenty-four. It is to that book I turn for my first story.

2 Dodson and Fogg – their honourable conduct

Everyone knows about the action which Mrs Bardell brought against Mr Pickwick for breach of promise of marriage. Everyone knows about the address of Serjeant Buzfuz to the jury. Everyone knows about the evidence of Sam Weller, the manservant of Mr Pickwick. But not everyone knows about the costs of the solicitors – Messrs Dodson and Fogg for Mrs Bardell and Mr Perker for Mr Pickwick. According to Mr Perker, Messrs Dodson and Fogg were 'very smart fellows; very smart indeed'. According to Mr Pickwick, they were 'great scoundrels'. They took up the case for Mrs Bardell knowing that she could not pay a penny of their costs. They instructed on her behalf Serjeant Buzfuz and Mr Skimpin. Those counsel, I am sure, did not inquire too closely whether they were to be paid and who was to pay them. When Sam Weller gave evidence, this was the interchange:

' "The ladies gets into a wery great state o' admiration at the honourable conduct of Mr Dodson and Fogg – them two gen'l'men as is settin' near you now." This, of course, drew general attention to Dodson and Fogg, who looked as virtuous as possible.

"The attorneys for the plaintiff", said Mr Serjeant Buzfuz. "Well! They spoke in high praise of the honourable conduct of Messrs Dodson and Fogg, the attorneys for the plaintiff, did they?"

"Yes", said Sam, "they said what a wery gen'rous thing it was o' them to have taken up the case on spec, and to charge nothing at all for costs, unless they got 'em out of Mr Pickwick."

At this very unexpected reply, the spectators tittered again, and Dodson and Fogg, turning very red, leant over to Serjeant Buzfuz, and in a hurried manner whispered something in his ear.

"You are quite right", said Serjeant Buzfuz aloud, with affected composure. "It's perfectly useless, my lord, attempting to get at any evidence through the impenetrable stupidity of this witness. I will not trouble the court by asking him any more questions. Stand down, sir." '

3 Not one farthing from Mr Pickwick

The jury found a verdict for the plaintiff for £750. As they went out, Mr Pickwick encountered Messrs Dodson and Fogg,

'rubbing their hands with every token of outward satisfaction.
   "Well, gentlemen", said Mr Pickwick.
   "Well, sir", said Dodson: for self and partner.
   "You imagine you'll get your costs, don't you, gentlemen?" said Mr Pickwick.
   Fogg said they thought it rather probable. Dodson smiled, and said they'd try.
   "You may try, and try, and try again, Messrs Dodson and Fogg", said Mr Pickwick vehemently, "but not one farthing of costs or damages do you ever get from me, if I spend the rest of my existence in a debtor's prison."
   "Ha, ha!" laughed Dodson. "You'll think better of that, before next term, Mr Pickwick."
   "He, he, he! We'll soon see about that, Mr Pickwick", grinned Fogg.'

4 Mr Pickwick goes to prison

At this point in the story Dickens breaks off and talks about the adventures of other members of the Pickwick Club. That takes up over seventy pages. So the casual reader loses the thread. I would take it up again where the sheriff's officer came with a warrant to arrest Mr Pickwick for non-payment of the damages and costs. He came with the old writ of 'ca-sa' – so described by Dickens. That is short for *capias ad satisfaciendum*. It authorised the sheriff to take the body of Mr Pickwick in execution until the amount was paid. Mr Perker advised Mr Pickwick to draw a cheque for it. But –

' "Perker", said Mr Pickwick, "let me hear no more of this, I beg. I see no advantage in staying here, so I shall go to prison tonight." . . .
   "You can go to the Fleet, my dear sir, if you're determined to go somewhere", said Perker.

"That'll do", said Mr Pickwick, "I'll go there directly I have finished my breakfast." '

5 The cobbler in Chancery

Dickens then describes the Fleet prison and its occupants. Most of them were in prison for debt. Dickens tells the story of a cobbler who had been there twelve years. He had been left a legacy by an old gentleman he worked for. The nephews and nieces had challenged the will in Doctor's Commons and the cobbler had been ordered to pay the money back and all the costs. (Dickens does not explain why he had to pay the costs.) Then the cobbler went on:

' "After that, we went into Chancery, where we are still, and where I shall always be. My lawyers have had all my thousand pound long ago; and what between the estate, as they call it, and the costs, I'm here for ten thousand, and shall stop here, till I die, mending shoes." '

6 Mrs Bardell in prison for costs

It is plain that Dickens had to get Mr Pickwick out of the Fleet somehow. He managed it after fifty more pages. He did it by means of the sheriff's officer again. Messrs Dodson and Fogg had got no satisfaction out of Mr Pickwick for their costs. So they turned round on their own client Mrs Bardell. They got her put in prison for not paying their costs. Their clerk went to see her:

' "Sad thing about these costs of our people, ain't it? your bill of costs, I mean."
"I'm very sorry they can't get them", replied Mrs Bardell. "But if you law-gentlemen do these things on speculation, why you must get a loss now and then, you know."
"You gave them a *cognovit* for the amount of your costs, after the trial, I'm told?"
"Yes. Just as a matter of form", replied Mrs Bardell.
"Certainly. Quite a matter of form. Quite." '

In Dickens' day everyone knew what a *cognovit* was. It was short for *cognovit actionem*. It was an acknowledgment that the claim for costs was justified, whereupon judgment was entered after trial. So Messrs Dodson and Fogg had got judgment against Mrs Bardell for her costs. They took her body in execution on *cognovit* for costs and cast her into the Fleet.

7 Free at last

So there she was in the Fleet. Here was an opportunity for Mr Pickwick's solicitor to intervene. Mr Pickwick was the soul of kindness. He would not wish Mrs Bardell to be imprisoned in the Fleet for the rest of her days. If only Mr Pickwick would agree to pay the costs of Dodson and Fogg (about £150) Mrs Bardell would forego her claim for £750 damages. This is what Mr Perker told Mr Pickwick:

' "I have seen the woman, this morning. By paying the costs, you can obtain a full release and discharge from the damages; and further – this I know is a far greater object of consideration with you, my dear sir – a voluntary statement, under her hand, in the form of a letter to me, that this business was, from the very first, fomented, and encouraged, and brought about, by these men, Dodson and Fogg; that she deeply regrets ever having been the instrument of annoyance or injury to you; and that she entreats me to intercede with you, and implore your pardon." '

Eventually the matter was settled on those terms. Mr Pickwick and Mrs Bardell went free. Messrs Dodson and Fogg got all their costs. That is the only reason why they ever took up the case. 'Those sharks', as Mr Pickwick called them.

2 Side effects in old days

1 'Mountains of costly nonsense'

There was one court and one class of case in which the suitors did
not have to pay their own costs. They came out of 'the estate'.
This was in the Court of Chancery. Much of the litigation in that
court was about the estates of persons who had died: or about the
succession to property on death or by will: or about trusts which
had been made of property or funds for children. In all these cases
lawyers were appointed to protect the interests of the estate
itself, of living persons, of persons of full age, of infants and of
unborn children. All sorts of points were argued – of the most
technical description. It used to take years before the estate was
finally wound up. And then at the end the court would order
costs of all parties to come out of the estate. That meant that all
the lawyers engaged got their costs in priority to any of the
beneficiaries. Often enough the estate had to be sold in order to
pay the costs. There would be little or nothing left for the
beneficiaries after the lawyers had had their costs out of it.

But the complete condemnation of the proceedings in Chan-
cery was given by Charles Dickens in the opening chapter of
Bleak House where he described the scene in Lincoln's Inn Old
Hall when the case of *Jarndyce v Jarndyce* was being heard:

'On such an afternoon, the various solicitors in the cause, some
two or three of whom have inherited it from their fathers, who
made a fortune by it, ought to be – as are they not? – ranged in
a line, in a long matted well (but you might look in vain for
Truth at the bottom of it), between the registrar's red table and
the silk gowns, with bills, cross-bills, answers, rejoinders,

injunctions, affidavits, issues, references to masters, masters' reports, mountains of costly nonsense, piled before them.'

2 The Duke refuses to pay

At common law every plaintiff or defendant had to pay his own costs to his own solicitor. It was quite wrong for anyone else to help him to pay them. No one was allowed to lend him money or promise to pay his solicitor or anything of that kind. No one was to back him in his cause. It was regarded as grossly mischievous. It was indictable as a crime. It was actionable as a wrong.

There was a celebrated case in 1784 about an election for a Member of Parliament for Colchester. The return showed George Jackson to have a majority over his opponent George Tierney. The loser, George Tierney, then brought a petition claiming that George Jackson had bribed some of the electors and should be unseated. The Duke of Portland supported the petition by George Tierney. He promised to pay the fees of solicitors and counsel. The petition failed. The Duke 'ratted'. He refused to pay the solicitors their fees. The solicitors sued the Duke. They failed. Lord Loughborough, the Lord Chancellor, said that 'every person must bring his own suit upon his own bottom and at his own expense', see *Wallis v Duke of Portland.*[1]

This rule operated very harshly against poor persons who did not have enough money to pay the lawyer's fees. So the practice grew up of lawyers taking up cases 'on spec' – as Dodson and Fogg did – or on contingency fees – as Mr Sprye did in 1849. He was a lawyer. He wrote this letter to General Sir Thomas Reynell:[2]

'. . . Now, almost all men are frightened at the idea of law proceedings to recover property, and consequently a system has grown up among men of business of conducting such cases on the arrangement that no law expenses are paid unless success attend the proceedings. In which case they are first paid out of the money recovered, and the party conducting the

1 (1797) 3 Ves Jun 494, on appeal (1798) 8 Bro Parl Cas 161.
2 *Reynell v Sprye* (1849) 8 Hare 222 at 230.

proceedings and furnishing the information is allowed for his compensation half of what is recovered, which is also to satisfy him for the risk of paying the law expenses, without perhaps succeeding.'

3 No contingency fees

That assertion by Mr Sprye was entirely wrong. English law has never sanctioned an agreement by which a lawyer is remunerated on the basis of a 'contingency fee', that is, that he gets paid the fee if he wins but not if he loses. Such an agreement was illegal on the ground that it was the offence of champerty. In its origin champerty was a division of the proceeds (*campi partitio*). An agreement by which a lawyer, if he won, was to receive a share of the proceeds was pure champerty. Even if he was not to receive an actual share, but payment of a commission on a sum proportioned to the amount recovered – only if he won – it was also regarded as champerty. Even if the sum was not a proportion of the amount recovered, but a specific sum or advantage which was to be received if he won but not if he lost, that too, was unlawful. It mattered not whether the sum to be received was to be his sole remuneration or to be an added remuneration (above his normal fee); in any case it was unlawful if it was to be paid only if he won and not if he lost.

4 Ambulance-chasers

Soon after the First World War there was instituted a system of poor persons' rules. There was a list of solicitors and counsel who volunteered to do poor persons' cases. This meant that the solicitors were paid their out-of-pocket expenses, such as conduct money for witnesses and costs of copying papers, but they did not get any fees or profit costs at all. The very first items in my fee book for my first year were for the interlocutory proceedings in a poor person's case: Settling defence; Advising on evidence; Brief on summons for particulars; Brief for defendant on trial. There was no fee for any of that work. It was all done in the hope that the solicitors might give me work in a paid case. But they never did. Later on I did several poor persons' cases – all for nothing – in the hope of getting experience – and getting to know solicitors.

Then there were firms of solicitors who were called 'ambulance-chasers'. On hearing of an accident, the clerk or the agents would seek out the injured person or his relatives and suggest that they might have a good cause of action for damages – and they would be ready to conduct the case. They were really conducting it 'on spec'. They had every expectation of winning or at least getting a good settlement. So they did not ask the injured person for any payment down. This practice was regarded by many as undesirable – even as unprofessional. The understanding was 'No cure, no pay'. The solicitors would get nothing unless they succeeded in the case. In our chambers we never accepted work on that basis. Every brief had to be marked with a proper fee. If the solicitor was regarded as at all doubtful, our clerk insisted on 'cash with brief'. In any case, win or lose, the solicitor was himself responsible for paying us the fees.

At that time there were not so many road accidents. Motor-cars had not become the peril which they are now. There was no compulsory insurance. At the trial of a personal injury case, you were not allowed to mention to the jury – or to the judge – that the defendant was insured. If you did, it was regarded as so prejudicial to the defendant that there would have to be a new trial.

That was all altered by the Road Traffic Act 1930. Insurance was made compulsory. Everyone knew that defendants were insured. Both judge and jury were much more ready to find negligence and to increase the damages.

3 The coming of legal aid

1 Only for the poor

The first Legal Aid Act was passed on 30 July 1949. No longer is any person bound to bring 'his own suit upon his own bottom and at his own expense'. Those who are *poor* – of small means – can bring their cases at the expense of the state. They can have them conducted by lawyers of their own choice – without making any contribution out of their own pocket. They make a 'nil' contribution, as it is called. If they win, they pocket the winnings. If they lose, they do not have to pay any of the costs of the other side.

So also for those who are a little better off – except for this difference. They have to make a modest contribution – such as they can easily afford without any hardship – towards the costs of their own solicitor.

In any case where swift action is needed, an 'emergency certificate' can be granted: without any inquiry as to means. All that is required is a brief outline by the solicitor.

But for those who are reasonably well off – the middle classes – there is no legal aid at all. They still have to pay their own costs – and also those of the other side if they lose.

I will first describe the main principles: and then afterwards the drawbacks of the scheme.

2 There must be reasonable grounds

The fundamental principle is that a person should only be granted legal aid if he has reasonable grounds for taking or defending the proceedings: and that each step taken on his behalf by his solicitor should only be taken if it is a reasonable step for him to take. It is particularly to be noticed that no account is to be taken of any hardship this may involve on the other side. The claim of the person may in the end turn out to be completely unfounded. It may be a bogus claim altogether. Nevertheless, if there appears – on the person's own story – to be reasonable grounds for it – or for any step taken in respect of it – then the state has to pay for it. The other side has to suffer.

I am afraid that this test of 'reasonableness' has been very generously interpreted. Any claim is considered to be reasonable – any step is considered reasonable – if it is one which it would be reasonable for a litigant to take if he had ample means at his disposal.

3 Poverty to be disregarded

Seeing that his poverty is to be disregarded, it follows that the litigant is regarded as having ample means to pay. This was shown in the case of *Re Saxton decd.*[1] where there was a question whether a document was genuine or not. The plaintiffs got legal aid. They said the document was a forgery. They had no real evidence to show it was a forgery, but they wanted it examined by a very experienced expert and refused to show this report to the defendants who were not legally aided. I said (page 971):

'It seems very hard on the defendants that the plaintiffs should be able to conduct their case at the expense of the state, including the cost of employing a handwriting expert to make highly skilled scientific tests, and yet not disclose the result to the defendants. For it means that the defendants, in order to meet the plaintiffs' case, will have to employ a handwriting expert of their own, who will also have to make scientific tests, all at great expense, which they will have little or no chance of recovering from their legally-aided opponents.

Yet the legislature has told us that we must ignore this aspect of the case. The courts must disregard the fact that

1 [1962] 1 WLR 968.

parties are legally aided and must exercise their discretion in the way in which it would be exercised if they were not legally aided.'

4 Counsel's opinion carries the day

This is what happens every day. A man goes to a solicitor saying that he wants to claim against another man for misrepresentation or for personal injuries. He puts forward a plausible story. Sometimes he may produce a witness; sometimes not. He has no money but seeks to get legal aid. The solicitor (or maybe his clerk) feels that he must accept the man's word for it. After all, the man is his client. If he is believed, the man has a cause of action. The solicitor (or more likely his clerk) puts the case before counsel. He advises in writing that, on the man's own story – if believed – he has a reasonable cause of action. On that advice the Area Committee grant legal aid. They really have no option.

5 'Chuck it, Smith!'

But if it had not been legally aided, the solicitor would have been much more chary about taking it on. He would say to his client, 'Chuck it, Smith!' That is the colloquial phrase in which G K Chesterton rebuked Mr F E Smith for hypocrisy:[1]

> 'Talk about the pews and steeples
> And the cash that goes therewith!
> But the souls of Christian peoples . . .
>   Chuck it, Smith!'

The solicitor would go on to say: 'You won't get away with this. You will be throwing good money after bad. And if you lose you will have to pay the costs of the other side.' The case would never have been started except for legal aid.

The difficulty arises, of course, because the Area Committee have to come to a decision on hearing one side only. They face up

1 *A Ballade of an Anti-Puritan.*

to that difficulty – as best they can. They do their work most carefully and well. They are entitled to, and do, consider the merits.

6 A barrister is sued

That was well shown when a man brought an action against a barrister for negligence. He applied for legal aid. It was refused. Lord Chief Justice Parker said:

'It seems to me that it is for the committee to consider the whole of the circumstances, and, in considering whether to grant legal aid for any particular proceeding, to take into consideration the nature of the action as a whole, and whether or not there are reasonable grounds for pursuing that action. If one looks at it from the point of view of the use of public money or from the point of view of the unfortunate defendant who is at risk in relation to costs when proceeded against under legal aid, it would be quite wrong if the committee were not entitled to take into consideration what I may call the merits of the action itself.'

As it happened, leading counsel did appear in that case – without fee – owing to the importance of having a decision on the point.

7 Value of the scheme

The scheme has proved of immense worth to the community. Many persons have recovered debts or damages by means of legal aid which they would not otherwise have done. Many points of law of great importance have been taken to the Court of Appeal and the House of Lords – and finally resolved – which would otherwise have been left unresolved. But it is capable of being abused, as I will show.

8 Charge on property recovered or preserved

When I said that a legally-aided person is not liable for costs, that is subject to an important modification. If he succeeds in recovering money or property, then he has himself to pay his costs in this way. The Legal Aid Fund has a charge on any money or property recovered or preserved. This is only fair. If he had not been legally aided, his solicitor would have had such a charge. So also should the Legal Aid Fund have a charge.

A familiar instance is when a person is injured in an accident and recovers, let us say, £30,000 damages. He was legally aided. So his solicitor is paid by the Legal Aid Fund – let us say £4,000. The Legal Aid Fund can require this £4,000 to be retained out of the £30,000.

But great difficulties have arisen in the many disputes between husband and wife about the matrimonial home. Each is legally aided. Each makes a 'nil' contribution. Each claims that the house belongs to him – or her – or that he or she has an equal share in it. Each recovers property from the other or it is preserved for him or her. In any case the house is subject to a charge for costs in favour of the Legal Aid Fund. These costs may be so great as to wipe out the whole value of the house, save for £2,500 allowed free by the regulations. Moral for husbands and wives: Settle any dispute about the matrimonial home before you go to court – or at any rate before you appeal – else the costs will take away the whole value of the house itself.

4 Drawbacks of the scheme

1 Running up costs

One of the problems about legal aid is that solicitors have an interest in running up costs – for their own benefit – contrary to the interest of the taxpayer – and of the other side. And there is no effective means of stopping them: except by the Area Committee imposing limitations on what they do. I feel I must draw attention to this but I would not like you to think it is widespread. I will only tell you of a case where the solicitors in the utmost good faith did work for which their costs were afterwards disallowed.

2 Jumping off the pier

A man went to the sea for a diving course. He jumped off the pier into the water. There was some civil engineering work being done on the sea-bed. He hit some obstruction. His leg was so badly injured that it had to be amputated. He said that it was the fault of the diving instructors. He said that they ought to have been aware of the danger and warned him not to dive or to jump into the water at that time. He applied for legal aid. He was granted it. The action was tried for four days. The judge dismissed his claim altogether. He said it was the man's own fault.

So there it was. The defendants had fought the case at their own expense. They had to pay their own costs out of their own pockets – without any chance of getting anything out of the man – as he was legally aided. On the other hand the man had nothing to pay. His solicitors would be paid by the Legal Aid Fund.

There was one check on his solicitors. Their costs were subject to what is called 'taxation'. That means that their costs could be reviewed by an officer of the court to see if they were reasonable or not.

Now when the solicitors put in their bill, they sought to recover the cost of a conference held at the pier four years after the accident. Counsel had advised them to hold it. It was attended by counsel and by solicitors as well as a diving expert and a surveyor. They thought that it was well justified. Maybe it was. But unfortunately for the solicitors the taxing officer took a different view. He thought that it had been a useless exercise. The sea-bed, he said, was entirely different from what it had been at the date of the accident four years before: and the civil engineering work had been completed. So he disallowed these costs of the conference. The solicitors appealed. I would repeat here what I said in the Court of Appeal:

'Seeing that there is no one to oppose, it seems to me that, on a legal aid taxation, it is the duty of the taxing officer to bear in mind the public interest. He should himself disallow any item which is unreasonable in amount or which is unreasonably incurred. In short, whenever it is too high, he must tax it down. Otherwise, the legal aid system could be much abused by solicitors and counsel. Not that it was abused in this case. But there is the possibility of it unless closely watched. I cannot help remarking that, in a legally-aided case, counsel's fees are not marked on the brief. Nor is there any negotiation about them between counsel's clerk and the solicitor. The barrister's clerk claims the fee at what he thinks the case is worth. Solicitors' fees are often left to a subordinate in the office or even to an outside costs clerk who may claim to be paid commission on the amount of the bill as drawn by him – not as taxed by the taxing master. Unless the principals keep close watch, there is a temptation for the clerks to claim fees that are unreasonably high. I do not suggest that they do so. But there is a temptation for them to say: "It will be knocked down. 10 per cent, comes off anyway. It is a legally-aided case. The Fund will pay." If the costs are passed without inquiry, the Fund will suffer. The public will have to pay more than they should. Very often the legal aid certificate is expressed in such wide terms as to give the solicitors a "blanket" authority to conduct the proceedings, covering all items concerned in the course of it – without going to the Area Committee for specific authority. No doubt the certificate in the present case covered everything done in preparation for trial and of the trial itself. In any such case it is of the first importance that the taxing officer should go through all the items and see that there is no over-charging in any respect. Lawyers must not think that, on getting a certificate for legal aid, they have a blank cheque to draw upon the Legal Aid Fund – as if it were a client with a bottomless purse – ready to pay for everything the lawyer can think of. The only safeguard against abuse is the vigilance of the taxing master. He has a difficult task. With no one to oppose it, he has to take much of the solicitor's word for granted – as to the work done. It would be easy for him to let everything through without question. But he must resist that easy course. He must be a watch-dog. He must bark when there is anything that arouses his suspicions.'

3 Settling cases

Another problem in legal aid cases is the immense superiority which is given to the legally-aided person when it comes to settling a case. He has this trump card in his hand. He can go on with the case at the expense of the state, whereas the other side has to pay out of his own pocket and would get no costs from the legally-aided person.

Many many times the defendants or their insurers have given way. It is far cheaper for them to pay the plaintiff a goodly sum than to pay all their own costs. So whilst the legal aid authorities often claim proudly their successes, it must be remembered that sometimes it is a success tainted with menaces.

4 The echo sounder

There are other cases where the grant of legal aid to one side may operate hardly against the other. Let me tell you of one where it might have done so but in the end did not.

An inventor invented an echo sounder. It was for use in large ships. They could tell the depth of water by the time it took for the echo to reach back from the sea-bed. He entered into an agreement with a big firm for them to exploit it. They were to exploit it if it came up to their requirements. But it failed to do so. So they refused to go on with it. He alleged that they were guilty of a breach of contract. He claimed damages, huge damages, because of the loss of profit he said he would have made.

He got legal aid. The trial was estimated to last for thirty days. He was himself insolvent. The big firm were ready to pay £40,000 to get rid of the claim altogether, rather than incur the expense of fighting the case over thirty days against a legally-aided plaintiff. He said he would accept the £40,000 provided that it was used to pay off his creditors. But he would not accept it if the £40,000 was to go to the Legal Aid Fund in priority to his creditors. He said in effect:

'Unless things can be settled on my lines, I insist on the action going on for trial for the thirty days – and that will put the big firm and the Legal Aid Fund to enormous expense in costs.'

The inventor did not get his own way. His solicitors acted very properly. They put everything before counsel, and on his advice before the Law Society and afterwards before the court. I would repeat what I said:

'This case brings out vividly the responsibility which attaches to legal advisers who conduct an action for a legally-aided person. They must remember that they are funded at the expense of the state, and that they are putting the defendant (who is not legally aided) to a great deal of worry and expense in contesting the case – a defendant who will not recover any of his costs even if he wins. This puts the legal advisers for the plaintiff in an extremely strong bargaining position. There is inequality of bargaining power. They should not abuse it at the expense of the defendant. Nor should they abuse it at the expense of the Legal Aid Fund. Whenever the question of a settlement comes up, the legal advisers for the plaintiff should consider any offer on the merits of the case itself, just as if they were acting for a private client of moderate means, not one who is wealthy enough to go to any expense, or one who is very much in debt already, against a defendant who is also of moderate means and will get an order for costs against the plaintiff if he wins. Once a figure is reached which is reasonable, they should settle the case at that figure. They should not try to manipulate its destination so as to avoid the statutory charge. In particular, they should not make the sum payable to the creditors of the plaintiff or to anyone other than the plaintiff. If they should do so, they will find that they will incur the displeasure of the court, which will see that their manipulations do not succeed.'

5 Pity the unassisted person

It is most unjust to an innocent person that he should have to fight a legally-aided person – and win – and yet have to pay his own costs. The villain of the piece – in the eyes of the innocent person – is the Legal Aid Fund. They have financed the claim – or the defence. Without legal aid the plaintiff might never have sued at all – or the defendant might never have put on a defence. The Legal Aid Fund have, beyond doubt, 'maintained' the claim or defence as the case may be. At common law they would be guilty, not only of a wrong, but of a crime. Yet under the Legal Aid Act 1949 they get away scot-free.

In 1964 the injustice was recognised by Parliament. But the statute gave a most inadequate remedy. If the unassisted person succeeded in the court of first instance he could only get his costs from the Legal Aid Fund in these circumstances: first, if he was the defendant in the case – not if he was the plaintiff; second, if it would cause him 'serious financial hardship' to have to pay his own costs.

These conditions have been found to be most unjust. Take the first condition. In many cases an innocent plaintiff (who is unassisted) has an unanswerable claim for debt or damages. There is no defence but the defendant puts up a cock-and-bull story to avoid payment. In one action on bills of exchange for

£4,000, the defendant simply did not admit his signature on the bills. But he got legal aid and took the case to appeal – where his defence was seen to be hopeless. The unassisted plaintiff got no costs against the Legal Aid Fund.

Take next the second condition. It 'must cause the unassisted party serious financial hardship'. These words were considered by the Court of Appeal in another case where I said:

'The words should be construed so as to exclude insurance companies; and commercial companies who are in a considerable way of business; and wealthy folk who can meet the costs without feeling it. But they should not be construed so as to exclude people of modest income or modest capital who would find it hard to bear their own costs.'

I must say that I see no justice whatever in this second condition. If the Legal Aid Fund support a hopeless case and put an insurance company or commercial company to much expense in defending it, why should not the Legal Aid Fund pay the costs? By not paying costs, the legally-aided person can exert a form of pressure: 'Pay me something or else I will go on with the case and you will not get any costs out of me.'

6 The surgeon pulled too hard and too long

Thus far I have spoken of the costs in courts only of first instance. In the Court of Appeal, things are much fairer. The court has power to award costs out of the Legal Aid Fund when it is 'just and equitable' (section 13 (2) of the 1974 Act). The Court of Appeal and the House of Lords now regularly make the Legal Aid Fund pay all the costs when they have supported an appeal, or resisted it, and lose.

One instance of this is where a child was born with severe brain damage. The mother put the blame on the surgeon. She said that in the course of carrying out a 'trial of forceps delivery' he pulled too hard and too long upon the child's head and that this caused the brain damage. She got legal aid to sue the surgeon and the hospital. No expense was spared. Two most eminent professors on each side. Eminent Queen's Counsel on each side.

The trial judge found the surgeon and the hospital negligent and awarded £100,000 damages. They appealed to the Court of Appeal. They won there. The mother appealed to the House of Lords. She lost there. So the surgeon and the hospital won both in the Court of Appeal and in the House of Lords. The Legal Aid Fund had to pay their costs in both those tribunals, but not their costs at first instance because there was no 'serious financial hardship' to them. The Legal Aid Fund had, of course, to pay the costs of the mother all the way through. The total costs of the case to the Legal Aid Fund came to £250,000.

7 The man who jumped out of the window

Another instance is where a man went into hospital because he had pain in his back. It got worse. He was very depressed about it. He went round the ward telling other patients. He told the nurses. They were sympathetic. He imagined that it was cancer and that he might die of it. So one night he decided to end it all. He wrote loving letters to his wife and family. He told them that he would be dead by the time they received them. He got out of bed, opened the window, and jumped out. He fell first on to a balcony. Then he leaped from it on to the ground below. He was very badly injured but was not dead. He was taken in and lived. But he was paralysed in all four limbs – a quadriplegic – bedridden for the rest of his days – with his wife having to spend all her time looking after him.

He got legal aid. He alleged that the nurses were negligent. They ought to have called in a psychiatrist: and he might have been able to do something to prevent him attempting to commit suicide. Doctors of eminence were called on both sides. The judge found in favour of the man and awarded him £200,000 damages against the hospital. The hospital appealed. The appeal was allowed. The man got nothing. The costs of the appeal had to be paid by the Legal Aid Fund – of both sides. Of the man's side because he had been granted legal aid. Of the hospital's side because it was just and equitable.

But the cost of the trial at first instance had to be borne – of the man's side – by the Legal Aid Fund. And of the hospital's side – by the hospital authorities – because it did not inflict 'serious financial hardship' on them.

No doubt it was quite right for legal aid to have been granted. The decision of the trial judge shows it – it was in favour of the injured man. But there are other cases where the event may show it to be unfortunate that legal aid was ever granted.

I remember a case where a baby was born prematurely. The hospital saved its life by giving it oxygen, but that resulted in it becoming blind. Legal aid was given. Much expense at first instance and on appeal. The claim failed.

8 Don't leave it to the unadmitted clerk

Only too often, I fear, the solicitors leave legal aid cases to their clerks. This is a mistake. It may involve them – or the other side – in much trouble. It was the cause of all the trouble on the sale of a photographic business. The owners agreed to sell it to a purchaser for £8,500, payable by instalments. The purchaser took possession of the business. He paid the first instalment but did not pay the rest. The owners sued for the balance. The purchaser had no money. He got legal aid. His defence admitted the claim but said that the agreement was induced by fraud and put in a counterclaim for fraud. The solicitors for the purchaser left it to a young articled clerk (not yet admitted) to fill in the legal aid form. He filled it in with a mistake. He only applied for legal aid to 'defend'. He did not apply for legal aid to 'counterclaim'. The certificate granted by the Committee followed the wording of the application. Thereafter both sides proceeded on the footing that legal aid had been granted for 'Defence and Counterclaim'. The whole fight was on the counterclaim: but owing to the mistake, the owners (who had suffered 'serious financial hardship') could recover nothing from the Legal Aid Fund.

I made this comment:

'So here we have presented to us at its most ugly the "unacceptable face" of British justice. The owners came to the courts of law to obtain sums from a debtor which were undoubtedly due to them. They were baulked by the grant of legal aid to the defendant. Their own costs came to £7,000. When they sought to recover those costs from the Legal Aid Fund, they were met by the plea: "You cannot recover them because a mistake was made in the legal aid certificate and it cannot be corrected". That plea has succeeded. I hang my head in shame that it should be so.'

9 Never work on a contingency fee

Legal aid has saved us from the 'ambulance-chasers' and from any danger of 'contingency fees'. That is much to be thankful for. The truth about them is vividly illustrated by a recent case.[1]

A motor vessel, owned by a company incorporated in Texas, USA, was engaged in carrying supplies to oil rigs in the North Sea. She was lying at Great Yarmouth in Norfolk. One of the crew was the plaintiff, a Portuguese. He was transferring oil from a drum to a tank – by a pipe with compressed air. A valve flew off and went into his neck. It penetrated his spinal cord. He was completely paralysed in his arms and legs – a quadriplegic. He was completely dependent on others for everything. Both by day and night.

He was in Stoke Mandeville hospital for nine months. He was well looked after there. The employers treated him very well. They continued to pay him his full salary. They arranged for members of his family to visit him from Portugal. They paid all their expenses. Their representative visited him regularly once a month to see to his welfare. After nine months, the doctors thought it would be better for him to be with his wife and family in Portugal. So his employers arranged for a specially fitted plane to take him back to Portugal. They also provided special equipment at his home in Portugal – so as to enable him to get about. Their representative in Lisbon visited him at his home – so as to do all they could for him and his family. His wife was

1 *Castanho v Brown and Root (UK) Ltd* [1980] 1 WLR 823, [1981] AC 557.

very good. She did everything for him. The only thing outstanding was the amount of compensation to be paid to him.

The Portuguese Consulate put him in touch with a good firm of solicitors in London. They issued a writ against the employers for negligence. The action was progressing well. The employers admitted liability. They were ready to settle the case by paying him £200,000 and costs. That would be ample compensation by English standards, or also by Portuguese standards.

But then a firm of solicitors from Texas came on the scene. They went over to Portugal and persuaded the man to drop the English proceedings and get the litigation to Texas. If the case was tried there the man could expect to get very high damages, perhaps as much as $5,000,000 (that is, about £2,500,000): and 40 per cent of that sum would go to the Texan lawyers. 40 per cent was the 'contingency fee' payable to the Texan lawyers if they won – and nothing if they lost. In short the Texan lawyers would get a very large sum out of it.

The trial judge here would not let the case go to Texas but in the Court of Appeal the majority of two thought it should go to Texas and that view was confirmed unanimously by five Law Lords. So two judges thought the claim ought to remain in England but seven others thought it should be transferred to Texas, if the American court would accept it. It was still going on in the American court a little while ago.

That case has a lesson for us in England. Never, never allow lawyers to work on the basis of a 'contingency fee'.

10 The case is settled

News has just come to hand that the case has been settled. The Texan company which owned the vessel was insured with a big American insurance company and also with Lloyd's and a syndicate of British insurance companies. They paid a sum of £1,500,000 damages to the man but of that sum he only received £800,000. I expect much of the remainder went to the lawyers. No doubt thay had considerable expenses but, even so, it was a very large sum indeed. The lawyers did exceedingly well out of it.

5 Criminal legal aid

1 No legal aid in former times

In former times there was no legal aid for any accused man. For many years he was not allowed counsel on a charge of felony – though he was on a misdemeanour. He was not even allowed to give evidence on his own behalf – not in any case either in felony or misdemeanour. All that he could do was to make a statement from the dock.

Blackstone condemned the rule by which he was not allowed counsel on his trial for a capital crime. He said[1] that it

> 'seems to be not at all of a piece with the rest of the humane treatment of prisoners by the English law. . . . And, to say the truth, the judges themselves are so sensible of this defect in our modern practice, that they seldom scruple to allow a prisoner counsel to stand by him at the bar, and instruct him what questions to ask, or even to ask questions for him, with respect to matters of fact: for as to matters of law, arising on the trial, they are *entitled* to the assistance of counsel. But still this is a matter of too much importance to be left to the good pleasure of any judge, and is worthy of the interposition of the legislature.'

2 Dock brief

By a statute passed in 1836 the accused was allowed to have counsel on a charge of felony – as well as on other cases. But

1 *Commentaries* IV, 355–356.

always at his own expense; so there was rarely counsel. When I was at the Bar there was a scheme – in difficult cases – of poor prisoner's defence – paid out of county funds. Otherwise, the only way of having counsel was by means of a 'dock brief'. To get it the accused had to find £1 3s 6d of his own money or from friends or relatives. Most young counsel starting at the Bar would go to Quarter Sessions or to Assizes – and sit in court when the prisoners were put up to plead – hoping that some of them would ask for a dock brief. The judge used to ask the prisoner:

'Have you got £1 3s 6d?'
Answer: 'Yes.'
'Then you can have any of the gentlemen sitting there.'

The accused could only see the backs of their wigs. So he had to take his chance. He pointed to one or other, hoping for the best. The judge (having been covertly told his name) said:

'Mr Smith, will you defend him?'

Mr Smith bowed and went down to the cells, saw the accused man and got his instructions. Often there was only half-an-hour for it. The case was then called on.

3 Legal aid now

Legal aid in civil cases dates from 1949. That is under the control of the Law Society. Legal aid in criminal cases only dates from 1967. It is paid by the Secretary of State for Home Affairs. It is under the control of the courts. But in point of practice legal aid is given almost automatically to every accused man who asks for it and says or pretends that he has not the wherewithal to pay. Not only when he denies his guilt, but also when he admits it and desires only to make a plea in mitigation of sentence. In many a magistrates' court there is a 'duty solicitor' on duty who will conduct the case for any person who desires it. Sometimes counsel are instructed too. In the Crown Courts counsel are nearly always employed.

Many people now think that the great increase in the number of cases tried by juries – and in the length of them – is due to legal aid. An accused person, who is obviously guilty, will plead 'Not Guilty': he is only too glad to put the prosecution to much expenditure of time and money. He has nothing to lose – and the outside chance that he may be acquitted. His lawyers – some of them – may encourage him in this attitude. It means more work for them and more fees. Often there is a case which could be disposed of in the magistrates' court. Instead of consenting to it being dealt with there, the accused and his lawyers will demand trial by jury. Again it means more work for the lawyers and more fees. Often there is a case with several persons accused. Each of them will be represented by leading counsel and juniors – each separately – each putting the same questions to the witnesses.

To put it bluntly – the beneficiaries of legal aid fall into two categories: first, the accused person, whether guilty or not; second, the legal profession. Some chambers have a dozen young barristers available to take briefs in small criminal cases. Each evening solicitors need a young barrister for this case or that. They ring up the barrister's clerk. He distributes the cases round to his young people.

4 Waiting time

In magistrates' courts accused persons are often given legal aid. They are often represented by solicitors and sometimes by counsel. But the unique factor is that the solicitors are paid for what is called 'waiting time'. Such a payment was never heard of before the introduction of legal aid. The solicitor or counsel got the brief fee for attendance. If he was kept waiting for his case to come on, that was just bad luck. It was the luck of the draw. It was not fair on the client that he should have to pay more than the proper fee for the solicitor or counsel to conduct the case. But with the legal aid scheme, there has been no client to worry about. So lawyers in the magistrates' courts have been paid £20 (now £15) an hour for waiting time. The result was vividly described in the *New Law Journal* of 30 July 1981:

'In one of London's more popular magistrates' courts (when the list was marked for 10.30 a.m.), I counted not less than eleven advocates awaiting the hearing of their cases at 12.45 p.m. . . . A number of us had to come back after lunch at yet more public cost. . . . Vast sums of money are wasted every day . . . by advocates hanging around being paid to do the crossword and chat with their friends.

. . . What can be done to accelerate summary justice in both London and the provinces and at the same time save costs? . . . One would be the elimination of the coffee break for justices . . . [and] the seemingly endless remands which are readily granted to both prosecution and defence.'

And so forth.

It appears that 'waiting time' accounts for 20 per cent of the payments to solicitors for costs in the lower courts. I often wonder whether it is possible for the court officer to know how accurate are the claims for 'waiting time'. No doubt he has to take the solicitors' word for it. Let us hope they are very conscientious about it.

6 Proposals for consideration

I Costs of unassisted persons

In thinking of the future, I would explain that legal aid is an extreme form of maintenance. It means that the state is maintaining litigation in which it has no legitimate interest or concern – save the sympathy which everyone has for any man who goes to law or is taken to it. Whereas the maxim of the Roman law was: '*Interest rei publicae ut sit finis litium*' (It is in the interest of the state that there should be an end of litigation), the maxim of English law under its new face is that: 'It is in the interest of the state that there should be an infinity of litigation – all paid for by the state'. No doubt it is in the interest of the legal profession, but for myself I do not think it is in the interest of the state.

I start by reminding you of the modern law about maintenance. I stated it in 1968 in this way:

'Much maintenance is considered justifiable today which would in 1914 have been considered obnoxious. Most of the actions in our courts are supported by some association or other, or by the state itself. Comparatively few litigants bring suits, or defend them, at their own expense. Most claims by workmen against their employers are paid for by a trade union. Most defences of motorists are paid for by insurance companies. This is perfectly justifiable and is accepted by everyone as lawful, provided always that the one who supports the litigation, if it fails, pays the costs of the other side. It is the universal experience in this court that if a trade union or an insurance company supports a case and fails, it pays the costs of the other side.'

The governing words are: 'provided always that the one who supports the litigation, if it fails, pays the costs of the other side'.

111

That is where the Legal Aid Fund at present goes free. It does not pay the costs when it fails. It ought to do so. Parliament ought at once to amend the Legal Aid Acts so as to make the Legal Aid Fund pay the costs at first instance – if it fails – irrespective of who starts the proceedings and irrespective of the question of 'serious financial hardship'. The court should have power to order it when it is 'just and equitable'. Recent cases have shown up the need for reform of the Legal Aid Acts and of the system itself.

The first thing is the immense power which the system puts into the hands of the legally-aided person as against the other side who is not legally-aided. The legally-aided person is backed by the unlimited financial resources of the state. He has the power to carry on the litigation indefinitely till the other side is exhausted. The certificate is often expressed in such wide terms that it covers the whole conduct of the suit, through all the interlocutory proceedings, right through to the end. It sometimes gives the solicitor a 'blanket' authority to consult experts and to call them at the trial. In some cases the expense is colossal, as in the medical negligence cases. If there are negotiations for a settlement, the legally-aided person can – and sometimes does – say to the other: 'Unless you settle on my terms, I will go on with the trial – at no expense to me – but at your expense entirely', with the result that unassisted defendants will often pay the demand of the legally-aided plaintiff rather than spend money on fighting the case; or an unassisted plaintiff will take much less than is due to him from a legally-aided defendant because it is not worth while spending any more money on the case. The most significant reform would be that, when the legally-aided person fails in his action or defence, the Legal Aid Fund should pay the costs of the unassisted party – just as any other litigant who fails.

2 A new principle for granting legal aid

The governing principle at present is that a person is not to be given legal aid unless he has reasonable grounds for taking or defending the proceedings. That seems fair enough. But there is this qualification to be made from the decided cases: You are to disregard the fact that one party is legally aided, or may be legally aided: and the other is not. This raises the question: How are you to regard any party who applies for legal aid? Or the other side who is opposed to him? I am afraid that in practice both are regarded as having unlimited means at their disposal. The plaintiff, who is granted legal aid, is able to employ experts of the highest rank and Queen's Counsel of the utmost eminence – just as if the expense made no odds to him – as indeed it does not – because it is the state who pays. The defendant, who is opposing the claim, is regarded as having as much means at his disposal as the largest insurance company or nationalised corporation or the National Health Service.

I think that it is wrong. Take the cases of which there have been several lately. I have already told you of the man who went into hospital: and whilst there, he tried to commit suicide. He failed, but injured himself so badly that he was rendered a quadriplegic for life. If legal aid had not been available – and he had been of modest means – he might not have sued the hospital at all. He would not have had the money to do it: and the risk of his failing – and having to pay the costs of the other side – would probably have been so great as to make it out of the question. Likewise in the other case of which I have told you where a mother had a premature baby – so weak it would have died unless given oxygen. No one of ordinary means could have contemplated the substantial risk of losing.

It seems to me that the grant of legal aid should not be dependent on the advice of counsel who writes: 'I think there are reasonable grounds for taking or defending proceedings'. The Area Committee should consider these questions: Is this a proper case in which the plaintiff's claim should be financed by the state? Is it a proper case in which the defendant should be put to the cost of defending it – at his own expense – without any hope of recovering it from any source if he wins?

3 What should be the income limit?

It is a remarkable thing that in the many cases in the courts lately against hospitals, the plaintiffs were all persons of little or no means – who have a grievance because the treatment did not turn out as well as they expected. They get legal aid – on the advice of solicitors – seeking large damages. None of the cases are brought by middle-class people who are not eligible for legal aid. They could not afford it for one thing. Another thing is that, by being better educated, they realise that operations involve risks and untoward consequences. They do not seek to make money out of misfortunes. I ask the question: Why should these persons in the lower income groups be given so great aid – to harass hospitals and impoverish them – when middle-class persons do not? Or more generally: Why should persons in the lower income groups be given legal aid – so as to harass persons in the middle-class bracket – who are not eligible for it?

The truth is that people in the middle-class bracket are now sorely hit by the cost of litigation. They are forced to give up good claims because they dare not risk the cost of enforcing them. A recent case was noted in *The Sunday Times*. A householder employed a big building firm to do work on his house. They did their work so badly on his house that it would cost him some thousands of pounds to put it right. They offered him £5,500. He felt he had to settle because he simply could not afford to fight on. After paying his own costs and doing the work, this left him £3,500 out of pocket. The newspaper comment was this:

> 'Lawyers are becoming more and more concerned about cases like this. The chairman of the Young Solicitors' Group said: "There is a certain group of people in this country who cannot afford to litigate. This is the middle range with incomes between £5,000 and £10,000." '

This leads me to suggest that legal aid should be extended to include all the middle range of incomes. Limited companies should still be excluded: and also those persons who are supported by insurance companies and trade unions.

4 Husband and wife

Cases between husband and wife – about custody and access to the children – or about the matrimonial home – are in a class by themselves. Often enough both sides are legally aided. Each tells a story to his solicitor which gives a reasonable ground for taking or resisting proceedings. One or other fails. Each side gets legal aid for appeal. The Legal Aid Fund pays the costs of both sides. I suggest that the Area Committee should ask themselves: Is it right that this litigation should be financed by the state? Often social conditions may give the answer 'Yes'. But not always.

5 Duty towards the Legal Aid Fund

Traditionally the duty of a solicitor is to his client – who retains him and pays him his fees and disbursements. But when his client is legally aided, I suggest that the solicitor owes a duty – not only to his client – but also to the Legal Aid Fund which pays him. His duty towards the Fund is not to involve the Fund in any unreasonable or unnecessary expense. He owes a duty also to the other side – not to use the legal aid as a means to oppress or harass the other side – or to extort an unreasonable settlement. He owes a duty to be absolutely honest – such as only to charge 'waiting time' when it is justified – and in keeping account of what he does and for what he charges. Unless he does so, his claim for payment cannot be checked at all.

These standards are so important that they should be inculcated as part of the training of every solicitor and legal executive. Any departure from them should be reported to the Professional Purposes Committee of the Law Society. As I put it in a recent case:

'I know that the legal aid system has done great good for a great many people. But the profession must remember that, when seeking legal aid, they are under a special responsibility to see that it is wisely and carefully administered. It is to be used only in cases where it is justified: and not to support thin cases of little merit: nor the uncorroborated word of dubious parties. It must not be used so as to incur extravagant or unnecessary expense: or so as to take unfair advantage of the unassisted party.'

Conclusion

Legal aid has conferred great benefits on a section of the community – those who only have modest means – and on the members of the legal profession – who are paid by the state for their services. But it has been accompanied by a vast increase in litigation, by congestion in the courts, by long delays before cases are heard, by the need for more and more judges and for more and more courts, and by an increase in the number of lawyers. It is far too late now to attempt to abolish it. All that can be attempted is to remedy the abuses which are incidental to it.

I should like to see the following:

1 Legal aid should be granted with circumspection, not without careful consideration of the consequences. It should not be used as an instrument of oppression against other parties who are not legally aided. It should not be used so as to exert undue pressure for a settlement. It should not be used so as to run up the costs in extravagant fees or expenses. It should not be used so as to delay or deny right or justice.

2 If a person who gets legal aid loses his case – or any issue in a case – against a person who is unassisted, the Legal Aid Fund should, as a rule, pay the costs of the unassisted person. Irrespective of who started the litigation and irrespective of the means of the unassisted person.

3 Legal aid should be extended so as to be available to persons in the middle range of incomes.

It is with all this in mind that I have written this Part. So as to make you think about it.

Part four

Personal injuries

1 The Royal Commission Report is shelved

The law as to personal injuries is in urgent need of reform. A Royal Commission has recently considered it. The Chairman was my dear friend Lord Pearson. Almost my exact contemporary. He was one of the best of judges of our time. Whilst still in the Lords in 1973 he undertook this most important task. He was supported by a very able team of commissioners representative of all interests. He continued it after his retirement in 1974 – without pay. No members of Royal Commissions are ever paid. Even so, it cost nearly £1½ million. I expect it was spent on their staff and offices and on investigations in other countries. The task took five years. Lord Pearson was very anxious to present a unanimous Report. He knew, as do we all, that unless a Report is unanimous it has very little chance of acceptance. He succeeded. The recommendations – numbering 188 – were unanimous in all but 19: and those 19 were very subsidiary. He was conscientious and careful, courteous and patient, able and intelligent – beyond compare. His Report[1] presented in 1978 is a monumental work.

Yet it has been 'shelved' by successive governments. Nothing has been done to implement it. I often wonder who reads the Reports of Royal Commissions. This Report was commissioned in 1973 by the Home Secretary of the day, a Conservative – Mr Robert Carr, MP.

It was presented in 1978 to the then Home Secretary who was Labour – Mr Merlyn Rees, MP. It was not a matter which should have raised any issue of party politics. I expect it was studied by some of the civil servants in the Home Office and maybe in the

1 Report of Royal Commission on Civil Liability and Compensation for Personal Injury (Cmnd 7054–1).

Lord Chancellor's Department. It may have passed round other government departments for information. I can say for sure that none of the judiciary were provided with it or read it or were asked for their comments on it. There has been a debate in the House of Lords on one section of it – on product liability. No doubt some members of the House read that section. But otherwise I doubt very much whether the whole of it has been read by more than a handful of them. No doubt many read the recommendations. But very few of them would have time to read the text of 388 pages of print. I suspect that the decision to 'shelve' it – that is, to put it on the shelf until there is more time to consider it – was taken by ministers on the advice of the civil servants.

At the very last moment as these pages are being revised, some attempt is being made to implement one or two recommendations of the Report, but these are very disappointing as I will tell you later (see Addendum, page 156).

2 Old days

The Royal Commission dealt with many things. I will confine myself mainly to road traffic: because it is the most important. The present law is based upon the law laid down in the nineteenth century. At that time traffic on the roads was by horses and carts – and pedestrians. But also there were many cases on the railways.

1 Negligence must be proved

When a person is injured or killed in a road accident, the law always was – and still is – loaded heavily against him. It is because the burden is on him to prove that the defendant was negligent. If he leaves the matter in doubt – so that it is uncertain whether the defendant was negligent or not – the plaintiff fails. It is this rule which operates so heavily under our present system. The plaintiff may be so badly injured that he cannot remember what happened: or he may be killed. There may be no witnesses. He gets nothing because he cannot prove negligence. Time after time in the old days juries used to find for the plaintiff – in cases where I should have thought there was evidence of negligence – but the judges set their verdicts aside. Thus, a woman was run over by a horse-drawn omnibus and killed. The driver admitted that he was not looking out at the time and had turned round to speak to the conductor. The jury found for the plaintiff, but the court set their verdict aside: see *Cotton v Wood*.[1] Again, a man crossing a public level-crossing at night was run over by a train and killed. It was admitted that the train driver did not whistle.

1 (1860) 8 CBNS 568.

The jury found for the plaintiff, but the House of Lords set aside the verdict: see *Wakelin v LSWR*.[1] Lord Halsbury said callously (page 45):

> 'In this case I am unable to see any evidence of how this unfortunate calamity occurred. One may surmise, and it is but surmise and not evidence, that the unfortunate man was knocked down by a passing train while on the level-crossing: but, assuming in the plaintiff's favour that to be established, is there anything to show that the train ran over the man rather than that the man ran against the train?'

In dozens of cases in my young days the judge used to throw out the case at the end of the plaintiff's evidence. 'No case to go to the jury', he would say. That was the end of it.

Nowadays these cases are no longer tried by juries. But the judges have still to apply the rule of law. The burden is on the plaintiff to prove negligence. A little child in the road is run over and killed: a grown-up is crossing the road and is rendered unconscious. There are no witnesses. The driver says it was not his fault. He was keeping a good look-out and had no chance to avoid the accident. No compensation is payable at all.

2 Contributory negligence was fatal

Even though the plaintiff did succeed in proving that the defendant was negligent, the law used to be that the plaintiff could not succeed – he could not recover a penny – if he was in any way at fault himself. If he could at the last moment have avoided the accident by taking reasonable care himself, he could recover nothing. In 1809 in *Butterfield v Forrester*[2] the defendant put up a pole halfway across the road. It was a dangerous obstruction. It was clearly negligent of him to put it there. It was getting dark – 'just when they were beginning to light candles'. The plaintiff came along the road riding his horse. He did not see the pole. He was thrown down with his horse and injured. He failed because it was said he did not take reasonable care himself.

1 (1886) 12 App Cas 41.
2 (1809) 11 East 60.

3 The donkey is hobbled

This harsh rule was mitigated by one of the most cited cases in our books at that time. It was the donkey case, *Davies v Mann*.[1] The plaintiff had a donkey. He left it to graze on some grass at the side of the highway. He tethered its forefeet so that it could only hobble. It could not go off any distance. The defendant came along with a waggon pulled by a team of three horses. It was going at a 'smartish pace'. It knocked down the donkey; the wheels passed over it. The donkey died. The jury found for the plaintiff. The court upheld the verdict. They did it because, although the owner of the donkey was at fault, the driver of the waggon was going too fast. He had the last opportunity of avoiding the accident.

> 'Were this not so', said Mr Baron Parke, 'a man might justify the driving over goods left on a public highway, or even over a man lying there, or the purposely running against a carriage going on the wrong side of the road.'

4 Parliament puts things right

For over 100 years those two cases were repeatedly cited in the courts. The question was asked: 'Which of the two had the last opportunity of avoiding the accident?' Countless cases were reported upon it – until eventually in 1945 there was passed the Law Reform (Contributory Negligence) Act. It said that, even if the plaintiff was at fault himself, he was not to be defeated; he was to recover such proportion of the damages as were just and equitable.

This reform was an outstanding success. Lord du Parcq made a funeral oration on the demise of the doctrine of last opportunity:

> 'How much has been swept away with the debris of the rule – what a mass of verbal refinements, of logic-chopping, of the results of pointless microscopical research! . . . I was a sinner myself when the occasion seemed to demand it. . . . I remember how Lord Justice Scrutton one day torpedoed my argument by

1 (1842) 10 M & W 546.

asking, "If two men walking in opposite directions with their eyes shut, run into one another, which of them has the last opportunity of avoiding the accident?" '

5 But still much uncertainty

Nowadays in many of the road traffic cases, both sides are to blame: and the damages are apportioned according to what is just and equitable. But this also may lead to great uncertainty. Take the case of *Baker v Market Harborough Industrial Co-operative Society Ltd.*[1] Early in the morning, when it was still dark, a motor-lorry came into collision with a motor-van. Both drivers were killed. No one witnessed the accident. The road-marks gave no clue as to who was at fault. Nor did the damage to the vehicles. Each driver sued the employers of the other driver. Neither could prove negligence. According to strict law, each claim should have been dismissed. But somewhat illogically both drivers were held equally to blame. Now suppose each driver had lived: and that each had brought a separate action against the employers of the other driver. Each might win his case and get full damages. That shows how uncertain are these cases.

6 No insurance in old days

At the time when the law was being formed, very few drivers were insured against third-party claims. There was no compulsory insurance. An injured person had to pay his own costs of bringing a claim. He would not sue unless the defendant was 'worth powder and shot'. That is why most of the cases in the nineteenth century were brought against railway companies. They had ample means to pay damages.

If the defendant was not a railway company but a private individual, or a small firm, then even if they were insured against liability, no one was to tell the jury that the defendant was insured. It was forbidden. It was thought that the jury would be influenced by sympathy to find for the plaintiff or to give him too much by way of damages.

1 [1953] 1 WLR 1472 at 1476.

7 The plaintiff is insured

In some cases the plaintiff insured himself against accidents, but if he did so the insurance moneys did not go in reduction of damages. Thus in *Bradburn v GWR*[1] a passenger was injured by the negligence of the railway company's servant. A jury awarded him £217 damages. But it appeared that he had insured himself against accidents and had received £31 from the insurance company. The railway company argued that that sum should be taken in reduction of the damages. The argument was rejected out of hand. Mr Baron Bramwell said: 'One is dismayed at the prospect'.

This ruling has been applied in many analogous situations. If a man is given sums by a charity, or if he gets a pension from his employers – as a result of the accident – it does not go in reduction of damages: see *Parry v Cleaver*.[2]

What is the reason for these rulings? It is because the defendant has committed a tort. He has done wrong. He should pay the full compensation to the plaintiff for the harm he has done him. He should not be allowed to reduce that compensation by saying: 'You have also got compensation from someone else.'

1 (1874) LR 10 Exch 1.
2 [1970] AC 1.

3 Modern times

Such is the law we inherit from times past. It is still the law we apply today. But things have changed so much that to my mind the law itself should be changed. The three great changes are: (1) the speed and danger of motor traffic; (2) the introduction of compulsory insurance; and (3) the introduction of social security benefits – for injury or disablement – on a substantial financial scale. I will consider all of these.

1 Motors are dangerous things

When I was a boy, all movement on the roads was by horse or on foot. There were the farm waggons going slowly along – with loads of hay – or bags of corn – drawn by two horses. There were the tradesmen's vans going more smartly – with one pony – but stopping every few yards to deliver their wares. There was the occasional gentleman's carriage driven by his coachman. There was the man on his horse coming to do business. So far as I remember there were rarely any road accidents. I never heard of anyone in our parts being injured or killed. The reason was that everything was slower. You could see what was coming. You could hear what was coming. You had time to take avoiding action. No need for split-second decisions. That was the sort of traffic for which the judges of the nineteenth century laid down the rules about liability for road accidents.

So it was for the first twenty years of this century. In 1910 motor-cars were a rarity. My wife's father had the first one registered in London – 'No. 1, London'. You got in the back like a trap. She drove it at the age of eleven. Snorting and smelling, these pre-war vehicles went only about 20 miles an hour. They often broke down. When they were coming, you could easily get out of the way. Even during the First World War my Field Company of Engineers had horses and waggon transport. No motor transport at all.

Now all is different. Motor vehicles are things that are dangerous in themselves. They traverse the roads at great speeds. They go round bends swiftly and silently. You do not hear them coming. They do not hoot. You do not have time to get out of the way. When any emergency arises, the driver has to make a split-second decision – to swerve or to go ahead or to brake. His decision is an exercise of judgment. Even if it turns out to be an error, it cannot always be said to be negligent. It is at most an error of judgment – without negligence. The error may – and sometimes does – kill or maim innocent people. They may be left without witnesses. Even if there are witnesses, they only catch – in that split-second – a brief glimpse of some little part of what happened. One witness sees one part. Another witness sees another part. By the time of the trial each witness has reconstructed in his own mind what he thinks he saw – not what he did see. A judge has to decide between their contradictory accounts. Often it is so close that he might as well toss up.

2 Compulsory insurance

In 1930 Parliament made a change of great importance. By the Road Traffic Act 1930 it made it compulsory for drivers to insure against liability to third parties: but they were only liable when they were proved to be negligent. This meant that the injured party could be sure of getting any damages that were awarded to him because, even though the driver himself had not the means to pay, the insurance company would do so. It also had much practical effect on the decisions of the courts. All juries came soon to know that the defendants were insured. So did the judges. The result was that they found for the plaintiff in cases where the defendant was only slightly to blame. They would make him liable even for an error of judgment. They also had no hesitation in awarding high damages as, after all, it was the insurance company who would pay. Nevertheless, there still remained one great drawback. The plaintiff still had to prove that the driver was negligent. If the plaintiff had no witnesses he could not recover because he could not prove it.

3 Social security benefits

One of the great revolutions of our time is the system of social security now consolidated in the Social Security Act 1975. By reason of it, many persons who are injured in a motor accident become entitled to benefits from the state. The principal ones are sickness benefit, industrial injuries benefit, disablement benefit, widows' benefit and children of deceased parents' benefit. The state pays out vast sums in weekly or monthly payments to injured or disabled.

By far the greater part of these benefits is payable by the taxpayer: not by contributions from the man or his employer.

Under our present system of liability for fault, the injured person does not have to give credit for the whole of these benefits, but only for one-half of them. They are to be deducted from any compensation given for loss of earnings or profits.

4 No need to prove negligence

In the present state of motor traffic, I am persuaded that any civilised system of law should require, as matter of principle, that the person who uses this dangerous instrument on the roads – dealing death and destruction all around – should be liable to make compensation to anyone who is killed or injured in consequence of the use of it. There should be no need for him to prove that he was negligent. There should be liability without proof of fault. To require an injured person to prove fault results in the gravest injustice to many innocent persons who have not the wherewithal to prove it. It is fault enough that the driver should use this dangerous instrument on the roads – thereby putting others at risk.

So I find myself in agreement with one of the best common law judges of my time – Mr Justice Swift – of whom Mr Justice Goddard said in 1938:[1]

'The late Swift J who, at the time of his lamented death, had an unrivalled experience of these cases, said, on more than one occasion, using the vigorous language which characterised him, that if Parliament allowed such potentially dangerous things as motor-cars to use the public streets, it ought also to provide that people who were injured by them through no fault of their own should receive compensation.'

1 *Hunter v Wright* [1938] 2 All ER 621 at 625.

4 No-fault liability

1 The Royal Commission considers it

All these matters were closely considered by Lord Pearson and the members of the Royal Commission. One of the most radical proposals was that there should be liability in motor-car cases even though the plaintiff could not prove the defendant to be at fault. Moreover, even if the defendant was not in any way at fault, the injured party should be compensated for any injuries he received. There should be a compensation fund established out of which all injured parties could be compensated. To enable this to be done, it would be necessary either for the insurance company to take on the responsibility or alternatively that the state itself should institute its own compensation fund. The Royal Commission came down in favour of the state providing its own compensation fund. After making all the calculations the Royal Commission thought it could be done by imposing a surcharge of 1p or 2p on every gallon of petrol.

This fund would, however, not be available for a man who was driving alone and was killed or injured himself when no other vehicle or pedestrian was concerned. In any such case any fault would be his alone. The scheme would be a no-fault liability scheme and not a no-fault insurance scheme. The driver would be in the same position as if he injured himself at home with his lawn-mower or garden tractor. His only recourse would be to seek such social security benefits as might be available.

2 Calculating the compensation

As I have said, at present when the injured party receives social security benefits he has to give credit only for half of them, but the Royal Commission proposed that if a system of no-fault liability were introduced – funded by the tax-payer in a petrol tax – the full amount should be deducted from the compensation. As the state had to provide the money in both cases it should not be made to pay double compensation in any sense. The Royal Commission envisaged the gradual extension of the social security benefits so that they covered the same field as no-fault compensation.

3 Should liability for negligence be continued?

If no-fault liability were introduced, I see no reason in principle for retaining liability for negligence. The injured party should get compensation from the compensation fund. He should get equivalent compensation, no matter whether he can prove negligence or not. The person who is lucky enough to be able to prove negligence should not get any more than the unlucky one who is not able to prove it. In either case the correct principle is fair compensation for the injury suffered. All injured persons should be treated on the same level.

But the Royal Commission recommended that liability for negligence, that is, tort, should be retained. They thought that those who could prove negligence should be allowed to prove it: because they might then be able to recover a much higher sum as damages than the compensation available from the no-fault fund. They would have to give credit, of course, for the sum received from the no-fault fund. '. . . The function of tort would become that of supplementing the no-fault compensation already provided by the state' (paragraph 279).

This seems to me to be contrary to principle. In either case compensation should be compensation for the injury suffered. The injury is the same no matter whether negligence can be proved or not. So the compensation should be the same.

I fear also that the retention of liability for negligence would mean that many a person would take gratefully his no-fault compensation and then (backed by legal aid) bring an action for negligence in the hope of getting more.

The right solution, to my mind, is to see that the no-fault compensation is assessed on a fair basis – and that compensation for negligence should be assessed on the same basis or at any rate on an equivalent basis. That would be fair by everyone. If high income-earners should have substantial compensation in actions for negligence, so they should have substantial compensation from the no-fault fund.

Any reform in the law bringing in no-fault liability should be accompanied therefore by a reform of the law as to damages for negligence, so as to make sure they are equivalent.

As I read the Report of the Royal Commission there were several members who thought that, on the introduction of the no-fault scheme, liability for negligence should be abolished. But they felt that it was not appropriate to abolish it all at once. They would prefer to see it 'wither away as no-fault compensation and social security provisions become more extensive'. That appears from the note by Professor Schilling (paragraph 949). In other words, they would prefer to see a gradual drawing together – by remodelling the two systems – 'no-fault' and 'tort' – so that in due course the compensation should be equivalent the one to the other.

5 Damages for personal injuries

1 'Fain to be trepanned'

The law governing damages is still derived from trial by jury. If a person was injured and sued another for negligence, the issues of liability and damages were always tried by a jury. There could be only one trial and one award. All the damages had to be assessed at one time. Once and for all. The plaintiff could never come a second time. It had to be one lump sum. There was no such thing as periodic payments, or payment by instalments. This was decided long ago in 1702.[1] Veal struck Fitter a heavy blow on the head. Fitter brought an action of trespass and recovered £11 damages for the 'beating and wounding'. Afterwards it turned out to be much worse than was at first realised. He was 'fain to be trepanned, and have a bone taken out of his skull, so that he thereby became maimed'. He therefore brought a second action. The defendant pleaded that it was barred because of the recovery of damages in the first action. The court held that the plaintiff could not bring a second action. Chief Justice Holt said (page 543):

'This is a new case, and none to be found that we know like it: for every man that recovers damages, it is supposed he has received according to the damage that he has received. If the plaintiff's surgeon had come at the last trial, and shewed that the plaintiff was not cured, the jury would have considered that matter; and then was his time to consider of the heinousness of the battery, and to give evidence of it. . . . And it

1 *Fitter v Veal* (1701) 12 Mod 542 at 543.

shall be intended here that the jury gave entire satisfaction for the battery.'

2 Not full but fair

In those days the amount of damages was entirely at large for the jury. No judge in his summing-up ventured to lay down any principles as to how they should calculate the award. Never was any amount interfered with by a higher court. But in the nineteenth century when there began to be many accidents on the railway, the judges began to direct the juries about it. One of the most famous was in 1852 when Mr Baron Parke laid down emphatically that they were *not* to give *full* compensation but only *fair* compensation: and they were not to use annuity tables. I would like you to notice it because of the difference today. These were the words of Mr Baron Parke as quoted by Mr Justice Brett in *Rowley v LNWR*:[1]

' "It would be most unjust", it is said, "if, whenever an accident occurs, juries were to visit the unfortunate cause of it with the utmost amount which they think an equivalent for the mischief done." And again, "Scarcely any sum could compensate a labouring man for the loss of a limb, yet you do not in such a case give him enough to maintain him for life. . . . You are not to consider the value of existence as if you were bargaining with an annuity office. . . . I advise you to take a reasonable view of the case, and give what you consider a fair compensation." '

3 Previously not itemised

When I was first a judge, that continued to be the rule. Until quite recently judges always used to give an award of damages in one lump sum. They never subdivided it. This is how I stated it in *Watson v Powles*:[2]

1 (1873) LR 8 Exch 221 at 230.
2 [1968] 1 QB 596 at 603.

'In the old days, when damages were assessed by juries, there could be no question of subdivision. A jury gave one award of general damages. In modern times, when damages are assessed by judges sitting alone, this court has discouraged judges from going too much into detail. When I was a judge of first instance, this court told me it was a mistake to subdivide the amount. On the whole I think this is right. There is only one cause of action for personal injuries, not several causes of action for the several items. The award of damages is, therefore, an award of one figure only, a composite figure, made up of several parts. Some of the parts may be capable of being estimated in terms of money, such as loss of future earnings. Others cannot truly be estimated in money at all but must proceed on a conventional basis, such as compensation for pain and suffering and loss of amenities. At the end all the parts must be brought together to give fair compensation for the injuries. If a man is awarded a very large sum for loss of future earnings, it may help to compensate him for his future pain and suffering. If he has no loss of earnings, he may be more generously compensated for pain and suffering. And so forth. Just as a jury in the old days would award an overall figure, so may a judge today.'

4 Now itemisation is with us

It is all altered now. It was altered because in 1970 Parliament declared that interest was to be added to judgments for personal injuries on such part as was appropriate. This meant that awards of damages had to be itemised by the judges. It has since become accepted practice that the judges have to divide up the damages into these four items:

1 Pecuniary loss and expenditure up to the date of trial.
2 Future expenditure.
3 Loss of future earnings.
4 Pain and suffering and loss of amenities.

As a result these four items have been treated much as if they were separate causes of action.

This has given rise to grave problems: How are you to assess the 'future expenditure' when you do not know what the future will hold? How are you to assess 'loss of future earnings' when you do not know what they would be and how long the man would have lived? and when you do not know what effect inflation will have? How far is there an overlap between one item and another? How can you assess pain and suffering and loss of amenities when it cannot be translated into money terms? It seems to me that, in trying to solve these problems, the judges have departed altogether from the approach of judges in the past. They have rejected the advice to give 'fair compensation'. They have attempted to give *full* compensation based on annuity tables and actuarial evidence, disregarding any overlap. They have clutched into the air and given immensely large sums for pain and suffering and loss of amenities. So great are the problems that I suggested there should be a reappraisal of them. The House of Lords agreed but said it was not for them to do it. I will now tell you all about it.

6 Living death

1 The lady doctor has a minor operation

The problem arises acutely when a person's brain is so badly injured that he or she suffers a 'living death'. The leading case is that of a lady doctor, Dr Lim Poh Choo. She had gone into hospital for a minor gynaecological operation. It was for dilatation and curettage. She was quite a healthy woman. She was put under a general anaesthetic. The operation was performed. She was moved from the operating theatre to the recovery room. Whilst she was still unconscious she began to go blue. The doctors call it cyanosis. This was a sign of trouble. It showed that her breathing had been affected. The recovery sister sent for help. They gave her oxygen, but nevertheless the cyanosis increased. Five minutes later her breathing stopped. This affected her heart. The blood stopped flowing to her brain. She suffered what the doctors call 'cardiac arrest'. The heart was massaged. After twenty-five minutes her breathing was restored to normal. She was brought back to life. The more's the pity of it! For it was to a living death. Her brain was severely damaged beyond repair. She was in a deep coma for two weeks. At length she recovered consciousness but could not talk. She had two epileptic fits. After four months she could speak a few words and could walk a little with help. At the trial five years later she was still helpless. Her mind had gone. She could speak a few words, but without meaning or sense. She could not dress or bath herself or attend to her toilet. In the words of the specialist, she showed 'evidence of dementia and gross physical disability due to severe cerebral damage. She will always need total care either at home or in an institution.'

Then by her mother (who was her next friend) she brought an action for damages against the area health authority. The judge awarded her nearly £250,000. It was a staggering figure. It was the highest sum awarded up to that time in the courts. The health authority appealed.

2 If she had died under it

If this lady had died under the operation – as in former times she would probably have done – then, even though it was due to the fault of the hospital, the damages would have been minimal. She had no relatives dependent on her. So there would be no payment under the Fatal Accidents Act. The only sum to be awarded to her estate would be a conventional sum of £750 for loss of expectation of life.

3 Her life now not worth living

But then, by reason of the advances of medical science, she was snatched back from death under the operation and was brought back to a life which was not worth living. The body was kept alive, but the mind had gone. The doctors and nurses, with the aids available today, said that they could keep the body going for the normal expectation of life. In her case thirty-seven years. But every moment of it distressing to her and those about her. Sadness and happiness would be all alike to her. Many might say: 'It were better she had died'.

Such cases are not uncommon; and we are faced with the problem: On what principles should compensation be awarded? The subject needs radical reappraisal.

4 Keep her in comfort

This is how I tried in my judgment to state the principle:[1]

1 *Lim Poh Choo v Camden Health Authority* [1979] 1 QB 196 at 216.

'It is a modern problem – the impact of modern science – in prolonging life in a body destitute of mind. To my mind on principle fair compensation requires that there should be ample provision in terms of money for comfort and care during the lifetime of the sufferer such as to safeguard him or her in all foreseeable contingencies, including the effect of inflation: that, if he or she has any dependants, they should be compensated for any pecuniary loss which they suffer by reason of his or her incapacity and inability to earn – just as if he or she had died and compensation was being awarded under the Fatal Accidents Act. Beyond that there can be conventional sums for pain and suffering and loss of amenities, but these should not be too large – seeing that they will do him or her no good – and can only accumulate during his or her lifetime to benefit others who survive after his or her death. This is reinforced by the views of Lord Pearson's Commission. Half of them thought there should be a statutory maximum of £20,000. The other half thought that there should not be a statutory maximum but that the Court of Appeal should exercise a restraining hand: see paras 391–392.'

5 Injury to the body politic

I then went on to consider the wider implication:

'I may add, too, that if these sums get too large, we are in danger of injuring the body politic: just as medical malpractice cases have done in the United States of America. As large sums are awarded, premiums for insurance rise higher and higher, and these are passed to the public in the shape of higher and higher fees for medical attention. By contrast, we have here a National Health Service. But the health authorities cannot stand huge sums without impeding their service to the community. The funds available come out of the pockets of the taxpayers. They have to be carefully husbanded and spent on essential services. They should not be dissipated in paying more than fair compensation. In many of these cases the National Health Service willingly provides full care, nursing and attention without charging anything for it. Surely this, too, should go to reduce the amount awarded against them. The damages should not be inflated so as to cover the cost of being kept in the most expensive nursing home. It has been known – I am not saying in this case – that when such damages have been awarded, the relatives have afterwards arranged to take advantage of the facilities afforded by the National Health Service – see Lord Pearson's Report, para 341 – and thus save money for themselves.'

In the result I would have reduced the award by nearly one-half. I would have reduced it to £136,596, but my two brethren declined to alter it.

6 The Lords part company

When the case reached the House of Lords the appeal was dismissed save on one minor point. The House refused to make the reappraisal which I requested. This is what Lord Scarman (who delivered the only speech) said:[1]

'The question, therefore, arises whether the state of the law which gives rise to such complexities is sound. Lord Denning MR in the Court of Appeal [1979] QB 196 at 216, declared that a radical reappraisal of the law is needed. I agree. But I part company with him on ways and means. The Master of the Rolls believes it can be done by the judges, whereas I would suggest to your Lordships that such a reappraisal calls for social, financial, economic and administrative decisions which only the legislature can take. The perplexities of the present case, following upon the publication of the Report of the Royal Commission on Civil Liability and Compensation for Personal Injury (1978) (Cmnd 7054) ("the Pearson Report"), emphasise the need for reform of the law.'

I take it from those remarks that the House of Lords require the judges to go by the present unsatisfactory state of the law, with all the problems it has created. They are not to tackle any of the

1 [1980] AC 174 at 182.

problems themselves. They are to await the time when the legislature intervenes. They are not to follow any of the recommendations of the Royal Commission until there is a statute upon it.

7 Should there be periodic payments?

To my mind it is wrong in principle that – in assessing future
pecuniary loss – either as to future expenditure or future loss of
earnings – a judge should have to look forward thirty or forty
years into the future and guess what is likely to happen. That is
inevitable so long as the judges are to make one award once for all
at the time of giving judgment. You can be quite sure that the
award is wrong. It will turn out to be much too much or much
too little. It cannot be right! The solution seems to be this:
Instead of a lump sum award, there should be a system of periodic
payments. If it were possible, the best way would be for all
expenditure to be paid as it is incurred: and all loss of earnings as
they are lost. I realise that that is not possible. But there is the next
best thing. At the trial the judge could fix the payments for the
first three years – index-linked – and then there should be a
review by the courts every three years thereafter – index-linked.
By this means care could be taken of cases where the man im-
proved or where he got worse: also of inflation and changes in
the value of money: also of his prospects of promotion or
changing his work. It has been said that

> 'the introduction of a system of periodic payments would meet
> with vehement opposition from almost every person or
> organisation actually concerned with personal injury litiga-
> tion' (see Cmnd 7054, para 572).

But the British Insurance Association told the Royal Commission
that, although they were not in favour of it, the commercial
insurance market could, if necessary, service a system of periodic
payments. And the majority of the Royal Commission recommended that provision should be made

> 'for damages in the form of periodic payments for future
> pecuniary loss caused by death or serious and lasting injury.

We are under no illusions as to the practical difficulties which would be posed by our recommendation.'

Even though there would be practical difficulties, the majority proposed ways in which they might be overcome.

I would add this: I was much concerned with pensions awarded for death or disablement attributed to or aggravated by war service. These were administered by the Ministry of Pensions with efficiency. I should have thought that no-fault compensation could be likewise well administered.

Whatever the difficulties, however, there is one telling reason why a system of periodic payments should be introduced in actions of liability for negligence. It would bring the compensation for liability for negligence more into line with the compensation for no-fault liability. Credit would be given for social security benefits – which are made by periodic payments. Credit would also be given for the periodic payments received under the no-fault scheme. In time it would mean that compensation for liability for negligence would wither away and be replaced by no-fault compensation.

7 When the person is killed

1 The stage-coach overturns

From the very earliest times there has been no sense or justice in the law of damages relating to death on the roads. On many occasions the legislature has tried to remedy it but it is still in need of reform.

The old law was bad but it was clear. It was expressed in the Latin maxim: *Actio personalis moritur cum persona* (A personal action dies with the person). If a pedestrian was killed in a road accident due to the negligence of the driver, his estate could recover nothing from the wrongdoer, nor could his dependants. If the man had not been killed but only injured and the driver had been killed, the injured man could recover nothing from the estate of the driver.

That was settled as long ago as 1808 in *Baker v Bolton*.[1] Mr Baker was a publican. His wife helped him very much in the conduct of his business. He was much attached to her. They were travelling as passengers in a stage-coach from Portsmouth to London. It overturned owing to the negligence of the driver. Mr Baker was only bruised but his wife was severely hurt. She was taken to hospital and died about a month later. He sued the proprietors of the stage-coach for negligence. Lord Ellenborough directed the jury:

'You can take into account the bruises which Mr Baker himself sustained, and the loss of his wife's society, and the distress of mind he suffered on her account, from the time of the accident till the moment of her dissolution. In a civil court, the death of

1 (1808) 1 Camp 493.

a human being cannot be complained of as an injury; and in this case the damages, as to her, must stop with the period of her existence.'

2 One reform after another

In 1846 there was an important reform by the Fatal Accidents Act of that year. If the man who was killed had a wife and children dependent on him, an action could be brought on their behalf to recover the money loss which they had sustained by his death.

This was good in its way. But it led to this extraordinary anomaly: It was cheaper to kill a man than to maim him for life. If he was only maimed, he could recover large damages. If he was killed, nothing could be recovered – except that, if he had any dependants, they could recover their money loss.

It also led to this even more extraordinary consequence: If the negligent driver was himself killed in the accident, nobody – none of those injured or killed – could recover anything from anybody.

The state of the law remained unremedied until 1934. In their very first interim report the Law Review Committee declared that

'The great frequency of deaths on the roads has made the reform of this part of the law a matter of most urgent national importance.'

So Parliament intervened. By the Law Reform (Miscellaneous Provisions) Act 1934 it was enacted that, on the death of any person

'all causes of action subsisting against or vested in him shall survive *against*, or, as the case may be, *for*, the benefit of his estate'.

That simple provision has led to many problems which the courts have attempted to solve – I fear without much success.

3 The prospect of happiness

This is illustrated by a leading case, *Benham v Gambling*.[1] Mr Gambling was driving his car and had with him his little child aged

1 [1941] AC 157.

two-and-a-half years. Mr Benham tried to overtake it. He failed. He ran into it and overturned it. The baby was badly injured. He was unconscious and died the same day. His father sued for damages on behalf of the baby's estate. It seems to me an extraordinary idea – that the dead baby's estate could recover damages. But the House of Lords held that the baby's estate could sue because the baby's life had been shortened. It had lost its 'expectation of life'. But then what value was to be put upon it? It was to be measured, said the House of Lords, by 'loss of prospective happiness'. How is that to be put into money? How can you possibly guess whether the child would have a happy life or a sad life? No doubt, as with most people, it would be half happy and half sad. So the two cancel out. The Lord Chancellor specially constituted a hearing with himself and five Law Lords. He said (pages 166 and 168):

> 'Such a problem might seem more suitable for discussion in an essay on Aristotelian ethics than in the judgment of a court of law. . . .
>
> Stripped of technicalities, the compensation is not being given to the person who was injured at all, for the person who was injured is dead. The truth, of course, is that in putting a money value on the prospective balance of happiness in years that the deceased might otherwise have lived, the jury or judge of fact is attempting to equate incommensurables.'

That happened to be the case of a baby of two-and-a-half years. But similar observations apply in the case of a grown man. The House did say that the figure should only be a small one. Damages of £200 were awarded. Later cases put it at £500. Later still at £750.

To my mind in point of principle there should be no award whatever for 'loss of expectation of life' or 'loss of the prospect of happiness'. It is not a thing that can be gauged in terms of money. Even if it could, it is a matter of such infinite speculation that it is not right to award any damages in respect of it. The Royal Commission recommended that damages for loss of expectation of life should be abolished.

8 Loss of future earnings

1 No compensation for 'lost years'

It is fair enough that an injured man should receive compensation
for his loss of future earnings. If he is so badly injured as to be
incapable of work and of earning wages – or only to be capable of
light work at reduced wages – he ought certainly to be compensated for his loss. But the problem that has arisen is when the injury
is so serious that his life has been shortened. Take a man of thirty.
If he had not been injured, he would have expected to live, say,
till seventy-five. But owing to his injury, he will probably die at
fifty. No doubt he should get damages for his loss of earnings
from age thirty to age fifty. But is he to get damages for loss of
earnings from age fifty to age sixty-five when he would have
retired? Those fifteen years from fifty to sixty-five are 'lost years'
– lost to him by reason of the accident. Ought damages to be
awarded for the 'lost years'?

In *Oliver v Ashman*[1] a boy of twenty months was injured in a
motor accident. His brain was so affected that he became a
low-grade mental defective incapable of work. His expectation of
life was reduced from sixty years to thirty years. The Court of
Appeal did not think it proper to allow any damages for the 'lost
years'. Lord Justice Pearson pointed out that any damages
awarded on that account (thirty years lost) would not go to him
or to his parents but to some remote next-of-kin. He said (page
243):

> 'Suppose there were a jury trial. Having in their deliberations
> arrived at a sum sufficient to cover the foreseeable financial

1 [1962] 2 QB 210.

146

needs of the plaintiff, the jury might reasonably be reluctant to add more money merely for the purpose or with the probable effect of increasing the surplus which would eventually descend to his next-of-kin whoever they might happen to be at the time of his death.'

2 Now there is compensation for them

That decision held the field for eighteen years. But then came the case of *Pickett v British Rail Engineering Ltd*.[1] Mr Pickett was a man of fifty-one, very fit, with a wife and two children. He worked for the railway, building railway coaches. It involved contact with asbestos dust. He became ill in 1974 at the age of fifty-one and died at the age of fifty-six. Whilst ill, he had started an action and got judgment. The House of Lords held that in this action he should be awarded damages for his 'lost years', that is, for the years from age fifty-six to sixty-five – during which he would have continued working had he not been ill. The House disapproved of *Oliver v Ashman*. That decision in *Pickett's* case was morally justified: because the widow and children had no claim under the Fatal Accidents Act. So it was only right that the earnings he would have received during the 'lost years' should go to compensate them.

3 The chickens came home to roost

But the chickens came home to roost. The curses which the House had sworn against *Oliver v Ashman* came back on their own heads – like chickens which stray during the day return to their roost at night. It was in *Gammell v Wilson*.[2] A young man aged twenty-two was killed outright in a motor accident. He had no dependants so there was no claim under the Fatal Accidents Act. The House held that his personal representatives could recover for the loss of earnings for the 'lost years', that is, for what he would have received if he had lived and worked all his expected working

1 [1980] AC 136.
2 [1981] 2 WLR 248.

life. If calculated actuarily, these would be colossal. Such damages would do no good to him at all. He was dead. They would only go to benefit his next-of-kin whoever they might be. That result was so ridiculous that Lord Diplock declared significantly (page 253):

'I join with your Lordships in thinking that it is too late for anything short of legislation to bring the like sense and justice to the law relating to damages for death recoverable by the estate of the deceased.'

4 Let the dependants claim

Lord Diplock did not make any suggestion for amendment. I would suggest that there should be no award of damages for 'lost years': but, if the man has any dependants, they should be given a separate cause of action to recover the pecuniary loss suffered to them owing to his premature death. This would mean that in the case of a child or young person being severely injured or killed, there would be no compensation at all for 'lost years'. It would only be available in the cases where a married man with dependants was injured or killed: and then only for the pecuniary loss suffered by the dependants for not being supported by him during the 'lost years'.

This is in accord with the recommendation of the Royal Commission (paragraph 435):

'The loss of the victim's income in the lost years is in practice felt by those dependent on him. We think it is in their hands that the right to recover damages should lie.'

5 The baby blind and paralysed

In a recent case[1] I tried to apply the principle (which I advocate) but without success.

James Croke was born in March 1972. At the time of the trial at first instance he was seven years old. He was a lovely little baby,

1 *Re C (a minor) v Wiseman* [1982] 1 WLR 71.

as bright as a button. But when he was only twenty-one months old, he became feverish with symptoms of croup. He was taken to the Northwick Park Hospital. There something went wrong in the treatment. Whilst the doctors were examining his throat, he suffered a cardiac arrest. It destroyed his brain beyond repair. As a result his brain does not function at all. He is blind. He is paralysed in all four limbs. He cannot stand. He cannot talk. He can only lie on his mother's lap or on the floor. Just like a baby of less than a year old. He has to wear nappies all the time, for he is doubly incontinent. There is no hope of any improvement. He does know his mother's voice and shows he loves her, just as a baby does. He is totally dependent on her for everything – for feeding, washing, changing and dressing – just like a little baby. Yet, while his brain does nothing, his body grows just as if he were a normal boy. For some years now he has been taken each day to a school for disabled children, the Whittlesea School at Harrow, where the headmistress says:

'He is greatly loved by all the staff at Whittlesea and we have tried to give him a quality of happiness in his life, as his disabilities are so great that he will need constant care and attention for the rest of his life.'

He is not likely to live long. The doctors put his expectation of life as between twenty and forty years.

Such is the tragic story of James Croke. By his mother as his next friend, he sued the hospital authorities for negligence. They admitted liability, but left the quantity of damages to the courts. In the Court of Appeal I said:

'The judge awarded £45,000 to this baby for loss of future earnings. To my mind there is something odd about giving this tiny baby two separate items of damages: one for cost of "future care"; the other for loss of "future earnings". "Future care" is awarded on the footing that he is completely incapacitated and has to be kept at great expense all his future life. "Future earnings" are awarded on the footing that he was not incapacitated at all and would be earning all his future life. I cannot think it right in principle that he should have both.

149

Never before has a child of two years claimed for loss of future earnings or received any.'

Then I considered cases where the baby

'. . . is killed in a motor accident or dies after a few days. All its years are "lost years". Why on earth should such a baby be given damages for loss of future earnings? It is dead. Any amount of damages would go to its parents, or if its parents are dead, to some remote relative. That would be absurd. If the English law were like Scottish law, they could be given a solatium. But not damages for loss of earnings. Such loss is far too speculative.'

Then I dealt with this baby:

'If this be so, then it must follow that if a baby of two years is not killed but is deprived of all brain power so that it can do nothing and earn nothing whatever, then that baby also has no claim for damages for loss of earnings either during its short-ened life or for the "lost years" thereafter.'

Finally, I said:

'If loss of future earnings is out, there should be ample provision for the cost of keeping this boy in the future so that he should have the best possible care for the rest of his expected life.'

My brethren awarded £206,224.72. I would have awarded £156,524.72. My figure was still a very large sum. If it were made into a trust fund for the benefit of the boy and well invested by the trustees on his behalf, it would be enough to keep him in care and comfort for the rest of his days. It would not, of course, compensate his father and mother for the tragedy which befell them. No money could do that. All the courts can do is to award a fair compensation – fair to both sides – and the figure I suggested was, I believe, fair.

I would only make this final comment: Would not the fairest thing have been, as I have indicated earlier, to have periodic payments to cover the boy's every need? It would meet the case of the boy dying in a year or two or living until fifty or sixty.

9 Pain and suffering and loss of amenities of life

1 'The sleeping beauty'

This item of pain and suffering and loss of amenities of life is the most intractable topic of all. In the old days when damages were assessed by a jury – without being split up into separate items – this item was swallowed up in the whole – like Jonah in the belly of the whale. Looking at the whale, you could not see whether Jonah was inside or not. But judges used to tell juries to take account of it. In *Phillips v LSWR*[1] where a surgeon was seriously injured in a collision between two trains, Mr Justice Field said:

'You will have to consider under the head of damages, first of all, the pain and suffering to him. That of course is a matter which you must take into account, as it is a fair matter for compensation. An active, energetic, healthy man is not to be struck down almost in the prime of life, and reduced to a powerless helplessness with every enjoyment of life destroyed and with the prospect of a speedy death, without the jury being entitled to take that into account, not excessively, not immoderately, not vindictively, but with the view of giving him a fair compensation for the pain, inconvenience and loss of enjoyment which he has sustained.'

That is excellent rhetoric. It was said in the early days of medical science. Nearly every word of it would apply to the case known as 'The sleeping beauty' (*Wise v Kaye*).[2] Veronica Wise was an attractive girl of twenty, full of life, living in a happy home,

1 (1879) 5 QBD 78 at 80.
2 [1962] 1 QB 638.

151

enjoying all the amenities of life, engaged to be married, in a good position with prospects of future advancement. Then – when she was a passenger in a car driven by her brother – it was in collision with a van driven by John Kaye. In a moment she was most seriously injured. She suffered serious injuries to the brain. She was rendered unconscious and never regained consciousness. She was taken to the Radcliffe Infirmary and by surgical skill, modern medicine and devoted nursing, she was kept alive. She remained alive for years. Her father, as her next friend, brought an action for damages. She was unconscious at the time of trial and would remain unconscious all the years till she died. What should be the damages for 'pain and suffering and loss of amenities of life'?

She was awarded £15,000. Never before has there been such difference between judges as to this head of damages. It was much discussed in the House of Lords in a similar case, *West v Shephard*.[1] Two of the greatest judges of our time, Lord Reid and Lord Devlin, would have awarded very little. Others affirmed the award of £15,000.

2 The problem is insoluble

The truth is, of course, that the problem is insoluble. You are attempting to assess in terms of money that which is incapable of being so expressed. Remember also that it is only to compensate the sufferer. It is not to punish the defendant. I ask the question: What is it that you compensate the sufferer for – over and above any pecuniary loss that he suffers? Just as we said when a person is killed, so also here where he is injured, you are compensating him for his loss of happiness – for his loss of enjoyment of life. So first consider what Lord Pearce said about it (page 368):

'The loss of happiness of the individual plaintiffs is not, in my opinion, a practicable or correct guide to reasonable compensation in cases of personal injury to a living plaintiff. A man of fortitude is not made less happy because he loses a limb. It may alter the scope of his activities and force him to seek his

1 [1964] AC 326.

happiness in other directions. The cripple by the fireside reading or talking with friends may achieve happiness as great as that which, but for the accident, he would have achieved playing golf in the fresh air of the links. To some ancient philosophers the former kind of happiness might even have seemed of a higher nature than the latter, provided that the book or the talk were such as they would approve. Some less robust persons, on the other hand, are prepared to attribute a great loss of happiness to a quite trivial event. It would be lamentable if the trial of a personal injury claim put a premium on protestations of misery and if a long face was the only safe passport to a large award.'

3 Replace it by a solatium

To my mind this item of damages is misconceived. The award for 'pain and suffering and loss of amenities' is not an award of compensation at all. It is an award in the nature of what the Scots call a solatium. As soon as this is realised we get rid of all the philosophical disputations. We can award a living plaintiff (who is fully conscious of what he has lost) a reasonable sum by way of solace to him. But we should award an unconscious plaintiff (who knows nothing of what he has lost) nothing by way of solace. It does him no good. It only goes to increase his estate when he dies. It goes to the next-of-kin.

The recommendations of the Royal Commission were in accord with this view but not on the same line of reasoning. They said (paragraph 382):

'We were struck by the high cost of compensation for non-pecuniary loss. It accounts for more than half of all tort compensation for personal injury, and for a particularly high proportion of small payments.'

I would suggest that the award should be by consent kept to a low level: and should be nothing in the case of unconscious or insensible plaintiffs.

Conclusion

I have shown, I hope, that our law as to personal injuries is entirely out of date. It evolved during the time when all civil actions were tried by juries and all damages were assessed by juries. It was formed in relation to horse transport and rail transport. It is quite inapplicable to transport by motor vehicles. These bring death and disablement on all sides. Many of those injured are unable to prove that the driver was negligent. It is imperative, as matter of justice, that there should be introduced a system for compensation to victims even though they cannot prove negligence: no-fault liability as it is called.

So far as damages are concerned the rule (that there is to be only one judgment for damages in one cause of action) is also quite inapplicable. It means that the court has to speculate as to what may happen in the future – and give one lump sum to cover all future expenditure and loss of future earnings – when no one can tell what the future may hold. It is more commensurate with justice that the injured person or his dependants should be compensated by periodic payments. These should be payable, as near as can be, according to the actual expenditure and actual loss of earnings – as and when they occur or are about to be incurred.

It is wrong to try to assess 'pain and suffering and loss of amenities' in terms of money – where there is no yardstick by which to measure the amount. There should be substituted the award of a solatium. It should not be awarded where the injured person is rendered unconscious or insensible so that no solatium will have any effect on his feelings.

All these objectives are to be found implicit in the Report of the Royal Commission. They recognise that, in point of principle, no-fault liability should in time supersede altogether liability for negligence. But it should be a gradual process. Liability for negligence should be retained but it should in time be encouraged to 'wither away'. Against any damages recoverable for negligence, the injured person should give credit for all payments receivable by him from the no-fault liability fund and for all social security benefits. These will wipe out all small claims for negligence, even at the present time. They will not wipe out immediately claims in negligence for serious injury or disablement. But in the course of time they should do so.

Such is, as I read it, the strategy underlying the Report of the Royal Commission. In this Part I have endeavoured to show that this strategy can be justified by reference to the principles of law as they should be.

Addendum

Scurvy treatment

Since I wrote the previous pages, there has been a development. It is most disappointing. The Government have taken the Report of the Royal Commission down – down from the shelf where it had lain for four years. This was because of mounting complaints. They have examined it and decided what to do about it. I expect it has been done – not by any minister – but by some clerks in some department or other. The result reminds me of the words of Horace:

> *'Parturient montes, nascetur ridiculus mus.'* (Mountains will be in labour, the birth will be a single laughable little mouse.)

Out of the monumental Report of the Royal Commission, the Government have produced a laughable little mouse – in the shape of nine clauses tucked away – amongst many other topics – in a bill for the Administration of Justice.

The Report warranted a full-scale bill on its own implementing most, if not all, of the 188 recommendations. Instead, only nine of them are to be implemented – by the interpolation of nine clauses into another bill. None of them is of major importance. Only two of them touch topics which I have discussed. One is designed to abolish damages for loss of expectation of life (chapter 7 (3)). The other is to overrule the House of Lords in *Gammell v Wilson* (chapter 8 (3)).

Apart from this, nothing is to be done. Nothing to remedy the injustice to the child or grown-up who is injured by another person's negligence but has no witnesses to prove it. Nothing done to institute a system of no-fault liability. Nothing done to introduce periodic payments. Nothing done to reappraise the principles on which damages are to be assessed. The plea of the House of Lords in the case of Miss Lim Poh Choo (chapter 6 (6)) has gone unanswered. Five years in the lives of Lord Pearson and his colleagues have been spent in vain. Scurvy treatment by an ungrateful Government.

Part five

Libel

Introduction

The law of libel is in a deplorable state. I say it because I know all about it. When I was a junior at the Bar I was instructed by *The Times* newspaper, *The Tatler* magazine and many others. I drew the pleadings, I dealt with discovery, I advised on evidence. I did everything. In my time on the Bench, I have sat on most of the important cases in the last thirty years. Some in the House of Lords. Many in the Court of Appeal. Often I have been rebuked. I am left discouraged. So I will set down the law as I think it should be. But first, a little history.

1 The Star Chamber

1 'The most honourable court'

As always I go back to the old common law. It knew a good deal about 'slander' – defamatory words spoken by word of mouth. You will find many actions for slander in the time of the first Elizabeth reported by Lord Coke. But you will find little about the printed word. The reason, I suspect, was that the original writing was governed by the common law: but the making of copies by printing was not. It had to be licensed. Any person aggrieved by a printed libel could only get redress in the Star Chamber. Lord Coke reports at least two there: *John Lamb's* case[1] and the case of the two physicians, *Dr Edwards v Dr Wooton*.[2] The reason given was that it is

'an offence to the King and is a great motive to revenge and tends to the breaking of the peace and great mischief'.

The Star Chamber was in its time a most effective instrument to restrain the abuse of power. Its true name was 'The Privy Council sitting in the Star Chamber'. It was housed in a long building with five gables. It stood between Westminster Hall and the river. It was manned by Privy Councillors who were assisted occasionally by a bishop or a judge or two. Coke wrote:

'It is called the Star Chamber in respect the roof of the court is garnished with golden stars. In all records in Latin it is *camera stellata*. . . . the most honourable court (our parliament excepted) that is in the Christian world.'

1 (1611) 9 Co Rep 59b.
2 (1608) 12 Co Rep 35.

The Star Chamber covered offences for which the common law provided no remedy. It could not inflict capital punishment. It had its own forms of punishment, such as pillory, whipping, loss of ears, *stigmata* in the face, and so forth. Shakespeare shows the confidence it had in his time in the opening sentence of the *Merry Wives of Windsor*, put into the mouth of Justice Shallow:

'I will make a Star-chamber matter of it; if he were twenty Sir John Falstaffs, he shall not abuse Robert Shallow, esquire.'

2 Prynne loses his ears

But later on the Star Chamber carried this too far. William Prynne, the strict and bigoted Puritan (sometime Treasurer of Lincoln's Inn), wrote a pamphlet directed against stage plays and cast aspersions on Charles I and his Queen. He was sentenced by the Star Chamber in 1634 to be imprisoned during life, to be fined £3,000, and to lose both his ears in the pillory. He was branded on the cheeks with the letters SL (seditious libeller). He asserted it to mean *Stigmata Laudis* (i.e. of Laud). A stigma was a mark made by burning with a hot iron. Archbishop Laud was against the Puritans and against Prynne in particular. No wonder that the Long Parliament abolished the Star Chamber: and with it, its jurisdiction in libel cases. No wonder that it beheaded Archbishop Laud.

2 The common law takes over

1 The Old Pretender causes trouble

After the Star Chamber the courts of common law took over jurisdiction in libel cases. At the end of the seventeenth century Chief Justice Holt laid down principles which have lasted well – particularly in civil actions for damages. He had a leading case which reflected the controversy about the Kingship. Who should be King? The new William III or the Old Pretender? It was defamatory to say of a man that he supported the Old Pretender and was against the new King. That appears from *Cropp v Tilney*.[1] You will remember that when James II was about to quit, his Queen Mary and their baby son James were escorted to France. This baby son was the Prince of Wales (afterwards known as the Old Pretender in contrast to his son Bonnie Prince Charlie, the Young Pretender). In 1693 we were at war with France. There was an election for Parliament. One candidate accused the other of saying these words in support of the Old Pretender:

'There is a war with France, of which I can see no end, unless the young gentleman on the other side of the water be restored.'

There was no mention by name of James's son. Could it be made actionable by means of an innuendo? In his pleading the plaintiff alleged that 'the young gentleman on the other side of the water' referred to the Prince of Wales. Chief Justice Holt held that the words could be made actionable by an innuendo. He did so in sentences which expressed the law as it is today. He said (page 226):

1 (1693) 3 Salk. 225.

'Scandalous matter is not necessary to make a libel, it is enough if the defendant induces an ill opinion to be had of the plaintiff, or to make him contemptible and ridiculous; as for instance, an action was brought by the husband for saying of him that he was "riding Skimmington", and adjudged that it lay, because it made him ridiculous, and exposed him. Every man understands who is meant by "the young gentleman on the other side of the water"; if words are false, the defendant may justify in an action, but not in an *indictment.*'

Even today some people, after the loyal toast, murmur, 'over the water'.

2 'Riding Skimmington'

That was a nice case quoted by Chief Justice Holt. In mediaeval processions they used to make fun of henpecked husbands. The man rode behind the woman with his face to the horse's tail. The man held a distaff (a cleft staff about 3 feet long which women used for spinning). The woman beat him across the jowls with a skimming-ladle. To say of a man that he was 'riding Skimmington' made him look ridiculous. It was actionable.

3 Men of the gown

But most of the libel cases of that time were treated as crimes. In the case of *R v Orme and Nutt*[1] the defendants were indicted for the crime of libel because they accused a group of people of being adventurers in a lottery. The jury found the writers guilty but the full court of Queen's Bench set it aside, saying (3 Salkeld 224):

'Where a writing which inveighs against mankind in general, or against a particular order of men, as for instance, men of the gown, this is no libel, but it must descend to particulars and individuals to make it a libel.'

In those days 'men of the gown' were of course the members of the legal or clerical professions.

That is still the law today. If a man writes, 'All lawyers are thieves', no lawyer can sue. Nor can the Law Society as

1 (1699) 1 Ld Raym 486, 3 Salk 224.

representing lawyers. But a defendant cannot always escape by writing of a group. If he writes, 'There are some "bent" lawyers in the west end of London' – and one of those lawyers can prove that the words were *intended* by the writer to refer to him – then that lawyer can sue. That was made clear by Lord Atkin in *Knupffer v London Express*.[1]

4 God save the King

The lawyers of the seventeenth and eighteenth centuries had a stronger word for some libels. They called them *libelli famosi*. Not meaning famous libels but infamous libels – notorious libels – libels of special gravity. These were always prosecuted by indictment: such as the trial of the Seven Bishops, or the trial of the publishers of *The Letters of Junius* defended by Thomas Erskine.

An example from an early date is the case of *R v Bear*[2] at the Devon Assizes in 1698. Bear was convicted and fined 500 marks. He wrote words supporting 'the young gentleman on the other side of the water' but added words apparently favourable to the King. He took exception to his conviction on the ground that the indictment only set out part of the words and not the whole. Chief Justice Holt rejected it, saying (page 417):

'Regularly, where a man speaks treason, *God save the King* will not excuse him.'

Blackstone said of these *libelli famosi* that[3]

'. . . they are malicious defamations of any person, and especially a magistrate, made public by either printing, writing, signs or pictures, in order to provoke him to wrath, or expose him to public hatred, contempt and ridicule. The direct tendency of these libels is the breach of the public peace, by stirring up the objects of them to revenge, and perhaps to bloodshed. . . . blasphemous, immoral, treasonable, schismatical,

1 [1944] AC 116 at 124.
2 (1698) 2 Salk 417.
3 *Commentaries* IV, 150–151.

seditious, or scandalous libels are punished by the English law, some with a greater, others with a less degree of severity.'

You may remember, too, that the information against John Wilkes was a criminal information that he caused to be printed and published a seditious and scandalous libel in *The North Briton*: and an obscene and impious libel in *An Essay on Woman* (*R v John Wilkes*[1]).

Thus at the close of the eighteenth century we find that serious libels were constantly tried and punished in the criminal courts: but also that the less serious libels were the subject of proceedings in the civil courts.

1 (1770) 4 Burr 2527.

3 The nineteenth century

1 A crime and a wrong

But when we come to the nineteenth century we find that all libels, no matter whether serious or minor, could be dealt with by either process – either on indictment for a crime and punished: or as a wrong for which damages were payable. This was clearly shown in the case of *Thorley v Lord Kerry*[1] where the church-warden of a parish wrote a letter to Lord Kerry and handed it – in an envelope unsealed to his servant – to take to Lord Kerry. The servant opened it and read in it the words (page 357):

> 'I sincerely pity the man (meaning Lord Kerry) that can so far forget what is due, not only to himself, but to others, who, under the cloak of religious and spiritual reform, hypocritically, and with the grossest impurity, deals out his malice, unchari-tableness, and falsehoods.'

Lord Kerry brought an action for libel. The jury awarded him £20. The churchwarden said that was erroneous. It was no libel. But Chief Justice Mansfield (*not* 'the great Lord Mansfield') said (page 364):

> 'There is no doubt that this was a libel, for which the church-warden might have been indicted and punished; because, though the words impute no punishable crimes, they contain that sort of imputation which is calculated to vilify a man, and bring him, as the books say, into hatred, contempt and ridicule; *for all words of that description* an indictment lies; and I should have thought that the peace and good name of individuals was

1 (1812) 4 Taunt 355.

sufficiently guarded by the terror of this criminal proceeding in such cases.'

The court held that an action would also lie for compensation in the shape of damages.

By 1878 we find the law well settled and stated by Mr Justice Lush in *R v Holbrook*:[1]

'Libel on an individual is, and has always been, regarded as both a civil injury and a criminal offence. The person libelled may pursue his remedy for damages or prefer an indictment, or by leave of the court a criminal information, or he may both sue for damages and indict. It is ranked amongst criminal offences because of its supposed tendency to arouse angry passion, provoke revenge, and thus endanger the public peace, but the libeller is not the less bound to make compensation for the pecuniary or other loss or injury which the libel might have occasioned to the person libelled.'

2 But not now

Now I would jump over about 100 years. By this time we find that no one ever prosecutes a newspaper for libel. The criminal remedy is very rare. In practice only the civil remedy remains.

In a recent case, there was an attempt to revive the criminal remedy. The magazine *Private Eye* published an article for which an information was laid against them. It was a private prosecution. It was in respect of an article about the disappearance of Lord Lucan. Now there is a distinction between a criminal libel and a civil libel. A criminal libel is so serious that the offender should be punished for it by the state itself. He should either be sent to prison or made to pay a fine to the state itself; whereas a civil libel does not come up to that degree of enormity. The wrongdoer has to pay full compensation in money to the person who is libelled and pay his costs: and he can be ordered not to do it again. But he is not to be sent to prison for it or pay a fine to the state. When a man is charged with criminal libel, it is for the jury to say on which side of the line it falls; that is to say, whether or

i [1878] 4 QBD 42 at 46.

not it is so serious as to be a crime. They are entitled to, and should, give a general verdict of 'Guilty' or 'Not Guilty'.

As it happened, in the *Private Eye* case the prosecution was not proceeded with. That is the last instance I remember of a prosecution for criminal libel.

3 The underlying policy

All this leads me to ask the questions: What is the policy of the law in regard to libel? What is the justification for taking legal proceedings against the perpetrators of it? In the old days our forefathers thought so badly of it that it ought to be punished as a crime. Not only those who sat in the Star Chamber but those who sat in the King's Bench. At bottom it was because of the deterrent effect of punishment. It stops them and others from doing it again or anything like it.

Now that in the passage of time libel is no longer prosecuted as a crime, are we to give weight in civil cases to a deterrent effect?

I ask: What is the reason why the law awards damages for libel? In some cases the libel causes a man 'special damage' as it is called. He loses his job or he loses business. But in the great majority of cases he loses nothing in money. He cannot prove that he suffered a heavy loss by reason of the libel. He is annoyed and angry – very angry indeed – but he does not think of taking revenge by force. He does not think of going to the editor and punching him on the nose. There is no breach of the peace or danger of it. Insofar as he is angry – insofar as his feelings are injured – money can do him no good. His anger cannot be measured in money terms. All that can be done on that score is to award him something by way of a solatium. But is that to be the limit of his damages? Should not it be the policy of the law to 'teach the newspaper a lesson'? Should not the law award damages – heavy damages in a suitable case – because of their deterrent effect? I can tell you from my own experience that that is how juries do assess damages in a libel case. If they think that the conduct of a newspaper is intentional and inexcusable, they do award a much larger sum than if it had been unintentional and due to an innocent mistake. The judge may tell them that they must not give punitive damages: but they do not take much notice of that – even if they know what it means.

4 The law takes a wrong turning

1 All about Artemus Jones

'There is Artemus Jones – with a woman who is not his wife.'

All lawyers know about Artemus Jones. His name was really Thomas Jones, but in his boyhood he had been called 'Artemus'. So Artemus he was in fact all his life. He was called to the Bar and practised on the North Wales Circuit – rarely going to London and never to Peckham.

Then the *Sunday Chronicle* came out with an article written by their Paris correspondent. It gave rise to the most famous case[1] in the law of libel. I had almost said the most infamous. It is certainly the most controversial. It concerned the most fundamental principles. So I will set out the newspaper's description of a motor festival at Dieppe.[2]

'Upon the terrace marches the world, attracted by the motor races – a world immensely pleased with itself, and minded to draw a wealth of inspiration – and, incidentally, of golden cocktails – from any scheme to speed the passing hour. . . . "Whist! there is Artemus Jones with a woman who is not his wife, who must be, you know – the other thing!" whispers a fair neighbour of mine excitedly into her bosom friend's ear. Really, is it not surprising how certain of our fellow-countrymen behave when they come abroad? Who would suppose, by his goings on, that he was a churchwarden at Peckham? No one, indeed, would assume that Jones in the atmosphere of London would take on so austere a job as the duties of a churchwarden.

1 *Hulton v Jones* [1909] 2 KB 444, [1910] AC 20.
2 [1909] 2 KB 444 at 445.

Here, in the atmosphere of Dieppe, on the French side of the Channel, he is the life and soul of a gay little band that haunts the Casino and turns night into day, besides betraying a most unholy delight in the society of female butterflies.'

Artemus Jones sued for a libel. The newspaper said that they knew nothing of him and did not intend to refer to him. They used the name simply as that of a fictitious character like John Roe or Richard Doe. There was evidence, however, that Artemus Jones himself had for six or seven years been a contributor to the paper. He had on several occasions published articles in the paper signed 'T.A.J'. So the jury may have taken the protestation of the paper with a grain of salt. They may have thought (although they ought not to have done so) that some people on the paper intended to make a bit of fun at the expense of Artemus Jones. The jury awarded Artemus Jones £1,750 (a large sum in those days). Their verdict was upheld by the Lords. The House was very poorly manned – only four of them. Not a single member had any experience of the law of libel in England. There were two Scots lawyers. One Divorce lawyer, and one Irish lawyer. They did not reserve judgment. They gave it on the second day straight off. That was less than respectful to a powerful dissenting judgment of Lord Justice Fletcher Moulton in the Court of Appeal. As it is, their judgments are impossible to reconcile as Master of the Rolls Sir Wilfrid Greene pointed out in a later case.

The case has also been taken as establishing the principle that the test in libel is objective. It depends on what the reader understood – not on what the writer intended. The Lord Chancellor Lord Loreburn said:[1]

'A person charged with libel cannot defend himself by shewing that he intended in his own breast not to defame, or that he intended not to defame the plaintiff, if in fact he did both.'

2 Intention does matter

As I am now writing extra-judicially, I make bold to say that I think the case of Artemus Jones was wrongly decided. I think

1 [1910] AC 20 at 23.

that liability should depend on the intention of the writer. If the real Artemus Jones had been a churchwarden at Peckham, he might have had a cause of action. It would then show that the words were intended of him. But the real Artemus Jones had never been anywhere near Peckham, nor so far as I know was he ever a churchwarden. Suppose the newspaper had put in David Jones. Could each David Jones in Wales – each Dai Jones – all the 10,000 of them – sue for libel?

I think the rule of law should be that, in order to be actionable, the words must be written 'of and concerning the plaintiff'. That means that the defendant intended them to refer to the plaintiff – or must be taken to have intended them to refer to the plaintiff. In other words, look to the intent of the writer. See if he intended to refer to the plaintiff – or if the circumstances are so strong as to lead to the inference that he did in fact intend to refer to him.

Also the pleading always said – and still says – that the defendant published the words 'falsely and maliciously'. I know that falsity and malice are presumed. But surely malice imputes an intent to defame. If the words are innocent in themselves – and not intended to be derogatory of the plaintiff – I do not see why the defendant should be held liable – simply because some third person puts a defamatory meaning upon them because of some special facts known to him and not to others.

3 'Liked having two wives at once'

The point came up for discussion in a case in which I was counsel for Harold Newstead (*Newstead v London Express Newspaper Ltd*[1]). Harold Newstead was a hairdresser in Camberwell, about thirty years old. He was a bachelor. The *Daily Express* published an article headed:

'WHY DO PEOPLE COMMIT BIGAMY?'

followed by the words:

'Harold Newstead, 30-year-old Camberwell man, who was jailed for nine months, liked having two wives at once.

1 [1940] 1 KB 377.

175

Married legally for a second time in 1932 – his legal wife is pictured right, above – he unlawfully married nineteen-year-old Doris Skelly (left, above). He said, "I kept them both till the police interfered".'

In that case I myself, acting for the plaintiff, relied on *Hulton v Jones*. I said that it did not matter that the words were true of Harold Newstead the bigamist. It did not matter that the newspaper intended to refer to the bigamist Harold Newstead, and not to my Harold Newstead, a bachelor. The newspaper were liable. I won on the law. The Court of Appeal accepted my argument. But it was a Pyrrhic victory. It was like the battle when Pyrrhus lost the flower of his army and exclaimed: 'One more such victory and Pyrrhus is undone'. So here although I won on the law, I lost before the jury. They only awarded my client Harold Newstead one farthing damages. Lord Justice MacKinnon as usual made a pungent comment (page 394):

'We sit here to administer justice, and not to supervise a game of forensic dialectics.'

4 An engagement is announced

The case of Artemus Jones laid the foundation for many odd decisions. The climax of absurdity was reached in 1929. I well remember the case (*Cassidy v Daily Mirror Newspapers Ltd*[1]) – we all thought it was wrongly decided at the time.

Michael Cassidy alias Corrigan described himself as a General in the Mexican army. He was indiscriminate in his relations with women. He went to a race meeting with a lady and told a press photographer he was engaged to marry her. The *Daily Mirror* published the photograph on their gossip page. Under it were the words:

'Mr M Corrigan, the race horse owner, and Miss [X], whose engagement has been announced.'

(The newspaper actually put the name of Miss X but it was not made public in the court.)

1 [1929] 2 KB 331.

Neither Mr Corrigan nor Miss X complained. But, to every-one's amazement, the real wife of Mr Cassidy alias Corrigan complained. She said it was a libel on her. She admitted that she and her husband did not live together but he visited her from time to time at the shop where she was employed. She called three of her acquaintances to say that on reading the article they thought that she (the real Mrs Cassidy) was not his wife but was masquerading as his wife. The jury found in her favour and gave her £500 damages. The Court of Appeal, by a majority, upheld the award. Lord Justice Greer dissented. I knew him and admired him greatly. He had a fine, almost saintly, face, and was one of the soundest of judges. In his dissenting judgment he said (page 350):

'If the decision of my brethren in this case is right, it would be right to say that I could be successfully sued for damages for libel (if, having been introduced to two apparently respectable people as persons engaged to be married, I repeated that statement in a letter to a friend) on the ground that my words meant that a lady totally unknown to me, who was in fact the wife of the man, was not his wife and was living in immoral intercourse with him. It seems to me wholly unreasonable to hold that my words could be construed as meaning anything of the kind.'

It is significant that in a later case Lord Justice Goddard said he agreed with Lord Justice Greer: see *Hough v London Express*.[1]

5 The dog-doping girl

Following on *Cassidy's* case an equally absurd result was reached in *Morgan v Odhams Press*.[2] The *Sun* newspaper published an article saying that a 'dog-doping girl' had been kidnapped by a gang. Mr Morgan called witnesses to say that they had seen him with her at lunch. The jury awarded him £4,750. All three of us in the Court of Appeal reversed it and gave him nothing. The House of Lords, by a majority of three to two, restored his £4,750.

1 [1940] 2 KB 507 at 516.
2 [1970] 1 WLR 820, [1971] 1 WLR 1239.

None of those absurd decisions would have been given if the test had been (as I think it should have been): 'Did the newspaper intend to refer to Mrs Cassidy?' The answer would have been 'No'. They knew nothing of the plaintiff. They published nothing 'of and concerning her'.

But there it is. The *Cassidy* case has been taken as deciding that, however innocent the words may be, a publisher is held liable because someone or other – knowing some other facts or matter, unknown to the writer – puts upon them a defamatory meaning. It has been known, in the words of the technical lawyers, as a 'secondary meaning'.

6 Parliament steps in

In 1952, as a result of the Report of Lord Porter's Committee on the Law of Defamation,[1] Parliament did something to give a remedy. A publisher could avoid liability if he knew nothing of the plaintiff and had no intention of defaming him; had acted innocently and without malice and had exercised reasonable care; and had made an offer of amends as soon as practicable. That puts a publisher under a very considerable burden of proof. I feel it would have been better to reverse *Hulton v Jones* altogether.

Another consequence of that Report was a rule in regard to secondary meaning. They realised the difficulties in which it put the defendant. So they recommended that in future, if the plaintiff relied on a secondary meaning, he should give particulars of the facts and matter relied on. A rule was made to that effect. It led to much trouble.

1 (1948) Cmnd 7536.

5 Technicalities beyond belief

1 'True' or 'false'?

It would be tedious in the extreme to go through the story. But the result was to lead to technicalities beyond belief. I will just tell you what happened. Nowadays in libel cases, the practitioners talk glibly of 'true innuendos' and 'false innuendos'; or about 'legal innuendos' and 'popular innuendos'. I always pretend I know the difference – and so I do – but I have to pull myself together to decide – which innuendo is 'true' and which is 'false'; and which is 'legal' and which is 'popular'. The distinction is, I believe, this: A 'true' or 'legal' innuendo is one which gives a secondary meaning to the words. A 'false' or 'popular' innuendo is one which gives the natural and ordinary meaning to the words. But that leaves open the question: What is a 'secondary meaning' as distinct from the 'natural and ordinary meaning'? The answer is that the 'natural and ordinary meaning' is the meaning which any ordinary reader would put upon the words without more ado – whereas a 'secondary meaning' is a meaning which is put by some person on to the words because of some extrinsic facts or circumstances known to him and not to the rest of mankind. To make confusion worse confounded, the House of Lords have held that each innuendo gives rise to a separate and distinct cause of action. Each must be separately and distinctly pleaded. If a secondary meaning is alleged, full particulars must be given of the facts and matters relied upon.

What a to-do, to be sure! We never had it in my days at the Bar. We got on very well with a simple pleading. We set out the words complained of. Then a simple innuendo: 'The said words meant and were understood to mean . . .', making it as strong as

179

the circumstances fairly permitted. We drew no distinction between natural and ordinary meanings – and secondary meanings. We rolled them all together in one innuendo. If you should look at the precedents in all the editions of Bullen and Leake's *Precedents of Pleadings* from the celebrated 3rd edition in 1868 to the 9th edition which I myself edited in 1935 with Mr (now Sir) Arthur Grattan-Bellew, you will find that all the precedents for 100 years follow that simple form. There was only one cause of action. There was never any suggestion that there were two or more. I could never understand why the House of Lords ever declared that there were two causes of action. There was only one publication and therefore only one cause of action.

Now let me come to the case, *Lewis v Daily Telegraph Ltd*,[1] which is responsible for all the technicalities.

2 The fraud squad come in

In 1958 the police were told something by an 'informer'. As a result they started to make an investigation into the affairs of a large public company called Rubber Improvement Ltd, whose chairman was Mr John Lewis who had been a Member of Parliament. The investigation was highly confidential. No word of it should have been leaked out from the police at all. If it did, it might cause infinite harm to the company. One of the police witnesses said:[2]

'It would be contrary to police orders and a breach of discipline to leak to the press about investigations being made by the fraud squad, and a very serious view would be taken by the fraud squad if there should be such a leak.'

But in this case it did leak out. The story was carried on the front pages. The *Daily Telegraph* put it in this way:[3]

1 [1963] 1 QB 340, [1964] AC 234.
2 [1963] 1 QB 340 at 361.
3 [1964] AC 234 at 237.

'INQUIRY ON FIRM BY CITY POLICE
Daily Telegraph Reporter

Officers of the City of London Fraud Squad are inquiring into the affairs of Rubber Improvement Ltd and its subsidiary companies. The investigation was requested after criticisms of the chairman's statement and the accounts by a shareholder at the recent company meeting.

The chairman of the company, which has an authorised capital of £1 million, is Mr John Lewis, former Socialist MP for Bolton.'

That newspaper story came as a shock to the company and its chairman. They had heard nothing of such an inquiry. It would obviously have a devastating effect. They issued a writ at once. In the statement of claim the innuendo was pleaded in these words (page 238):

'By the said words the defendants meant and were understood to mean that the affairs of the plaintiffs and/or its subsidiaries were conducted fraudulently or dishonestly or in such a way that the police suspected that their affairs were so conducted.'

If that innuendo was well stated – if that was the meaning to be put upon the words – the newspapers had no hope of justifying it. They could not prove the truth of the innuendo.

As it happened, there was an inquiry held. At that inquiry it was found that there was nothing wrong with the affairs of the company or with its chairman. The police took no steps against them.

3 The judge sums up

The case was tried by Mr Justice Salmon – a judge of the highest quality who had much experience at the Bar and on the Bench of libel cases. He left it to the jury in these words (pages 241–242):

'How would the ordinary man understand this? The two views which have been canvassed before you are these: Mr Faulks (for the newspaper) has said: Well, the ordinary man is not very

181

suspicious; he would just regard it as a piece of intelligence, the police are looking into it, and it would not really produce any other effect upon his mind. Mr Milmo (for the company) says: Well, the ordinary man seeing this "City Police. Officers of the City of London Fraud Squad are inquiring into the affairs of Rubber Improvement Ltd" – the ordinary man, not being any more suspicious than his neighbour, would immediately say to himself, says Mr Milmo – either he would say to himself: "There is fraud here, or the police would not be looking into it" or, he would say to himself: "At any rate, there is enough in this for the police to suspect that there is fraud". I cannot really help you. Those are the two rival contentions. It is for you to say what it means. When you read the newspapers, what would you have thought when you read that? You see, the only way you can get at what the ordinary man and woman think is by getting a jury of 12 people together, who are ordinary men and women, and asking them what they would have thought.'

I must say that I think Mr Justice Salmon summed up entirely correctly. He did it in the way which judges have done for the last 100 years. He left it to the jury. They put upon the words the meaning contained in the pleaded innuendo. The majority of the House of Lords held that the words themselves did not bear that meaning. The House included a Scots Lawyer, a Chancery lawyer, a Divorce lawyer and a Commercial lawyer. The other was one who had had great experience in libel cases with juries. He was my dear friend Lord Morris of Borth-y-Gest. He dissented. He thought the words did bear the innuendo. He said (page 269):

'No responsible newspaper would dare to publish, or would be so cruel as to publish, the words in question unless the confidential information, which in some manner they had obtained, was not information merely to the effect that there was some kind of inquiry in progress but was information to the effect that there was fraud or dishonesty. Some reasonable readers might therefore think that the words conveyed the meaning that there must have been fraud or dishonesty.'

4 The jury award damages

The jury awarded damages of £75,000 to the company and £25,000 to Mr Lewis. The majority of the House thought these were excessive. Lord Morris of Borth-y-Gest did not feel strong enough on it to dissent on the amount of damages.

I can hazard a guess why the jury awarded such high damages. They must have felt that the newspaper had been guilty of a gross abuse of power. They had obtained access to information of the most confidential kind. And then it was used to cast the gravest discredit on a large public company and its chairman. It caused them great damage. The jury clearly felt that this sort of thing should not go on. They expressed it in the only way open to them – by the award of damages.

5 If I had been there

I ask myself: If I had been sitting in the Lords, would I have interfered with that verdict of the jury? I leave you to give the answer.

I hope that I would not have been party to the ruling that each innuendo gives rise to a separate cause of action. In that very case (page 279) Lord Devlin said that principle 'seems in modern times to be of dubious value'. And the Committee on Defamation presided over by Mr Justice Faulks in 1975 have recommended that

> 'A claim in defamation based on a single publication with or without a plea of legal innuendo should constitute a single cause of action giving rise to one award of damages only.'[1]

1 (1975) Cmnd 5909, para 119(b).

6 Inordinate length

1 Three little pigs

The technicalities have been so many that the cases take an inordinate length of time. Let me give you some instances. Here is another consequence of *Cassidy's* case. It is *Boston v Bagshaw*.[1] Three little pigs were put up for sale. They were pedigree and earmarked. A man wearing a brown smock was amongst the bidders. They were knocked down to him for £103 19s. He gave his name as 'Boston of Rugeley'. He took them off in a trailer and was never seen again. He never paid for them. The auctioneer told the police and wrote letters to other auctioneers warning them. The police gave notice too on television that they wanted to interview him. They said that the man gave his name as Boston and said that he came from Rugeley.

Now there happened to be a real Mr Boston of Rugeley. He was a farmer of good standing, well-known in the district. No one would have dreamt that it was him. But he brought an action against the auctioneers for libel. He failed, but only after this disastrous sequence described by Lord Diplock (page 1135):

'This is an ordinary simple case of libel. It took 15 days to try: the summing-up lasted for a day: the jury returned 13 special verdicts. The notice of appeal sets out seven separate grounds why the appeal should be allowed and 10 more why a new trial should be granted, the latter being split up into over 40 sub-grounds. The respondents' notice contained 15 separate grounds. The costs must be enormous. Lawyers should be ashamed that they have allowed the law of defamation to have

1 [1966] 1 WLR 1126.

184

become bogged down in such a mass of technicalities that this should be possible.'

If it were not for the cases of *Artemus Jones* and *Cassidy*, that case would never have been started. Neither the auctioneers nor the police nor the television people had any intention to refer to the well-known farmer at Rugeley.

2 Fair comment

I cannot cover in this Part the whole law of libel – not even the main principles of it. I can only draw attention to some parts of it which deserve the attention of reformers. Particularly insofar as newspapers are concerned. It is much to be desired that newspapers and television should be free to bring to the notice of the public any matter of public interest or concern. The law recognises this already by the defence of 'fair comment on a matter of public interest'. In order to make good their defence the newspapers have to prove two things: first, that the facts were truly stated; second, that the comment was fair. But even this defence had, until recently, become darkened by the clouds of obscurity.

3 'Double think'

This was shown in a case, *Slim v Daily Telegraph*,[1] where there was a dispute about a path by the river Thames at Hammersmith. There was a public right of way along it. The local council put up a notice, 'No Cycling'. It was signed by the clerk, Mr Slim. Later on Mr Slim retired from the council and became legal adviser to a limited company, Vitamins Ltd. They sought to use the path as access for their vehicles. Then, strangely enough, the notice about 'No Cycling' was removed and some of the local residents seem to have thought that Mr Slim had a hand in it because now that he was employed by Vitamins Ltd he was taking their side. One of the local residents then wrote to the *Daily Telegraph* a letter which they published. It was headed 'Double Think'. The letter said:

1 [1968] 2 QB 157.

185

'. . . Upstream at Hammersmith the peace of Upper Mall is threatened by a claim of Vitamins Ltd, a factory nearby, to the vehicular right of way. If this is approved, this narrow stretch of the riverside with its period houses may become a thorough-fare for heavy lorries and a dangerous place for a walk.

. . . what gives cause for concern is that already at the western end of Upper Mall a council notice forbidding even cycling has been removed. If this has made local residents a little cynical, they must be forgiven.

For many years this notice was signed by one Horace Slim, the reigning town clerk. It is now the same Mr Slim, as legal adviser to Vitamins Ltd, who claims the right to drive lorries along this very path.'

This letter was followed by another in like vein. Mr Slim brought an action for libel against the *Daily Telegraph*. The letters were undoubtedly defamatory, but the matter was clearly one of public interest. The defendants were protected if the letters were fair comment. Otherwise they were liable.

So the simple issue should have been: Fair comment or not? But it became submerged in pleadings which covered 83 pages, in correspondence which filled 300 pages, in evidence which covered six days, in argument which covered two or three days, and a judgment which filled 35 pages.

The judge held that the letters bore the imputation that Mr Slim had brought improper pressure to bear on the council employees and was not fit to remain a solicitor. The judge awarded him £3,500.

The Court of Appeal reversed the judge's decision. We held that the newspaper was entitled to the defence of 'fair comment on a matter of public interest'. I hope that our judgment in that case will have done much to clear up the defence of 'fair comment' and to enable newspapers to rely upon it in any proper case. Perhaps I may re-state the underlying principle now.

4 'Write to the newspaper'

In considering a plea of fair comment, it is not correct to canvass

186

all the various imputations which different readers may put upon the words. The important thing is to determine whether or not the writer was actuated by malice. If he was an honest man expressing his genuine opinion on a subject of public interest, then no matter that his words conveyed derogatory imputations: no matter that his opinion was wrong or exaggerated or prejudiced: and no matter that it was badly expressed so that other people read all sorts of innuendos into it; nevertheless, he has a good defence of fair comment. His honesty is the cardinal test. He must honestly express his real view. So long as he does this, he has nothing to fear, even though other people may read more into it. I stress this because the right of fair comment is one of the essential elements which go to make up our freedom of speech. We must ever maintain this right intact. It must not be whittled down by legal refinements. When a citizen is troubled by things going wrong, he should be free to 'write to the newspaper': and the newspaper should be free to publish his letter. It is often the only way to get things put right. The matter must, of course, be one of public interest. The writer must get his facts right: and he must honestly state his real opinion. But that being done, both he and the newspaper should be clear of any liability. They should not be deterred by fear of libel actions.

7 Fair information

In many cases, however, the newspapers are not able to rely on 'fair comment' because they cannot prove that the facts stated are true. Where this is the case, there is sometimes a need for the newspapers to be granted a privilege – a qualified privilege – for them to give fair information to the public when it is in the public interest for them to do so. This privilege may be defeated if the newspaper is actuated by malice, but otherwise it should avail the newspaper.

1 The dismembered body

The point arose in a strange case, *Webb v Times Publishing Co.*[1] In 1949 a dismembered body was found in the Essex marshes. Someone had cut up a body, parcelled it up and thrown it out of an aircraft. It was the body of Stanley Setty. In the next year, 1950, Donald Hume was tried at the Old Bailey for the murder of Setty. Hume's wife gave evidence that she had never met Setty in her life. Hume was acquitted of murder but afterwards pleaded guilty to being an accessory after the fact.

Ten years later, in 1959, *The Times* published this account about a court case in Switzerland. Their correspondent there had attended the trial and picked out the spice. It was said to be libellous of Mrs Hume.

1 [1960] 2 QB 535.

'HUME ADMITS KILLING STANLEY SETTY

Body dismembered and thrown from aircraft

Winterthur, Switzerland, September 24

Donald Brian Hume, who is on trial on a charge of murdering a Swiss taxi driver, told the court here today that he robbed the Midland Bank in Brentford, London, and shot a clerk. He also admitted killing Stanley Setty, a car dealer, out of jealousy, sawing off his limbs and making them into parcels to be dropped from an aircraft. . . . Asked if he was married and had a child Hume replied, "Yes, but it was not mine. The father was Stanley Setty".'

I do not suppose that Mrs Hume was a reader of *The Times*. Someone else read it and told her. They thought she had a good claim for libel – owing to the last words, 'The father was Stanley Setty'. She issued a writ. She insisted that she had never met Setty in her life. Her husband, Donald Hume, was the father of her child. She had divorced him in 1951. In her statement of claim she said that the words in *The Times* meant and were understood to mean that she had committed adultery with Setty and had given perjured evidence at the Old Bailey trial.

What defence was available to *The Times*? It was no defence for them to say, 'We only reported what Donald Hume had said'. If a newspaper publishes the words, 'Mr A says Mr B is a thief', it is no defence for them to prove that Mr A said it. They must prove that Mr B is a thief.

The Times could not rely on fair comment, because they could not prove that the facts were true. They could not rely on the privilege of 'fair report of judicial proceedings' because that privilege only applies to English proceedings. But this is the importance of the case. Mr Justice Pearson raised this question (page 565):

'Could there be a plea of "fair information on a matter of public interest" which would be co-ordinate with the familiar plea of "fair comment on a matter of public interest"?'

The judge held that in this case there was a qualified privilege. So

The Times were not liable in the absence of malice. And no malice was proved.

2 The Bishop launches out

Further support for this development is to be found in the case about an approved school called Court Lees (*Cook v Alexander*[1]). A teacher, Mr Cook, at the school wrote letters to the papers criticising the way in which the school was conducted. He said that the boys were punished – by beating – with excessive severity. An inquiry was held. The school was closed. The staff lost their employment.

The matter was raised in the House of Lords. The Bishop of Southwark attacked Mr Cook. The *Daily Telegraph* reporter gave what journalists call a 'parliamentary sketch'. It was in these terms:

'BISHOP ATTACKS COURT LEES "CRUSADER"

. . . Dr Mervyn Stockwood, Bishop of Southwark, launched a scathing attack on Mr Ivor Cook, the master whose revelations prompted the inquiry. [Debate p. 27.]

Dr Stockwood's own startling revelation was that Mr Cook had sent more boys to the headmaster for discipline – which usually meant corporal punishment – than any other master.

. . . He then read out some of the charges involved, to the amusement of the House. One boy had spat in a public place; another swept drain debris across Mr Cook's clean shoes; a third had worn socks in bed.

"This is the apostle in the crusade against corporal punishment", he commented with scorn.'

The *Daily Telegraph* had no defence on the ground that this was a 'fair report of parliamentary proceedings'. It was not a report in the proper sense at all. But the Court of Appeal held that there was a privilege of the nature of 'fair information on a matter of public interest'.

1 [1974] 1 QB 279.

3 A parliamentary sketch

That case raised distinctly the question: What is the position of a parliamentary sketch? When making a sketch, a reporter does not summarise all the speeches. He selects a part of the debate which appears to him to be of special public interest and then describes it and the impact which it made on the House. A parliamentary sketch is privileged if it is made fairly and honestly with the intention of giving an impression of the impact made on the hearers. In these days the debates in Parliament take so long that no newspaper could possibly report the debates in full, nor give the names of all the speakers, nor even summarise the main speeches. When a debate covers a particular subject matter, there are often some aspects which are of greater public interest than others. If the reporter is to give the public any impression at all of the proceedings, he must be allowed to be selective and to cover those matters only which appear to be of particular public interest. Even then, he need not report it verbatim word for word or letter by letter. It is sufficient if it is a fair presentation of what took place so as to convey to the reader the impression which the debate itself would have made on a hearer of it. Test it this way: if a member of the House were asked: 'What happened in the debate? Tell me about it', the reporter's answer would be a sketch giving in words the impression it left on him, with more emphasis on one thing and less emphasis on another, just as it stuck in his memory. Such a sketch is privileged, whether spoken at the dinner-table afterwards, or reported to the public at large in a newspaper. Even if it is defamatory of someone, it is privileged because the public interest in the debate counterbalances the private interest of the individual.

4 To be worked out

This privilege of fair information needs to be worked out from case to case. But it would afford a new and valuable protection to a newspaper or to the television people. Just look back at the case of the three little pigs. The warnings given by the auctioneers – and the description given by the television people – were all of

191

them 'fair information on a matter of public interest'. They should be protected by qualified privilege. They should not be held liable in the absence of malice.

I would like to see this principle emerging: If the newspaper or television receive or obtain information fairly from a reliable and responsible source, which it is in the public interest that the public should know, then there is a qualified privilege to publish it. They should not be liable in the absence of malice.

5 A dangerous new provision

Another defence is in danger. It is the defence of a 'fair and accurate report'. It has long been open to the newspapers to publish a fair and accurate report of legal proceedings. But in 1981 Parliament inserted a new provision, section 4(2), in the Contempt of Court Act 1981 which gave a new power to courts and tribunals. It enables them to give orders to the press. Judges or magistrates or even chairmen can give orders to newspapers that they are not to publish this or that speech or evidence which takes place in the courtroom – nor indeed any part of the proceedings. They can give them orders if they think it necessary in the interests of the administration of justice.

The scope of this new section came under discussion in a case[1] of four men charged with gun-running. It was expected to bring in evidence about plots to assassinate political figures. The accused asked for the proceedings not to be reported. The magistrates at Horsham made a blanket order. They directed that the press were not to publish any part of the proceedings before them – at that stage. The National Union of Journalists were so upset by this order that they brought it up to the Court of Appeal – so as to test the ruling of the magistrates.

I thought the section was to be given very limited application– and I said so. My colleagues did not agree. They thought that it did give a wide power to the courts to postpone the reports of legal proceedings. Leave was given to appeal to the House of Lords. In the hope that my view may prevail, I venture to set out what I said:

1 *R v Horsham Justices, ex parte Farquharson* (1981) Times, 14 November.

'This interpretation is, in my mind, necessary so as to ensure two of our most fundamental principles. One is open justice. The other is freedom of the press. It is of the first importance that justice should be done openly in public: that anyone who wishes should be entitled to come into court and hear and see what takes place; and that any newspaper should be entitled to publish a fair and accurate report of the proceedings – without fear of a libel action or proceedings for contempt of court. Even though the report may be most damaging to the reputation of individuals, even though it may expose wrongdoing in high places, even though it may be embarrassing to the most powerful in the land, even though it may be political dynamite, nevertheless it can be published freely – so long as it is part of a fair and accurate report. The only case in which it will be punishable as a contempt of court is when the court makes an order postponing publication in the legitimate exercise of its power in that behalf.

6 A monumental fraud

'The most illuminating case is that of William Cooper Hobbs.[1] It was in 1925 when we still had Grand Juries. It was for them to decide whether or not there was a true bill. If they found a true bill, the man would be tried by a Petty Jury during those very sittings. On the 3rd February 1925 the Recorder of London in his charge to the Grand Jury said:

"There can be no doubt, I should say – it is for you to judge – that Hobbs was a party to a gigantic fraud, as monumental and perhaps as impudent a fraud as has ever been perpetrated in the course of our law."

The newspapers that very evening and the next day made big headlines:

"HOBBS'S PART
'NO DOUBT PARTY TO A MONUMENTAL FRAUD' "

– omitting the words, "it is for you to judge".

1 [1925] 2 KB 158.

'On the 6th February 1925 William Cooper Hobbs applied to attach *The Evening News* and the editor for contempt of court. He put it on the ground that it was a serious prejudice to his trial which would be held in a few days. On the 10th February 1925 the application was heard by Lord Hewart CJ, together with Mr Justice Salter, one of the best common law judges, and Mr Justice Fraser who was of the highest authority on the law of libel and of publication in newspapers. They held that the article was a fair and accurate report of judicial proceedings and that it was not a contempt of court. If the Recorder had directed the press that they should not publish his charge to the Grand Jury it would no doubt have been a contempt of court for them to do so.'

7 Wrong to make a blanket order

Then I turned to section 4(2) which enables the court to prohibit some things being reported:

'I cannot think that Parliament in section 4(2) ever intended to cut down or abridge the freedom of the press as hitherto established by law. All it does is to make clear to editors what is permissible and what not. In considering whether to make an order under section 4(2), the sole consideration is the risk of prejudice to the administration of justice. Whoever has to consider it should remember that at a trial judges are not influenced by what they may have read in the newspapers. Nor are the ordinary folk who sit on juries. . . . The risk of their being influenced is so slight that it can usually be disregarded as insubstantial – and therefore not the subject of an order under section 4(2).

Returning to our present case, I cannot see any risk of prejudice to the administration of justice. Let me assume that, in the course of the evidence, there will be talk about political assassination of one kind or another. It is probably irrelevant to the charges. It may be damaging to the reputation of some person or other. It may be embarrassing to some group or other. But it is most unlikely to influence the administration of justice. I do not think it would influence any judge or juror who might read it and who might – weeks or months later – sit on the trial. So I think the magistrates were wrong to make the blanket order as they did at the outset of the hearing. The Divisional Court was quite right to set their order aside.'

8 Exemplary damages before 1964

1 Awarded to deter wrongdoing

Until the year 1964 the judges of England had always directed juries that in actions of tort for wrongdoing, whenever the conduct of the defendant was grossly improper or reprehensible, they could take it into account in awarding damages against him. It was accepted by the profession as settled law. But in 1964 Lord Devlin in the House of Lords said that this was erroneous. Damages for tort, he said, should be confined to compensation in money for the wrong done. Punishment should be left to the criminal law. That smacks too much of legal theory for my liking. Much wrongdoing is actionable as a tort in the civil courts. It is also punishable as a crime in the criminal courts. Libel is a good instance. The injured person is to receive compensation in money. The wrongdoer is to be punished by a fine. Why should it not all be done in one proceeding? even though the fine – if you call it such – goes to the injured person and not to the state. The important thing is for the legal system to act as a deterrent to wrongdoing. It can do this effectively – in suitable cases – by increasing the award so as to be an example to others – to teach the wrongdoer a lesson, especially where, as in libel cases, the criminal remedy has become very rare.

2 The pocket-book filled the mouth of the sack

At any rate, that is the way the English courts have looked at damages for wrongdoing down the centuries. It was established, I should have thought, once and for all, by one of the most celebrated cases in our history – *Wilkes v Wood*.[1] The plaintiff, John Wilkes, was said to have written an article in *The North Briton* which attacked private persons and persons in public station in the land. He was to be prosecuted for libel in the criminal court. But in those proceedings the prosecutor would have to prove that Wilkes was the author of the article. In order to get this proof Lord Halifax, the Secretary of State, issued a 'general warrant' authorising his house to be searched. The warrant was executed by Mr Wood and others. This is what they did. They rummaged all the papers together they could find in and about the room. They fetched a sack and filled it with the papers. The smith came and opened four locks of the lower drawers of a bureau. They took out all the papers in those drawers and a pocket-book belonging to Mr Wilkes. They put them all into the sack. The pocket-book filled the mouth of the sack.

John Wilkes brought a civil action against Wood. He claimed damages for trespass. Mr Wood relied on the 'general warrant'. Lord Chief Justice Pratt held that the Secretary of State had no power to issue general warrants. He held that Mr Wood was liable in damages for trespass. He gave this memorable ruling (page 18):

> 'Notwithstanding what Mr Solicitor-General has said, I have formerly delivered it as my opinion on another occasion, and I still continue of the same mind, that a jury have it in their power to give damages for *more* than the injury received. Damages are designed not only as a satisfaction to the injured person, but likewise as a punishment to the guilty, to deter from any such proceeding for the future, and as a proof of the detestation of the jury to the action itself.'

The jury awarded John Wilkes £1,000. That would be a fortune in those days. I suppose the equivalent today would be £25,000.

3 Beef-steaks and beer

Besides searching John Wilkes's house, the officers also arrested one of the men who printed *The North Briton*. They 'kept him in

1 [1763] Lofft 1.

custody about six hours, but used him very civilly by treating him with beef-steaks and beer, so that he suffered very little or no damages': see *Huckle v Money*.[1] The jury awarded the printer £300 damages – a sum perhaps equal to £7,500 today. There was an appeal on the ground that it was excessive. Lord Chief Justice Pratt said (page 206):

> 'If the jury had been confined by their oath to consider the mere personal injury only, perhaps £20 damages would have been thought damages sufficient. . . . I think they have done right in giving exemplary damages. To enter a man's house by virtue of a nameless warrant, in order to procure evidence, is worse than the Spanish Inquisition; a law under which no Englishman would wish to live an hour; it was a most daring public attack made upon the liberty of the subject.'

Lord Devlin would have us treat those cases as entirely exceptional. They are to be confined, he says, to 'oppressive, arbitrary or unconstitutional action by the servants of the government': see *Rookes v Barnard*.[2] But why so confine it? The servants of the government are not the only people who are guilty of oppressive, arbitrary or unconstitutional action. I will tell you of a case (*Loudon v Ryder*[3]) we had in 1953.

4 A young lady is beaten

A young lady of twenty-one owned a flat in a London mews. It had been left to her by her father who had died. Her mother seems to have become friendly with a Polish émigré who had taken the name of Ryder. He spoke in broken English. Together the mother and Ryder plotted to break into the flat and turn the young lady out. They had no right or title whatever to do so. It was the young lady's flat, left to her by her father. They got their gardener to help them. They tried the door. It was locked. They got a ladder. The gardener went up it part way but when he saw the young lady, he came down the ladder. Then Ryder, the Pole, went up. The young lady got a pail half full of water and threw it down

1 (1763) 2 Wils 205.
2 [1964] AC 1129 at 1226.
3 [1953] 2 QB 202.

towards him. It had no effect. He advanced up the ladder with an
iron instrument, broke one of the small panes of glass close to the
fastening of the window and jumped into the kitchenette. He
shouted, 'Get out'. She screamed for help. An electrician, who
was working in the mews, heard her cries. He went up the ladder
to rescue her. This is what he saw when he got inside (page 210):

> 'She was holding up her arms and Ryder was beating her hands.
> I caught hold of him by the shoulders. He had not seen me
> until then, and his face changed and he started cringing in the
> corner and asked me what I was doing there: "What are you
> doing here? It is nothing to do with you". I told him that he
> had no business to be doing things like that in England.'

The young lady claimed damages for trespass and assault. The
case was tried by Mr Justice Devlin (as he then was) and a jury.
He summed up in the way in which judges have always summed
up ever since the days of Lord Chief Justice Pratt. He told the jury
that they could award exemplary damages 'so as to show the
defendant that he cannot do that sort of thing with impunity'.
The jury awarded a total of £5,500, made up of £1,500 for
trespass, £1,000 for assault and £3,000 exemplary damages.

Mr Ryder appealed. His appeal was dismissed. Lord Justice
Singleton said: 'I can see no fault in the direction given by
Devlin J'. Lord Justice Hodson and I agreed.

Now I am sorry to find that in the House of Lords in *Rookes v
Barnard* Lord Devlin said (page 1229) that

> '*Loudon v Ryder* ought, I think, to be completely overruled. . . .
> The case was not one in which exemplary damages ought to
> have been given as such.'

This looks to me like a piece of retrospective legislation. *Loudon v
Ryder* was right at the time it was decided. It was in complete
accord with the law as laid down for hundreds of years. It ought
not to have been overruled.

5 Was it not a forcible entry?

Beyond doubt Ryder was guilty of forcible entry contrary to a statute passed as long ago as 1381 which, translated from the Norman-French, said:

'None from henceforth make any entry into any lands and tenements but in case where entry is given by the law: and in such case not with strong hand, nor with multitude of people, but in peaceable and easy manner. And if any man from henceforth do to the contrary, he shall be punished by imprisonment.'

That Act is still on the Statute Book. Ryder was certainly in breach of it. He entered 'with strong hand' and 'with multitude of people'; he used 'actual violence and struck terror' into the breast of the occupier – to use the phrases in the case. Was not Ryder guilty of an oppressive, arbitrary and unconstitutional action? Just as much as the officers who broke the locks of John Wilkes's bureau? or detained the printers' man for six hours? Why should not a jury give exemplary damages in *Ryder's* case just as they did in those cases? Why should the jury not say in *Ryder's* case as the electrician did: 'You have no business to be doing things like that in England', and to award damages according to the principle laid down by Lord Chief Justice Pratt

'to deter from any such proceeding for the future, and as a proof of the detestation of the jury to the action itself'?

6 Poisoning the barley

To prove my point, just think of what happened in 1818. The case was *Sears v Lyons*.[1] A man mixed poison with barley and threw the poisoned barley on to his neighbour's land – intending that his fowls should eat it – as they did. Many died. It was contended for the defendant that the plaintiff was not entitled to greater damages than the value of the fowls and that the jury could not take into their consideration the malicious intention conceived by the defendant. Mr Justice Abbott (afterwards Lord Chief Justice Tenterden, one of the best of judges) directed the jury:

'It has always been held that for trespass and entry into the

1 (1818) 2 Stark 317.

house or lands of the plaintiff, you the jury may consider not only the mere pecuniary damage sustained by the plaintiff but also the intention with which the act has been done, whether for insult or injury. You are not confined in this case to the mere damage resulting from throwing poisoned barley but may consider also the object with which it was thrown.'

The fowls were only worth £1 or £2, but the jury awarded damages of £50 – that is, the equivalent of £1,000 today.

Lord Devlin does not mention that case. He would have difficulty in fitting it into his theory.

7 The conduct of F E Smith

From long experience I know that judges always left the damages at large to the jury, telling them they could take everything into account. Not only the conduct of the defendant but also of his counsel at the trial. The jury always found the damages in one lump sum. The Court of Appeal never interfered with the verdict except in extreme cases. I always like the way in which Lord Justice Hamilton put it in *Greenlands v Wilmshurst*:[1]

'It is said that the defendant's counsel set the jury against him by the impetuosity of his attack on the plaintiffs and that the jury could inflame the damages for that. Still, in my opinion by no formula or manipulation can £1,000 be got at. For any damage really done, £100 was quite enough: double it for the sympathy: double it again for the jury's sense of the defendant's conduct, and again for their sense of Mr F E Smith's. The product is only £800. I am aware that "In libel the assessment of damages does not depend on any definite legal rule": per Lord Watson in *Bray v Ford*.[2] There must be some reasonable relation between the wrong done and the solatium applied. The verdict is excessive and cannot stand.'

(You must understand that Mr F E Smith KC (afterwards Lord Birkenhead, the Lord Chancellor) was the most effective counsel of the day.)

1 [1913] 3 KB 507 at 532.
2 [1896] AC 44 at 50.

9 Exemplary damages after 1964

1 The gallant Commander Broome RN

Then there is the problem case of *Broome v Cassell*.[1] I have told about this in some detail in *The Discipline of Law* (pages 308–312) together with the description in *The Family Story* (pages 117–118) so I will not repeat it all here. I feel myself that it was a case where the jury under the former system of law were fully entitled to award exemplary damages. The libel was a gross calumny on a brave man – done without any justification or excuse – after being warned that it reeked of defamation. £40,000 was not a penny too much – in the eyes of the ordinary citizen – though it was to some who live in an ivory tower.

2 Lord Wilberforce gets it right

I would only add one word more here. I would ask those who are interested in the subject to 'read, mark, learn and inwardly digest' the speech of Lord Wilberforce in the House of Lords in *Broome v Cassell* [1972] AC 1027 in the eight pages 1113–1120. He disposed of the theory that the purpose of the law of tort is solely compensatory – and not punitive – in this passage (page 1114):

'It cannot lightly be taken for granted, even as a matter of theory, that the purpose of the law of tort is compensation, still less that it ought to be – an issue of large social import – or that there is something inappropriate or illogical or anomalous (a question-begging word) in including a punitive element in

1 [1971] 2 QB 354, [1972] AC 1027.

202

civil damages, or, conversely, that the criminal law, rather than the civil law, is in these cases the better instrument for conveying social disapproval, or for redressing a wrong to the social fabric, or that damages in any case can be broken down into the two separate elements. As a matter of practice English law has not committed itself to any of these theories: it may have been wiser than it knew.'

He supported the old system in this passage (page 1116):

'My Lords, I think there was much merit in what I understand was the older system, before *Rookes v Barnard*. I agree with the Court of Appeal that in substance, though not perhaps philosophically or linguistically, this was clear and as explained above I doubt if there was any confusion as to what the judge should do. It was to direct the jury in general terms to give a single sum taking the various elements, or such of them as might exist in the case, into account including the wounded feelings of the plaintiff and the conduct of the defendant, but warning them not to double count and to be moderate. . . . As evidence that modern practice corresponds I could not desire more than the passage, based on considerable experience, in the judgment of Salmon LJ in this case, *Broome v Cassell*.'[1]

He disposed of *Rookes v Barnard* by showing that Lord Devlin cannot have intended it to apply to libel cases (page 1119):

'Defamation is normally thought of as par excellence the tort when punitive damages may be claimed. It was so presented in argument by counsel for the respondent (arguing against punitive damages) and he was an acknowledged expert in the subject. Every practitioner and every judge would take this view. . . .

It is difficult to believe that Lord Devlin was intending to limit the scope of punitive damages in defamation actions so as to exclude highly malicious or irresponsible libels. At least if he intended to do so at a time when the media of communication are more powerful than they have ever been and certainly not motivated only by a desire to make money, and since elsewhere

1 [1971] 2 QB 354 at 387–388.

the judgment shows him conscious of the need to [impose a] sanction [on] the irresponsible, malicious or oppressive use of power, I would have expected some reasons to be given.'

3 Aggravated damages

Lord Wilberforce also drew attention to the fact that even Lord Devlin admitted that a jury might give 'aggravated damages' for the wounded feelings of the plaintiff in having the libel published about him. Lord Devlin explained that many cases (in which judges spoke of exemplary damages) were really cases of aggravated damages. Lord Wilberforce did not think much of that explanation. He said of it (page 1115):

'. . . to do so seems to attribute a high degree of confusion of thought or inaccuracy of expression to judges of eminence . . .'.

All I would say about 'aggravated damages' is that it is an open-ended expression which contains a considerable punitive element. The feelings of the plaintiff are wounded by the disgraceful conduct of the defendant. By giving him damages for injured feelings you are at the same time awarding him damages for the disgraceful conduct of the defendant. Nowadays judges (in order to keep on the right side of the House of Lords) tell the juries that they may award aggravated damages but not exemplary damages: and that they can award one lump sum to cover all his compensation. In practice this often includes as much for aggravated damages as it would previously have done for exemplary damages. So why all this fuss? Let me tell you of our latest case.[1] It is a good illustration of some of the points I have been making.

4 A wealthy benefactor of the Liberal party

It all arose because Mr Jeremy Thorpe was the leader of the Liberal party in Parliament. A man called Norman Scott alleged that he had had a homosexual relationship with Mr Thorpe.

1 *Hayward v Thompson* [1981] 3 WLR 470.

Then whilst Mr Scott was walking with his dog on Exmoor, an airline pilot, Andrew Newton, came in close and shot the dog. He said that he had been paid £5,000 to shoot Mr Scott but instead he shot the dog. Then the *Sunday Telegraph* came out with this article on the front page:

'TWO MORE IN SCOTT AFFAIR

By Christopher House, Crime Correspondent

The names of two more people connected with the Norman Scott affair have been given to the police. One is a wealthy benefactor of the Liberal party and the other is a businessman from the Channel Islands.

Both men, police have been told, arranged for a leading Liberal supporter to be "reimbursed" £5,000, the same amount Mr Andrew Newton alleges he was paid to murder Mr Scott.'

Now there was a wealthy benefactor of the Liberal party. He was Mr Jack Hayward, a staunch Englishman of unimpeachable character. Mr Hayward said that the article imputed that he was a party to a plot to murder Mr Norman Scott. He brought an action for damages. The crime correspondent, Mr House, gave evidence that, at the time of this article, he did not know Mr Jack Hayward or anything of him. He got his information from an informant. He did not give his name. Journalists never do. The jury found that it was a libel on Mr Hayward. They awarded him £50,000 damages. There was an appeal to the Court of Appeal.

5 The intention of the journalist

In the course of my judgment I ventured to emphasise that in my view the intention of the journalist was the most important factor. In a way I was seeking to try to depart from *Hulton v Jones* and to emphasise, as I have said, what I think the rule of law should be.

'One thing is of the essence in the law of libel. It is that the words should be defamatory and untrue and should be published "of and concerning the plaintiff". That is, the plaintiff should be aimed at or intended by the defendant. If the defendant intended to refer to the plaintiff, he cannot escape liability simply by not giving his name. He may use asterisks or blanks. He may use initials or words with a hidden meaning. He may use any other device. But still, if he intended to refer to the plaintiff, he is liable. He is to be given credit for hitting the person whom he intended to hit.'

6 The amount of damages

I also sought to depart in some ways from *Rookes v Barnard.*

'So long as journalists insist on keeping secret their sources of information (for which they are now to get statutory authority in section 11 of the Contempt of Court Act 1981), I think they must take the rough of it together with the smooth. They cannot expect the jury to believe that they got their information from a trustworthy informant on whom they were entitled to rely – when they refuse to give his name. They cannot expect the jury to believe that it was not solicited or not paid for or rewarded by them – when they will not disclose how they got it. They cannot expect the jury to be sympathetic to them when they "lose" their notebooks: so that they cannot be disclosed to the court. The assessment of damages is peculiarly the province of the jury in an action of libel. If they take a poor view of the conduct of any of the defendants – be it journalist, sub-editor, editor or proprietor – they are entitled to fix whatever sum they think fit in aggravation of damages without distinguishing between them – so long as they do not wander off into the forbidden territory of exemplary damages.'

7 Put technicalities aside

Then I dealt with the technicalities:

'As the argument of Mr Bateson (for the defendants) proceeded, I could not help feeling: How unfortunate it is that our law of libel has become so technical and so complicated. He submitted that the judge ruled wrongly on this point or on that: misdirected the jury on this point or that: or failed to direct them on this distinction or that: and that there should be a new trial on one or other of those grounds.

To my mind in an action for libel a Court of Appeal should pay no regard to any supposed misdirection by the judge – on law or on fact – unless it was plainly such as to lead to a substantial miscarriage of justice.'

10 Trial by jury – or by judge?

1 Lord Justice Lawton adds his aid

In the Part of this book dealing with 'Trial by jury', I said that there are some cases – often of much importance – which 'are quite unsuitable to be tried by a jury selected at random'. I added that, if it were practicable, 'I should like to see revived a panel of special jurors for commercial frauds and like cases'.

Those observations apply with especial force to libel cases – to which I would add the pungent observations of Lord Justice Lawton in a memorandum to the Faulks Committee on Defamation:

'Once the issues become complicated and the doing of justice requires inferences to be drawn from proved facts, then I feel certain juries begin to flounder and do one of two things: either they work on "hunches" (and the "hunch" can often be that of the know-all on the jury) or they do what they think the judge wants them to do – and they may get this wrong if the judge has given a well-balanced summing-up which doesn't disclose in any way what he thinks about the case. The difficulties which can face juries in defamation cases are illustrated by one aspect of the recent "Mafia" case.[1] In that case an important issue, but only one of many, was this:- why did the plaintiffs, who were a public company, make a takeover bid for Butlins Holiday Camps? A good deal of evidence was led about the commercial and financial consideration which influenced the making of the bid. The jury heard evidence from

---

[1] *Associated Leisure Ltd v Associated Newspapers Ltd* reported on an interlocutory point in [1970] 2 QB 450.

the plaintiff's directors, accountants, stockbrokers and merchant bankers, all of whom were cross-examined at length. Who were the jurors? Nearly all manual workers living in the inner south-eastern London suburbs.'[1]

2 The editor came in person

To my mind the right solution is that which was proposed by the Faulks Committee. There should no longer be a right on either party to have trial by jury. It should lie in the discretion of the judge. He should hold a pre-trial inquiry to decide whether there should be trial by jury or not: and either party should have an appeal to the Court of Appeal without the need for obtaining leave. You would, I am sure, find that in all proper cases there would still be trial by jury. The Court would follow guide-lines laid down in the case, *Rothermere v Times Newspapers*,[2] in which Mr Bernard Levin in *The Times* had criticised Lord Rothermere and his colleagues. *The Times* wanted trial by jury. Lord Rothermere wanted trial by judge alone. The editor, Mr Rees-Mogg, came in person and argued the case before us. I said (pages 452–453):

'It is one of the essential freedoms that the newspapers should be able to make fair comment on matters of public interest. So long as they get their facts correct, they are entitled to speak out. The editor of *The Times* sees this case as a challenge to this freedom. He asks that this challenge should be tried by a jury. He himself came before us. He reminded us of the right given by our constitution to a defendant who is charged with libel, either in criminal or in civil proceedings. Every defendant has a constitutional right to have his guilt or innocence determined by a jury. This right is of the highest importance, especially when the defendant has ventured to criticise the government of the day, or those who hold authority or power in the state. . . .

Looking back on our history, I hold that, if a newspaper has criticised in its columns the great and the powerful on a matter

1 (1975) Cmnd 5909, para 464.
2 [1973] 1 WLR 448.

of large public interest – and is then charged with libel – then its guilt or innocence should be tried with a jury, if the newspaper asks for it, even though it requires the prolonged examination of documents.'

But there it is. Although the Faulks Committee recommended that the judge should have a discretion, Parliament has not implemented the recommendation.

11 Legal aid

Defamation cases are the only cases in which no legal aid is available. There is a good deal to be said for refusing legal aid in them. Take a slander case. One says he was spoken ill of across the garden fence. He was accused of stealing apples. That gives rise to a reasonable cause of action. But it is not a case for legal aid. No public money should be spent on petty quarrels of that kind. Take a libel case where the only publication alleged is dictated to a typist. There is a reasonable cause of action but it involves issues of malice and so forth – with the plaintiff raking up all the evidence he can to support a charge of malice. That is not a case for legal aid.

But there are some cases which would seem very appropriate for legal aid to be given. I would like to see it applied where there is a reasonable case for the plaintiff and where the Area Committee feel that it is a suitable case for the state to pay the costs. If the Area Committee were given liberty to grant legal aid in such a case it might be desirable. But unsuitable cases should be rigorously excluded. If this were done, I would agree with the recommendation of the Faulks Committee that legal aid should be extended to cover defamation cases.[1]

1 (1975) Cmnd 5909, para 581.

Conclusion

Both judges and text-writers alike have deplored the state of the law of libel. In *Slim v Daily Telegraph* Lord Justice Salmon said:[1]

> 'Any attempt to rationalise the law of libel would have proved a daunting task even before 1964.'

He added that it has not been made any easier by two cases in the House of Lords in that year 1964: *Lewis v Daily Telegraph*[2] and *Rookes v Barnard*.[3] Lord Justice Diplock said that the law of libel 'has passed beyond redemption by the courts'.

1 Throw out Artemus Jones

I venture to suggest that things went badly wrong when the House of Lords in *Hulton v Jones*[4] decided in 1910 (contrary to the view of Lord Justice Fletcher Moulton) that the intention of the writer or publisher is immaterial. His meaning does not matter. All that matters is the meaning put upon the words by the readers. Not all readers by any means. But only some readers. According to *Hulton v Jones* if only a few readers, out of some odd piece of information, or by some quirk of their own, put upon the words a secondary meaning, defamatory of the plaintiff, he can recover damages from the writer or publisher, no matter how innocent he may be of any intention to defame anyone.

This is quite contrary to sound principle, especially when you

1 [1968] 2 QB 157 at 179.
2 [1964] AC 234.
3 [1964] AC 1129.
4 [1910] AC 20.

212

remember that libel always was and still is a crime. It is established by a host of authorities that *mens rea* – a guilty mind – or a guilty intent – is an essential ingredient of every offence unless some reason can be found for holding that it is not necessary: see *Sweet v Parsley*.[1] The indictment for a crime – the pleading in an action – always alleged that the words were published 'falsely and maliciously of and concerning' the prosecutor or the plaintiff as the case might be. How can the publication be said to be 'of and concerning' the plaintiff when the defendant did not know of his existence? How can the defendant be said 'falsely and maliciously' to have had a guilty intent when he was quite innocent of any intent to defame anyone?

It is a direct consequence of *Hulton v Jones* that we have all the cases on secondary meanings giving absurd results, such as *Cassidy's* case and *Morgan v Odhams Press*, and all the cases about 'true' and 'false' innuendos, such as *Lewis v Daily Telegraph*.

I would like to see the House of Lords take *Hulton v Jones* by the scruff of the neck and throw it out of the courts, and start afresh.

Powerful support for this view is to be found in an article written by Professor Sir William Holdsworth in the *Law Quarterly Review* of January 1941. He called it 'A Chapter of Accidents in the Law of Libel'. Since that time we have had – not a chapter – but a whole book. There has been a pile-up like on a motor-way. I regret to say, however, that in 1975 the Faulks Committee did not recommend the abolition of the rule in *Hulton v Jones*: see Cmnd 5909, paragraph 123. They left it as Lord Porter's Committee had left it years before.

2 'Fair information on a matter of public interest'

On broad principles, too, it is of the first importance that the newspapers and the media should be free. So long as this freedom is exercised in the public interest – and, I may add – for the public interest – it should not be subject to undue restraint. If they intentionally defame a person – without justification or excuse –

1 [1970] AC 132 at 149.

let them be made liable in damages. But if they are quite innocent, let them go free.

On principle, too, I would add this: If things go wrong in society and it is in the public interest that they should be made known and righted, then the newspapers and the media should be protected by a privilege. So long as they act fairly and publish information which the public have a right to know or ought to know, the newspapers and media should not be liable in the absence of malice. That is why I would like to see qualified privilege granted, not only to fair comment, but also to 'fair information on a matter of public interest' as suggested by Mr Justice Pearson in *Webb v The Times*:[1] such as information about a crime that has been committed and the police are looking for the man. They name someone whom they want to 'interview'. Or someone is 'helping the police with their inquiries'. Even though some of the information may afterwards turn out to be erroneous – even though the facts may turn out not to be truly stated – and may be defamatory of an individual – nevertheless the public interest in the flow of information should not be hampered or hindered: provided always that a correction is made as soon as the error is discovered.

3 Throw out *Rookes v Barnard*

But if the newspapers or media abuse their power – if they get information by bribery or corruption – or if they distort information which they have – and publish it scandalously – no matter whether it be for profit or not – then I think this gross abuse should be punished. It used in times past to be punished by proceedings in the criminal courts. But now that such proceedings have fallen into disuse, I think it can and should be punished by an award of exemplary damages. Our legal system should be framed so as to deter the powerful from abusing their power – no matter whether it is the government or their servants – or nowadays the newspapers and the media – who are just as powerful, indeed more powerful, than the servants of government. That is why I think the House of Lords went wrong in *Rookes v Barnard*. If they

1 [1960] 2 QB 535 at 565.

had kept to the old law – as stated by Lord Chief Justice Pratt in *John Wilkes's* case – we should not have had all that trouble in *Broome v Cassell*. The jury would have awarded one lump sum of £40,000 and costs. That would have been the end of it. As it was, the case went to the House of Lords – where Lord Wilberforce afterwards showed pretty plainly that it was wrong – and Captain Broome (as he then was) had to bear half his own costs in the Court of Appeal and the House of Lords. I have always thought that was most unfair to the gallant Captain. It was indirectly a means of depriving him of much of the £25,000 exemplary damages which the jury awarded him – and which, I suspect, most of the House felt that he ought not to have had.

4 Another Report shelved

Is there any hope of these suggestions bearing fruit? I fear not. In 1975 the Faulks Committee on Defamation made many valuable recommendations. But they have not been implemented. What is the use of appointing Committees if their Reports are shelved? Will you find anyone to serve on Committees in the future if that is their fate? So, as things stand, the law of libel will remain in its deplorable state for a long time to come. It is past redemption by the courts. Parliament will fear to tread. So I rush in. As Pope said in his *Essay on Criticism*, 'Fools rush in where angels fear to tread'.

5 Summary

To summarise, may I suggest:

1 That liability for libel should depend on the intention of the publisher – on the natural and ordinary meaning – and not on any secondary meaning.
2 That the distinction between 'true' and 'false' innuendos should be abolished.
3 That there should be a defence of 'fair information on a matter of public interest'.

4 That exemplary damages should be allowed in libel actions.
5 That all technicalities should be abolished.
6 That trial by jury be discretionary.
7 That legal aid be available.

Part six

Privacy and confidence

1 Two human rights in conflict

We are here concerned with a conflict between two fundamental human rights: the right of privacy; and the freedom of the press. Each is contained in the European Convention on Human Rights which has been signed by the United Kingdom, but not yet enacted as part of our law.

The first of these human rights is the right of privacy:

'*Article* 8
1. Everyone has the right to respect for his private and family life, his home and his correspondence.
2. There shall be no interference by a public authority with the exercise of this right except such as is in accordance with the law and is necessary in a democratic society in the interests of national security, public safety or the economic well-being of the country, for the prevention of disorder or crime, for the protection of health or morals, or for the protection of the rights and freedoms of others.'

The other of these human rights is the freedom of the press:

'*Article* 10
1. Everyone has the right to freedom of expression. This right shall include freedom to hold opinions and to receive and impart information and ideas without interference by public authority and regardless of frontiers. This Article shall not prevent states from requiring the licensing of broadcasting, television or cinema enterprises.
2. The exercise of these freedoms, since it carries with it duties and responsibilities, may be subject to such formalities,

conditions, restrictions or penalties as are prescribed by law and are necessary in a democratic society, in the interests of national security, territorial integrity or public safety, for the prevention of disorder or crime, for the protection of health or morals, for the protection of the reputation or rights of others, for preventing the disclosure of information received in confidence, or for maintaining the authority and impartiality of the judiciary.'

You will notice there that each of these human rights is subject to large exceptions: and that each of them may come into conflict with the other. Thus freedom of expression may be subject to restrictions so as to preserve the right of confidence. How are these two human rights to be reconciled? That is what I wish to discuss in this Part.

2 Our case-law

Our English law on this subject is not set out in any statute. It is contained in our law books. I can best explain it by telling you of some of our leading cases.

1 The royal etchings

The case of the royal etchings, *Prince Albert v Strange*,[1] is the foundation of the law about privacy and breach of confidence. I referred to it in a speech which I made in the House of Lords in 1961 and told something of it. It is in *The Family Story* (page 188) but as it is so pertinent to the present discussion I hope you will forgive me if I tell you more about it now.

In 1849 people did not take family photographs. Instead, Queen Victoria and her husband, Prince Albert, made sketches. They made drawings of the children and of their close friends. They were so pleased with them that they had impressions made of them by means of a private press. There were about sixty-three different sketches of which impressions were made. They kept them in their private apartments at Windsor. They employed a printer called Brown to make the impressions. He employed a man, Middleton, who took them surreptitiously and sold them to a man called Judge. Then Judge took them to a publisher, Strange, who made reproductions of them and prepared a catalogue with this title:

1 (1849) 1 Hall & Twells 1.

'A Descriptive Catalogue of the Royal Victoria and Albert Gallery of Etchings

Every purchaser of this catalogue will be presented (by permission) with a *fac-simile* of the autograph of either Her Majesty or of the Prince Consort, engraved from the original, the selection being left to the purchaser. Price sixpence.'

Strange said that he struck off 51 copies only and then broke up the type. He did not sell any or offer them for sale: because he heard that the Queen and the Prince disapproved of it. So he submitted to an injunction about the impressions themselves. He did, however, want to publish the catalogue. The Prince sought an injunction to restrain him from publishing the catalogue. Strange disputed it. The only question was about the right to publish the catalogue.

The Lord Chancellor, Lord Cottenham, granted an injunction. He said that the information (from which the catalogue was compiled) must have originated in a breach of trust, confidence or contract in Brown or some person in his employ: and that an injunction should be granted to stop the publication of such confidential information.

2 The physician's diary

In that case the Lord Chancellor quoted the case of *Wyatt v Wilson* which came before the court in 1820 when King George III had just died. Lord Eldon said:

'If one of the late king's physicians had kept a diary of what he had heard and seen, this court would not in the king's lifetime, have permitted him to print or publish it.'[1]

That observation is significant. It is the first instance I know of a right of privacy as distinct from a right of confidence. The King had not given any confidential information to the physician. But by publishing the diary, the physician would infringe the King's right of privacy. King George III, as you will remember, went off his head. Suppose the physician had written in his diary: 'The

1 (1820) 1 Hall & Twells 25.

222

King walked into the garden and behold, like the Emperor in the fable, he had no clothes' and proposed to publish it. Lord Eldon would, I am sure, have granted an injunction to restrain the publisher. To bring it to modern times: Suppose a photographer with a long-distance lens took a picture of a prominent person in a loving embrace in his garden with a woman who was not his wife. Surely an injunction would be granted to stop it being published. The only cause of action, so far as I know, would be for infringement of privacy.

A recent instance, in February 1982, is where some newspapers published a photograph of the Princess of Wales on holiday – in a bikini – when everyone knew that she was expecting a baby. That was a gross infringement of privacy. The newspapers afterwards apologised but surely it was contrary to law.

3 The Duke and Duchess talk privately

Now let me leave royalty and descend to dukes and duchesses. It is the case where Margaret, Duchess of Argyll, sued Ian Douglas, Duke of Argyll, and joined as defendant a Sunday newspaper, *The People* (*Duchess of Argyll v Duke of Argyll*).[1] The Duke and Duchess had married in 1951 and were divorced in 1963. During the early years of their marriage, they discussed – as all married couples do – their personal affairs freely between themselves. They discussed 'our attitudes, our feelings, our hopes, aspirations and foibles, our past lives and previous marriages'. The Duke then came to an arrangement with *The People* by which they were to publish articles based on information supplied by him. The Duke told *The People* all sorts of things which the Duchess had told him. He told *The People* her secrets relating to her private life and *The People* proposed to publish them.

The Duchess moved for an injunction to restrain the Duke and *The People* from publishing her secrets. Mr Justice Ungoed-Thomas granted it, not only against the Duke, but also against *The People*. The decision was based on breach of confidence – broken by the Duke – and knowingly aided and abetted by *The People*.

1 [1967] 1 Ch 302.

But the reason I mention the case at this stage is this: Suppose the husband had not broken any confidence. Suppose the husband and wife – or any other couple – were in a hotel bedroom which had been 'bugged' by a device which recorded all their private conversations: that it was all on tape and was to be published by *The People*. The bugger (if I may use that word) would not have been guilty of a breach of confidence: because he had not been entrusted with any confidence. But surely he would have been guilty of an infringement of privacy. The hotel might sue him for trespass in placing the device there, but the couple could only sue for infringement of privacy.

I suggest that any unreasonable intrusion upon the plaintiff's seclusion or solitude or into his private affairs is an infringement of his right of privacy.

So it would be an infringement for anyone – the police or anyone else – to tap a person's private conversations on the telephone: or to have any secret listening device. Any such conduct could only be justified or excused if it could be brought within such reasons as national security or the prevention of crime.

4 The golfer's piece of chocolate

In my young days Cyril Tolley was the amateur golf champion of England. But Fry's, the chocolate manufacturers, without his permission put an advertisement in the newspapers. There was a caricature of Mr Tolley hitting one of his most vigorous drives with a carton of Fry's chocolate sticking prominently out of his pocket. Beneath it were the words:

> 'The caddy to Tolley said, "Oh, Sir!
> Good shot, sir, that ball see it go, Sir!
> My word, how it flies,
> Like a cartet of Fry's,
> They're handy, they're good and priced low, Sir!"'

In the case, *Tolley v J S Fry & Sons Ltd*,[1] some of the judges thought that the advertisement was defamatory of Mr Tolley

1 [1930] 1 KB 467, [1931] AC 333.

because it imputed that he was being paid money for it: and was thus departing from his amateur status. But two of the judges thought it was not defamatory of him. Now suppose those two were right. Suppose it was not a libel. Was it not an infringement of his right of privacy? Nevertheless Lord Justice Greer denied it. He said:[1]

'I have no hesitation in saying that in my judgment the defendants in publishing the advertisement in question, without first obtaining Mr Tolley's consent, acted in a manner inconsistent with the decencies of life, and in doing so they were guilty of an act for which there ought to be a legal remedy. But unless a man's photograph, caricature, or name be published in such a context that the publication can be said to be defamatory within the law of libel, it cannot be made the subject-matter of complaint by action at law.'

That dictum has been taken as a denial of any right of privacy in English law. Surely, in Lord Justice Greer's own words, 'there ought to be a legal remedy'. I suggest that there is one. If the defendant indulges in publicity which places the plaintiff in a false light in the public eye, it is an infringement of his right of privacy.

1 [1930] 1 KB 467 at 478.

3 Breach of confidence

1 It is actionable

Ever since *Prince Albert v Strange* the courts have restrained a breach of confidence. They will restrain the recipient from breaking it by communicating it to another. They will likewise restrain anyone else who uses it or seeks to use it, knowing that it originated in confidence. I sought to sum it all up in *Seager v Copydex* where I said:[1]

'The law on this subject does not depend on any implied contract. It depends on the broad principle of equity that he who has received information in confidence shall not take unfair advantage of it. He must not make use of it to the prejudice of him who gave it without obtaining his consent.'

Whilst that is the approach of a court of equity, I see no reason why breach of confidence should not be regarded as a tort. It is in the same class of wrongdoing as inducing a breach of contract – which is always regarded as a tort. It should not only be restrained by injunction. Any breach should give rise to an action for damages.

2 There is the public interest to consider

The power of the courts – to restrain a breach of confidence – or to give damages for it – is subject to an important limitation. A breach may be justified or excused if it is done in the public interest. Time after time the courts have to balance the two

1 [1967] 1 WLR 923 at 931.

226

competing interests: on the one hand there is the public interest in ensuring confidentiality; on the other hand there is the public interest in having information disclosed. These two public interests reach their climax in investigative journalism. To this I will return later.

But meanwhile I wish to establish this broad proposition: that it is a matter of balancing the competing public interests. I propounded it in a leading case, *D v National Society for the Prevention of Cruelty to Children*,[1] to which I am coming. It was not accepted by the House of Lords at the time. But I believe it points the way for the future. So I would develop it here.

3 Talk of privilege

The trouble about this whole subject is that it has got mixed up with talk of 'privilege'. We speak of Crown privilege, legal professional privilege, public interest privilege, and all sorts of privileges. In this context the lawyers are using the word 'privilege' in a very special sense. They use it as a right to keep things secret – to keep things back from your opponent or from the court – so that they cannot get to know of them.

In this discussion I am going to abandon any talk of privilege. I am going to show how the leading cases fit into my proposition about competing public interests. First, I will tell you of those cases where confidentiality has prevailed, and the courts have not allowed it to be broken. Then I will tell you of cases where the courts have allowed breaches of confidence because they are outweighed by the public interest in disclosure. They are all leading cases within the last few years.

1 [1978] AC 171.

4 Confidentiality prevails

1 Bingo clubs want a licence

The case which started the modern trend was *R v Lewes JJ*.[1]
Previously we had always talked about Crown privilege. Now
the House of Lords spoke of public interest. It made the public
interest the decisive factor.

In 1967 the gaming clubs in England were having a very
profitable time. They had found a way to avoid the Gaming
Acts. The courts had let through their devices. The prospects
were so promising that new clubs were springing up all the time –
with all sorts of evil consequences. So Parliament intervened.
'Enough', it said, 'of these devices. We are tired of this continual
battle between the gaming clubs and the law – with the clubs
always one jump ahead. We will try a new way altogether.' In
1968, Parliament enacted the Gaming Act 1968. It enacted that
there was to be no gaming at all except in premises licensed for
the purpose: and before any person could even apply for a
licence, he had to be certified as one who could be trusted.

A company in Sussex applied to the Gaming Board for a
licence to carry on five bingo clubs. The Board made inquiries of
the police about the company and its director, Mr Henry Rogers.
The police sent a letter to the Gaming Board reporting very
unfavourably about the director. The letter was very confidential
for the information of the Gaming Board. Somehow or other the
director got hold of a copy of the letter. He said that the information in it was false and was a libel on him. He instituted proceedings for criminal libel – very rare, as I have previously pointed
out. In those proceedings he had to prove the sending of the

1 [1973] AC 388.

letter and the receipt of it. He claimed that it should be produced in the interest of justice – so as to enable him to prove it in the criminal proceedings that he had started. But the House of Lords held that it was in the public interest to keep the letter confidential and that it should not be disclosed in the criminal proceedings. Lord Reid said (page 402):

> 'On balance the public interest clearly requires that documents of this kind should not be disclosed, and that public interest is not affected by the fact that by some wrongful means a copy of such a document has been obtained and published by some person.'

I have often wondered why Mr Rogers brought criminal proceedings for libel. Why did he not bring a civil action?

2 Was the baby battered?

The next case to stress the public interest was the one I have mentioned, *D v NSPCC*.[1] A mother had a baby girl only fourteen months old. She put her to sleep in her cot and went downstairs, waiting for her husband to come back from work. There was a knock at the door. She answered it. A man produced a visiting card showing that he was a representative of the National Society for the Prevention of Cruelty to Children. She thought he was coming for some charitable purpose for the Society. She asked him in. He asked her how the baby was. She said: 'Very well'. He said: 'We have an allegation that you have been beating your child'. She said: 'You must be mad'. She was terribly upset. She went upstairs and awakened the baby. She took her out of her cot and showed her to the inspector. The baby looked fine. The mother was distraught. She telephoned the doctor. He came and examined the child. The doctor said she was a perfect baby. The inspector gave the impression both to the mother and the doctor that he thought the allegations were true, although not proved. Her husband then came in. He, too, was

1 [1978] AC 171.

very upset. He said that it was essential that they be told the name of the informant, but the inspector would not give it.

The mother and father took proceedings against the NSPCC. They claimed damages because of the shock to the mother at the allegations made against her. They also asked to be given the name and address of the informant.

The NSPCC told the court that they always gave an assurance to informants that any information they received would be treated as confidential. They issued a leaflet containing this provision:

> 'Do you know of a child who may be suffering because of misfortune, ignorance, neglect or ill-treatment? . . . If so please tell your nearest NSPCC Inspector at (giving his or her address). Your name, and the information you give for the purpose of helping children, will be treated as confidential. Your immediate action may prevent a child from suffering.'

In giving judgment, I put it as a question of holding the balance. I said (page 192):

> 'In the scales on the one side I put the reasons why it is in the public interest that the name and address of the informant should be given. There is only one reason which is of any weight at all. It is that it will assist the mother in her action for damages. It will enable her to bring in the informant as a defendant and to investigate the circumstances in which the information was given. . . .
>
> In the scales on the other side I put the reasons why it is in the public interest that the name and address should not be given.
>
> There are several. The first is that the Society should be able to continue its good work. If it is to be compelled to disclose the names, its sources of information will dry up. The second is that confidences should be respected. The law should not compel the Society to break faith with those who have placed their trust in it. The third is that grave injustice may be done to the informant if he or she is to be the object of resentment by the mother, or harassed by an action for libel or slander, when

she is not shown to have done any wrong at all, but has done all for the best.

Weighing these considerations one against the other, I think the balance comes down decisively against the name being disclosed. I find myself in complete agreement with the judge, who put it thus:

> "When one looks at the duty which has been laid by Parliament on the defendants, and bears in mind the great public interest that children should not be neglected or ill-treated, in my mind there is no doubt at all that the public interest in protecting the defendants' sources of information overrides the public interest that [the mother] should obtain the information she is seeking in order to obtain legal redress." '

I was in a minority in the Court of Appeal. The House of Lords supported my conclusion (that the NSPCC need not disclose the name of the informant) but put it on a narrow ground.

3 The unsuccessful candidate

That case was soon followed by two which threw up an important point consequent on modern legislation. They were *Science Research Council v Nassé* and *Leyland Cars Ltd v Vyas*.[1]

A lady employed by a Research Council complained that she had been passed over. She had not been selected for interview: whereas two of her male colleagues had been selected, and one of them was appointed. She complained that she had been discriminated against because of her sex. She wanted to see – not only her own confidential reports – but also the confidential reports on her two colleagues.

Likewise, an analyst of Asian origin employed by Leyland Cars Ltd applied for a transfer. He and three white candidates were interviewed. He was not successful. Two white candidates were given a transfer. He complained that he had been discriminated against because of his colour. He wanted to see – not only his own confidential report – but the confidential reports on the white candidates.

1 [1979] 1 QB 144, [1980] AC 1028.

231

Those cases were of wide concern. They would apply to applications for places at universities, to those who sit for degrees, and so forth. Is every applicant who complains of unfair treatment to be entitled to see the marks of his competitors or the reports upon them? Again it is a question between competing interests – of holding the balance. This is the answer I gave in the Court of Appeal:[1]

'In holding the balance . . . it is very important in the public interest that confidential reports should not be disclosed. Not only would their disclosure be a gross breach of faith with the makers of them, but once the subjects of the reports got to know of the disclosures, it might lead to much disturbance and unrest. Furthermore, in the long run, if the tribunals made a practice of ordering discovery (as they have done in the two cases before us) the likely result would be that the makers of the reports would make them in future by word of mouth: or write the reports in a colourless and neutral fashion, rendering them useless for the purpose in hand. So great is it in the public interest that these reports should be kept confidential that I do not think the tribunals should ever make an order at large or in general terms for the disclosure of confidential reports. They should not order the disclosure of all the references on applicants for employment, or of all the reports on candidates for entry to universities, or anything of that kind. The very furthest they should go is to order disclosure of specific documents in respect of specific individuals, where that is shown to be essential in the interests of justice: and so essential that it warrants overriding the confidence in which they were made.

Such cases must be rare.'

Then I stated the principle so as to keep it to holding the balance, but letting it be held by the chairman of the tribunal:

'The industrial tribunals should not order or permit the disclosure of reports or references that have been given and received in confidence except in the very rare cases where,

1 [1979] 1 QB 144 at 173.

after inspection of a particular document, the chairman decides that it is essential in the interests of justice that the confidence should be overridden: and then only subject to such conditions as to the divulging of it as he shall think fit to impose – both for the protection of the maker of the document and the subject of it. He might, for instance, limit the sight of it to counsel and solicitors on their undertaking that it should go no further.'

I was glad to find that the House of Lords were eventually in agreement with us in the Court of Appeal. They only took exception to my saying 'very rare cases'. They preferred to let it depend upon the discretion of the chairman. So be it. It is for him to hold the balance. This was reinforced by the next case where it was held that the court can look at disputed papers in order to hold the balance.

4 The Burmah Oil Co at the bottom of the market

In this case we discussed Crown privilege again but decided it on balancing the competing public interests. It marks the beginning of the end of Crown privilege. It is the important case of *Burmah Oil Co v Bank of England.*[1]

In 1975 the Burmah Oil Co was in a precarious position. Its condition was becoming serious. To save it from going into liquidation, it was forced to sell 80,000,000 shares in the British Petroleum Co to the Bank of England at £2.30 a share. It turned out to be the lowest price ever. The market soon recovered and in a few months the shares were worth nearly three times as much at £6.85 a share. The Burmah shareholders said that the deal was most unfair and that undue pressure was brought to bear by the government. In the interlocutory proceedings, Burmah wanted to see the confidential documents passing between the government and the Bank of England. The Chief Secretary to the Treasury made an affidavit claiming Crown privilege for many of these confidential documents. I was against it. I regarded it as a matter of weighing the competing interests. I said:[2]

1 [1979] 1 WLR 473, [1980] AC 1090.
2 [1979] 1 WLR 473 at 489.

'Weighing the competing interests in the balance here, I think the public interest would be best served by the disclosure of the documents to the other side in this litigation – with safeguards against the information in them being spread further than is necessary.

We have been able to inspect samples of the documents for which public interest is claimed. . . . Then we have to balance the competing interests. On the one hand, the public interest in keeping the deliberations of government secret. On the other hand, the public interest in seeing that justice is done between the parties. As between these two I have no doubt that priority should be given to the doing of justice between the parties. If there are some aspects which ought not to be exposed to public glare, there are ways and means available to the court to see that the information contained in them does not go beyond those immediately concerned, as is done often in cases concerning trade secrets.'

5 May the judge take a peep?

My brethren, however, did not agree: and their view was upheld by the House of Lords. The important point is, however, that the House of Lords did test it by weighing the competing interests: and they did it by looking at the confidential documents themselves – so as to decide where the public interest lay. Lord Edmund-Davies said:[1]

'A judge may well feel that he cannot profitably embark on such a balancing exercise without himself seeing the disputed documents. May he take a peep? . . .
. . . A judicial peep seems to be justifiable and may, indeed, prove vital if the judge is to be enabled to arrive at a just conclusion in the matter of discovery. . . .'

Lord Scarman added wise words as to the reasons for protecting the 'secrecy', that is, the confidentiality of government documents or discussions. He, too, thought it necessary to do the balancing exercise. He said (page 1145):

1 [1980] AC 1090 at 1129.

'The reasons given for protecting the secrecy of government at the level of policy-making are two. The first is the need for candour in the advice offered to ministers: the second is that disclosure "would create or fan ill-informed or captious public or political criticism". Lord Reid in *Conway v Rimmer*[1] thought the second "the most important reason". Indeed, he was inclined to discount the candour argument.

I think both reasons are factors legitimately to be put into the balance which has to be struck between the public interest in the proper functioning of the public service (i.e., the executive arm of government) and the public interest in the administration of justice. Sometimes the public service reasons will be decisive of the issue: but they should never prevent the court from weighing them against the injury which would be suffered in the administration of justice if the document was not to be disclosed. And the likely injury to the cause of justice must also be assessed and weighed. Its weight will vary according to the nature of the proceedings in which disclosure is sought, the relevance of the documents, and the degree of likelihood that the document will be of importance in the litigation. In striking the balance, the court may always, if it thinks it necessary, itself inspect the documents.'

In the result the House, by a majority of four to one, inspected the documents. They did the balancing act. With some hesitancy, they decided that the documents were not of such significance that they should be disclosed. They were not necessary for fairly disposing of the case.

This ruling is an illustration of the general principle: that in every case it is a matter of balancing the competing public interests involved.

6 Can the privilege be waived?

I cannot leave the *Burmah Oil* case without remarking on one relic of the old Crown privilege. It was often said that it could not be waived. The reason was because it seemed unfair that the

1 [1968] AC 910 at 952.

Crown could waive the privilege when they wanted to use the documents in support of their own case – but insist on the privilege if it supported the opponent's case. That argument was legitimate when Crown privilege was looked upon as a privilege – a right – of the Crown. But it does not apply at all when it is replaced by a balancing of competing interests. I stand by what I said on this submission in the Court of Appeal:[1]

'It is often said that Crown privilege, or public interest privilege, cannot be waived: so much so that the Crown cannot itself make use of a document even though it is in its interest to do so. I cannot believe this is correct. It is obvious to every beholder that unless a minister or his department comes to the court and asserts the privilege, the court allows the document to be used in evidence. The court has no material on which to assert a public interest privilege – unless a minister comes and informs the court of it. And, even when he does come, the court will not grant the privilege unless it is satisfied that it exists. By consciously or unconsciously failing to assert it, the Crown can to my mind effectively waive the privilege. . . .

. . . If the Crown is genuinely concerned to have the truth ascertained, and justice done, they should waive any Crown privilege in all commercial transactions, save when "overborne by the gravest considerations of state policy or security".'

7 Fishing expeditions

Finally, I would draw attention to two decisions of the Court of Appeal, *Gaskin v Liverpool City Council*[2] and *Neilson v Laugharne*.[3] These illustrate what lawyers call 'fishing expeditions'. This is when the plaintiff wants to see all the papers of the other side in order to discover whether he has a cause of action.

In the first case, *Gaskin v Liverpool City Council*, a man, nearly twenty-one, sought to sue the Council. His mother had died

1 [1979] 1 WLR 473 at 487–488.
2 [1980] 1 WLR 1549.
3 [1981] 1 WLR 537.

when he was six months old. He was taken into the care of the Council. They put him out with foster parents and afterwards to various institutions. He had a bad record. He was sent to various approved schools. He was sent to Borstal. He was afterwards arrested on a criminal charge and was sent to prison for six months.

Then he turned round on the Liverpool City Council and said it was all their fault. He got legal aid. His solicitors wanted to see all the files – containing all the confidential reports on him from the beginning. They did it so as to bolster up a claim for damages. This is what I said (page 1552):

'As always in these cases, it is a matter of balancing the public interests. The judge did balance them in accordance with the tests which have been laid down in the authorities. At the end of his judgment he said:

"I am left in no doubt that it is necessary for the proper functioning of the child care service that the confidentiality of the relevant documents should be preserved. This is a very important service to which the interests – also very important – of the individual must, in my judgment, bow. I have no doubt that the public interest will be better served by refusing discovery and this I do." '

In the second case, *Neilson v Laugharne*, a man left his home for the weekend. Whilst he was away the police went to the justices and got a search warrant for drugs. No doubt they had reasonable ground for suspecting that controlled drugs were on the premises. They searched for drugs but found none. They found some suspicious circumstances but nothing to warrant a charge being brought against him.

When Neilson got back, he saw that someone had been into the house. He got legal aid and sued the police for damages for trespass. Meanwhile the police had held an investigation of their own. The Complaints Board decided that the police had done nothing wrong. Neilson's solicitors then demanded to see all the statements made to the Complaints Board. The Court of Appeal refused. I said (page 544):

'This modern development shows that, on a question of discovery, the court can consider the competing public interests involved. The case is decided by the court holding the balance between the two sides. One of them is asserting that, in the interest of justice, the documents should be disclosed. The other is asserting that in the public interest they should not be disclosed.'

Then I went on to hold the balance:

'On the one hand we have a man who is suing the police for damages. He has got legal aid and demands to see all the statements taken by the police. He – or rather his solicitors – want to see the police statements so as to find out something, if they can, to back him up. On the other hand there are the police who, for aught that appears, apart from this man's complaint, have acted perfectly properly.'

Then this was the conclusion:

'If this man has any case at all, he must make it out on his own showing – supported by witnesses whom he can find himself. He should not be allowed to delve through these statements so as to make out a case – which he would not otherwise have.'

At this point I would refer back to the Part of this book on legal aid. No doubt in each of these last two cases, on the plaintiff's own story, if believed, there was a reasonable cause of action. But would it not have been better if the test had been: Is this a proper case for the grant of legal aid? I should have thought that it ought not to have been granted in either case.

5 Confidentiality overruled

So far I have told you of cases where the plaintiff was not allowed to see confidential documents. In each of them, the decision turned on a balancing exercise. The public interest in preserving confidentiality had to be weighed against the public interest in doing justice in the instant case. In some of these cases there was a reference to 'privilege' but this tends to confuse rather than to illuminate the task of 'holding the balance'.

Now I will turn to cases where the courts have ordered that confidential information or documents be disclosed. Again you will find that it is a balancing exercise so as to see whether the public interest lies in preserving confidentiality or in overriding it.

1 'This is the heir; come, let us kill him'

You will all remember the parable in the Bible (*St Matthew* 21:38):

> 'But when the husbandmen saw the son, they said among themselves, "This is the heir; come, let us kill him, and let us seize on his inheritance." '

It had an exact parallel in a case in 1743. It was *Annesley v Earl Anglesea*.[1] There were two brothers in Ireland. The elder brother, Earl Annesley, owned the family estates. He died, and the younger brother entered and took possession of them. But the elder brother had left a son who claimed to be the heir and entitled to the estates. The son brought an action against his uncle (the younger brother) so as to get the estates. Then, whilst the action

1 (1743) LR 5 QB 317 *in notis.*

was pending,. the son accidentally shot a man in a shooting accident. The uncle then went to his lawyer and said to him:

'I want you to prosecute the son for murder. I will spend £10,000 to get him hanged. The estates will then be mine.'

The lawyer did not prosecute the son. The son was not hanged. The case went on. The question was whether that statement of the uncle to his lawyer could be given in evidence. It was, of course, spoken in complete confidence and ordinarily would be protected from disclosure by what is now known as legal professional privilege. But the court held that the lawyer was bound to give it in evidence. It tended to show that the uncle knew that the son was the lawful heir. The son won. As was said in a later case:

'There is no confidence as to the disclosure of iniquity.'

The public interest in disclosure outweighed the public interest in preserving confidence.

2 'Laundries in Price Shock'

That case had its counterpart in modern times – in what is called investigative journalism. It is *Initial Services Ltd v Putterill*.[1]

A firm of launderers had a sales manager. He did not like the way they carried on business. So he left, taking with him a lot of documents in the company's file. He handed them to reporters of the *Daily Mail*. That newspaper studied the papers and came out on its front page with a big headline:

'LAUNDRIES IN PRICE SHOCK

The *Daily Mail* has discovered a liaison system between a group of firms in the laundry business. By this system they are keeping up prices and getting a great deal of extra profit.'

Then on the next day:

'NOW THE BOARD OF TRADE MOVES IN

The Board of Trade began investigations yesterday into the

1 [1968] 1 QB 396.

confidential system of "Inter-company liaison" operated by leading industrial laundries supplying linen-hire services.'

The firm of launderers issued a writ against the sales manager and the *Daily Mail*, claiming damages for breach of confidential information and delivery up of confidential papers. The launderers failed.

It was held by the Court of Appeal that the confidence was overridden. It was because the conduct of the firm of launderers was of such a nature that it ought in the public interest to be disclosed to others.

So here again we have the competing public interests to be balanced one against the other.

3 Has a journalist a privilege?

Then comes the leading case on this topic, *Attorney-General v Mulholland*; *Attorney-General v Foster*.[1] It was investigative journalism again. I told all about it in *The Due Process of Law* (pages 27–30) when I described how two journalists were sent to prison because they had refused to answer questions put to them by Lord Radcliffe. I venture to re-state the principle (see [1963] 2 QB 477 at 489) again here:

'It is said that however relevant these questions were and however proper to be answered for the purpose of the inquiry, a journalist has a privilege by law entitling him to refuse to give his sources of information. The journalist puts forward as his justification the pursuit of truth. It is in the public interest, he says, that he should obtain information in confidence and publish it to the world at large, for by so doing he brings to the public notice that which they should know. He can expose wrongdoing and neglect of duty which would otherwise go unremedied. He cannot get this information, he says, unless he keeps the source of it secret. The mouths of his informants will be closed to him if it is known that their identity will be disclosed. So he claims to be entitled to publish all his information without ever being under any obligation, even when

1 [1963] 2 QB 477.

241

directed by the court or a judge, to disclose whence he got it. It seems to me that the journalists put the matter much too high. The only profession that I know which is given a privilege from disclosing information to a court of law is the legal profession, and then it is not the privilege of the lawyer but of his client. Take the clergyman, the banker or the medical man. None of these is entitled to refuse to answer when directed to by a judge. Let me not be mistaken. The judge will respect the confidences which each member of these honourable professions receives in the course of it, and will not direct him to answer unless not only it is relevant, but also it is a proper and, indeed, necessary question in the course of justice to be put and answered. A judge is the person entrusted, on behalf of the community, to weigh these conflicting interests – to weigh on the one hand the respect due to confidence in the profession and on the other hand the ultimate interest of the community in justice being done or, in the case of a tribunal such as this, in a proper investigation being made into these serious allegations. If the judge determines that the journalist must answer, then no privilege will avail him to refuse.'

That principle was accepted by the House of Lords as correct in the *Granada* case to which I am coming.

4 The journalist goes to prison

In that *Mulholland* case it came down again to a balancing exercise. Where did the public interest lie? In maintaining the confidence of the journalist in his source of information? or in making him disclose it?

Mulholland did not disclose the name of his informant. He was sentenced to six months' imprisonment. He served it. That raises the crucial question: Is it right to order a journalist to give his source of information – when he feels so strongly that he would rather go to prison than name his informant? It is like the case of the twelfth juryman (of whom I have told you): 'I would rather die in prison than give a verdict against my conscience'. Does it not throw doubt on the way the courts decided the case of

Mulholland? Would not the public interest be better served by not ordering the journalist to name his source – rather than make him a martyr by sending him to prison?

5 Confidential reports are to be disclosed

Now I would say more about 'legal professional privilege'. As I showed in the *Annesley* case, that, too, can be overridden where the public interest so requires. The House of Lords so held in *Waugh v British Railways Board*.[1]

A railway driver was killed in a collision between two locomotives. An inquiry was held immediately after the accident. Then a report was made on a form which had at the top the words:

'(For the information of the Board's Solicitor:

This form is to be used by every person reporting an occurrence when litigation by or against the BRB is anticipated. It is to be provided by the person making it to his Immediate Superior Officer and has finally to be sent to the Solicitor for the purpose of enabling him to advise the BRB in regard thereto.)'

The Railways Board submitted that that heading entitled them to claim 'legal professional privilege' to keep to themselves the report and not to disclose it to the widow's solicitor. The Court of Appeal by a majority upheld the plea of privilege. I dissented. I thought the report ought to be disclosed. The House of Lords upheld my dissenting judgment. My judgment has not been reported, but the transcript (28 July 1978) is held in the Bar library. As it is very pertinent to our present discussion, I would venture to quote from it here:

'I take it to be axiomatic that the object of the law is to do justice. To achieve justice, this report ought certainly to be available to the court of trial. The court has to decide this issue: What was the cause of the accident? In preparation for the trial, the report ought to be disclosed to the widow's advisers. And at the trial it ought to be available for either side to be

1 [1980] AC 521.

243

given in evidence. Just see how valuable it is. The inquiry was held by two senior responsible railway officers expert and experienced in railway matters. It was held within two days of the accident when everything was fresh in the memories of the witnesses. Each witness gave his account clearly in answer to questions put to him. Each question and answer was taken down in handwriting. Each witness signed his statement in verification of it. Such a statement so taken is the best evidence that ever was, or could be, available to ascertain the truth. Every wise judge trying a case would give great weight to it.

Yet, strange to relate, until a few years ago that best of evidence was excluded. There was a rule of law which prevented any such statements being given in evidence. It was the rule which prohibited the giving of hearsay.'

Then I went on to say that the hearsay rule had been abolished by the Civil Evidence Act 1968:

'Section 4 makes the statements of witnesses, made at such an inquiry as this, freely admissible in evidence at the trial of the subsequent case. So, by waiving any claim to legal professional privilege, the Railways Board themselves can adduce in evidence the statements of witnesses given to the inquiry.

This means that today we are faced with a strange anomaly. Although the Railways Board are at liberty to use these statements at the trial, if they wish, in support of their own case, nevertheless they can keep them back if they think they may hurt their case, or do them no good. They can refuse to disclose the statements to the widow and her advisers. This seems to me to be most unjust. If this injustice is to be allowed to continue, it can only be because of "legal professional privilege". This privilege calls for reconsideration today, just as much as the hearsay rule did. Indeed the abolition of the hearsay rule makes imperative the reconsideration of the privilege rule.'

We did reconsider the rule about legal professional privilege. I said that it 'is not a rule in aid of justice. It is a rule in aid of litigation – which is a very different thing – and it is, moreover, a rule in aid of *one side* in litigation – which can operate very unfairly against the other side.'

Then I stated the principle which we should apply:

'We should only grant the privilege to material which comes within the words "wholly or mainly" for the purpose of litigation. We should not extend it further. If material comes into being for a dual purpose – one to find out the cause of the accident – the other to furnish information to the solicitor – it should be disclosed, because it is not then "wholly or mainly" for litigation. On this basis all the reports and inquiries into accidents – which are made shortly after the accident – should be disclosed on discovery and made available in evidence at the trial.'

The House of Lords approved this principle but substituted the word 'dominant' for my words 'wholly or mainly'.

I go on to the latest cases on confidence – especially in respect of investigative journalism.

6 All about the 'mole'

1 The *Granada* case

This is the most controversial case of modern times. It is *British Steel Corporation v Granada Television*.[1] It covers 80 pages of the Law Reports.

Someone in the British Steel Corporation got access in some way to a large number of confidential documents. Many of them were marked 'Secret'. This employee of British Steel has been called the 'mole' because he works underground secretly and no one knows what he is up to. This 'mole' came up to the surface and handed the documents to an unnamed journalist employed by Granada Television. (His name was not given so I will call him the 'unnamed' journalist.) The unnamed journalist told the 'mole': 'Thank you very much for these papers. I promise you I will not tell anyone your name or that you gave them to me.'

When the unnamed journalist examined them, he thought that they contained dynamite. It could be used to blow up British Steel. He took them along to the head of current affairs in Granada and said to him: 'Look what I have got hold of. I will not tell you how I got them. But they are top-secret papers of British Steel.'

Granada's head of current affairs got his specialists to go through them. He got their assessment. He decided that there were a number of points which were of considerable public interest that should be ventilated. He thought a programme could be constructed which would be critical of British Steel: and that it would be a good thing to invite Sir Charles Villiers, the chairman of British Steel, to take part. Sir Charles did so. The programme was shown.

1 [1980] 3 WLR 774.

British Steel felt that the programme was very unfair to them. They issued a writ against Granada Television. I must omit here a good deal of the story and come to the main point. British Steel eventually sought an order on Granada ordering them to disclose the name of the 'mole' who handed the secret papers to the journalist who handed them to Granada Television. All the courts ordered Granada to name the 'mole'. The only dissent was by Lord Salmon in the House of Lords.

There was, however, a significant difference in the reasons that were given. I stated (page 804) the principles which would entitle a newspaper (which goes in for investigative journalism) to refuse to give the name of its informant. These commended themselves to Lord Salmon who said (page 842):

'It seems to me that the principles which Lord Denning MR has laid down in the present case and with which I agree and the many authorities which he has cited in support of those principles, if they are as correct as I believe them to be, make it wrong to dismiss this appeal.'

I repeat the principles here in the hope that some day they may be accepted as correct.

2 The underlying principles

'After studying the cases it seems to me that the courts are reaching towards these principles. The public has a right of access to information which is of public concern and of which the public ought to know. The newspapers are the agents, so to speak, of the public to collect that information and to tell the public of it. In support of this right of access, the newspapers should not in general be compelled to disclose their sources of information. Neither by means of discovery before trial. Nor by questions or cross-examination at the trial. Nor by subpoena. The reason is because, if they were compelled to disclose their sources, they would soon be bereft of information which they ought to have. Their sources would dry up. Wrongdoing would not be disclosed. Charlatans would not be exposed. Unfairness would go unremedied. Misdeeds in the corridors of power – in companies or in government departments – would never be known. Investigative journalism has proved itself as a valuable adjunct of the freedom of the press. Notably in the Watergate exposure in the United States: and the Poulson exposure in this country. It should not be unduly hampered or restricted by the law. Much of the information gathered by the press has been imparted to the informant in confidence. He is guilty of a breach of confidence in telling it to the press. But this is not a reason why his name should be disclosed. Otherwise much information, that ought to be made public, will never be made known. Likewise with documents. They may infringe copyright. But that is no reason for compelling their disclosure, if by so doing it would mean disclosing the name of the informant.'

3 Adequate remedies available

Then I went on to say that there were adequate remedies available to the plaintiff.

'In all these cases the plaintiff has his remedy in damages against the newspaper – or sometimes an injunction: and that should suffice. It may be for libel. It may be for breach of copyright. It may be for infringement of privacy. The courts will always be ready to grant an injunction to restrain a publication which is an infringement of privacy. That was well shown when Mr Strange published drawings which Queen Victoria made for her private amusement: see *Prince Albert v Strange*.[1] So let the plaintiff sue the newspaper: without getting the name of their informant. I know that in some cases it might be relevant and useful – in the interests of justice – for a plaintiff to get to know the name of the newspaper's informant – so as to prove malice, for instance – but the plaintiff will have to forego this advantage in deference to the interest which the public has in seeing that newspapers should not be compelled to disclose their sources of information.'

Then, remembering the *Mulholland* case, I went on:

1 (1849) 1 Hall & Twells 1.

'Nevertheless, this principle is not absolute. The journalist has no privilege by which he can claim – as of right – to refuse to disclose the name. There may be exceptional cases in which, on balancing the various interests, the court decides that the name should be disclosed. . . . Have we any yardstick by which to determine which cases are exceptional?'

I would still stand by every word of that passage.

4 After the weekend

It may interest you to know that whilst preparing my judgment I was at first disposed to decide against British Steel and in favour of Granada. I thought that British Steel ought to make proper inquiries within their own organisation – so as to find out who was the 'mole' who was in their employ and working underground. It was up to British Steel to find it out for themselves. I actually wrote a paragraph in my draft on those lines refusing to order Granada to disclose the name. But over the weekend – actually on the Bank Holiday, 5 May 1980 – I came to my decision: I felt that Granada had not behaved with due respect. So I made a second draft (which now appears in the Law Reports), ordering Granada to disclose the name.

5 Lord Wilberforce does a balancing exercise

The House of Lords affirmed the decision of the Court of Appeal. Lord Wilberforce did a balancing exercise and came down, on balance, against Granada. He said (page 827):

'I come then to the final and critical point. The remedy (being equitable) is discretionary. Although, as I have said, the media, and journalists, have no immunity, it remains true that there may be an element of public interest in protecting the revelation of the source. . . . The court ought not to compel confidence bona fide given to be breached unless necessary in the interests of justice. . . . There is a public interest in the free flow of information, the strength of which will vary from case to case. In some cases it may be very weak; in others it may be very strong. The court must take this into account. . . . Granada had, on its side, and I recognise this, the public interest that people should be informed about the steel strike, of the attitude of British Steel, and perhaps that of the government towards settling the strike. . . . The courts, to revert to Lord Denning MR's formulation in *Attorney-General v Mulholland*; *Attorney-General v Foster*,[1] had to form their opinion whether the strong public interest in favour of doing justice and against denying it, was outweighed by the perfectly real considerations that Granada put forward. I have reached the conclusion that it was not.'

6 Would Granada obey the court order?

After the House of Lords made its order, there was much speculation as to what Granada would do. Would Granada give the name of the 'mole'? Would they obey the court order? It appeared that none of the directors or senior staff of Granada knew the name of the 'mole'. The only person who knew it was a minor member of Granada's staff – the unnamed journalist (whose name Granada kept to themselves) to whom the papers were handed. He refused to give the name of the 'mole'. He had promised not to disclose it.

Suppose in those circumstances Granada did not give the name of the 'mole' – explaining the reasons. Would they be guilty of a contempt of court? I should think not. The secretary of Granada would say in his affidavit: 'None of the directors or officers knew the name of the informant. I have made inquiries of the journalist and he refuses to name the informant.' On such an affidavit being made, there would be no contempt of court by the company. In order for a contempt to be committed – it being a criminal offence – there would have to be disobedience by the directors or senior officers of the company. Disobedience by a minor employee of Granada (the unnamed journalist) would not be a contempt by the company itself: see *Tesco Supermarkets Ltd v Nattrass*.[2] As it

1 [1963] 2 QB 477.
2 [1972] AC 153.

250

happened, there was no need for the point to be tested in the courts. British Steel themselves eventually – by their own efforts – discovered the 'mole' in their employ. It was none of the directors or senior staff at all. It was a humble employee who was entrusted with the destruction of papers. Instead of destroying those secret papers of British Steel, he handed them to the unnamed journalist employed by Granada. The order of the court to Granada was not an order to that unnamed journalist. He was not a party to the proceedings. He was not guilty of any contempt – in refusing to tell his superiors the name of the 'mole'.

These new facts – which were not before the courts during the argument – give rise to further thought. Was it right to make an order on Granada which they could not fulfil? Before the courts made any such order, ought not they to have considered whether it could be made effective?

It tends much to the discredit of a legal system in a country if its Parliament makes laws or its courts make orders which they cannot enforce. Take the prohibition laws of the United States. They could not be enforced. They had to be repealed. So also if the courts make an order on a newspaper or television company to name an informant. It may not be able to be enforced because the company is not responsible for what its journalists do or do not do. If it comes to a balancing exercise, therefore, it may not be in the public interest that the courts should make such an order.

7 I think again

On reconsideration, therefore, I think that in cases of investigative journalism, save in most exceptional circumstances, the newspaper or television company ought not to be ordered to disclose the source of information: first, because it impedes the flow of information concerning matters of public interest; and second, because such an order is apt to be a mere *brutum fulmen* – which Addison in *The Spectator* described as 'an empty Noise, when it has not the sound of the Oaken Plant in it'.

Now we have section 10 of the Contempt of Court Act 1981. It says that

'No court may require a person to disclose, nor is any person guilty of contempt of court for refusing to disclose, the source of information contained in a publication for which he is responsible, unless it be established to the satisfaction of the court that disclosure is necessary in the interests of justice or national security or for the prevention of disorder or crime.'

Those words – 'necessary in the interests of justice' – are virtually a repetition of my judgment in *Attorney-General v Mulholland*; *Attorney-General v Foster*[1] which was approved by the House of Lords in *British Steel Corporation v Granada Television*.[2] So the section appears to leave the law just as it was before. And my comments on it stand.

8 Private Eye

As I go through the proofs, we have a welcome decision.[3] Mr Jack Lundin, a journalist, got some information about a casino. He did a valuable piece of investigative journalism. He exposed the wrongdoings of the casino. It was published in *Private Eye*. As a result the casino lost its licence. A police sergeant was prosecuted. The judge ordered the journalist to give the source of his information. He refused. The Attorney General applied to commit the journalist. The Divisional Court acquitted him, because it was not 'necessary' to know the source. The decision was not based on section 10 of the new Act as it was not yet in force. It was based on the common law. I anticipate that in future it will be very rare for a journalist to be ordered to name his source.

1 [1963] 2 QB 477 at 489–490.
2 [1980] 3 WLR 774 at 827.
3 *Attorney General v Lundin* (1982) Times 20 February (not yet reported).

7 'The Primodos Affair'

1 Babies are born deformed

A very recent case was in the Court of Appeal. It is *Schering Chemicals v Falkman Ltd*.[1] It is not going to the Lords. No leave was asked. It is all about a drug called Primodos. It has some similarity to the *Thalidomide* case.[2] You can read all about that case in *The Due Process of Law* (pages 45–49). This drug, Primodos, was a drug given to pregnant women – and in consequence babies were born deformed. It was supposed to be a test for pregnancy – to tell a woman whether she was pregnant or not. But many women thought it would act as an abortifacient – to stop the baby getting any further – to bring on her period. The drug was sold in millions to women all over the world. Then some researchers found out that it might harm the unborn child. The evidence was so strong that the Committee on the Safety of Medicines in London issued a 'yellow warning' about it. In due course the makers withdrew the drug from the market.

The newspapers and media gave the subject full coverage. Papers came out with headlines: 'Drug company ignored deformity risk for 10 years', and so forth.

The makers decided to launch a campaign to mitigate the effect of this publicity. They employed a firm to train their executives. A course was held. It was done on the basis that the course was confidential to the participants.

1 [1981] 2 WLR 848.
2 *A-G v Times Newspapers Ltd* [1973] QB 710, [1974] AC 273.

2 A film is made

One of the participants was David Elstein. He conceived the idea of making a television film about the drug. He got Thames Television to take it up. He got a bright young lady to do much research in the scientific journals and in the press. All of it was what lawyers call 'in the public domain'. Anyone of the public could use it if he took the trouble to look for it. The researchers also saw women who had taken the drug. They saw professors who had studied its effect. Out of all this fresh material Thames Television made the film called 'The Primodos Affair'. They were quite frank about it. They told the makers of the drug that they were going to show the film.

The makers had a preview of it. They thought that it might harm them. So they went to court. They asked for an injunction to stop the showing of the film on the ground of breach of confidence. Each member of the Court of Appeal did the balancing exercise. The majority thought that Mr Elstein was in flagrant breach of his duty to honour the confidence entrusted to him at the course. They granted an injunction. But I went the other way.

3 Freedom of the press

In the course of my judgment I ventured to deal generally with the freedom of the press. I said (pages 865–866):

'Freedom of the press is of fundamental importance in our society. It covers not only the right of the press to impart information of general interest or concern, but also the right of the public to receive it. It is not to be restricted on the ground of breach of confidence unless there is a "pressing social need" for such restraint. In order to warrant a restraint, there must be a social need for protecting the confidence sufficiently pressing to outweigh the public interest in freedom of the press. No injunction forbidding publication should be granted except where the confidence is justifiable on moral or social grounds: *Duchess of Argyll v Duke of Argyll*;[1] or, I will add, on industrial

1 [1967] 1 Ch 302.

254

grounds: the *Granada* case;[1] and, in addition, where the *private* interest in maintaining the confidence outweighs the *public* interest in making the matter known to the public at large.

A neat problem was set out in the Report of the Committee on Privacy:[2]

"Suppose a newspaper comes into possession of information, which it knows to be confidential and obtained surreptitiously by the newspaper's informant, that a particular firm is about to discharge 10,000 employees. It approaches the firm who will neither confirm nor deny the report but immediately proceeds to apply for an injunction to prevent publication of the information. Perhaps the newspaper would have a defence, but it cannot be asserted with certainty."

I hope that the courts in such case would refuse an injunction.[3] The public interest in receiving the information would outweigh the private interest of the firm in keeping it secret. So in our present case, the *public* interest in the drug Primodos and its effects far outweighs the *private* interest of the makers in preventing discussion of it. Especially when all the information in the film is in the public domain, and where there has already been considerable coverage in newspapers and on television; and when the publication cannot in any way affect the course of justice in the pending actions. Nor affect the sale of Primodos because it has long been withdrawn from the market.

It comes back to this. Prior restraint is such a drastic interference with the freedom of the press that it should only be ordered when there is a substantial risk of grave injustice.

I stand as ever for the freedom of the press, including television, except when it is abused . . . I see no abuse here. Even if there was any abuse, it was not such as to warrant the injunction of a prior restraint. I think that the judge ought to have refused the injunction on 27 August 1980. I would allow the appeal accordingly.'

It is no doubt presumptuous of me, but I still think I was right.

1 [1980] 3 WLR 774.
2 (1972) Cmnd 5012, p. 298.
3 In a similar case the Court of Appeal did refuse an injunction. It was *Sun Printers v Westminster Press Ltd* February 1982 (not yet reported).

I hope that in the future others may come to think so too. That is one of my reasons for writing this book.

4 Was there a contempt of court?

'The Primodos Affair' has, however, another aspect on which we were all agreed. It was submitted that the showing of the film would be a contempt of court. The whole court rejected this.

Now in one aspect the *Primodos* case was stronger than the *Thalidomide* case. In the Thalidomide cases the actions by the parents against Distillers were dormant, whereas in the Primodos cases, the actions by the parents were active and very active.

In the Thalidomide cases all that had happened was that the writs had been issued and served; appearances had been entered; but nothing more had been done in the actions. So far as the courts were concerned, the 266 actions had gone soundly to sleep and had been asleep for three to four years. No one had awakened them. So the litigation had remained dormant. It was still dormant when the *Sunday Times* started in September 1972 publishing its articles on the Thalidomide children. It was still dormant when the appeal was heard.

That was one of the reasons why the Court of Appeal held that the articles were not a contempt of court. They dealt with a matter of the greatest public interest and contained comments which the newspaper honestly believed to be true. They did not prejudice pending litigation because that litigation was dormant – and had been dormant for years.

5 No judge would be influenced

In the Primodos cases five parents had started actions. They had been set down for trial. The date of trial had been fixed. The film, 'The Primodos Affair', was to be shown in the intervening period – whilst waiting for the trial itself. The actions were active indeed.

Now despite this activity, the court held that the showing of the film would not be a contempt of court. One thing was that the actions would be tried by a judge sitting alone. He might or might not have seen the broadcast, but even if he had he would not be influenced by it. As Lord Salmon said in the *Exclusive Brethren* case (*Attorney-General v BBC*):[1]

'I am and have always been satisfied that no judge would be influenced in his judgment by what may be said by the media. If he were, he would not be fit to be a judge.'

Next, the witnesses would not be influenced by the broadcast. As Lord Justice Shaw said in the *Primodos* case:[2]

'If among the witnesses to be called are some who have a part in the documentary, there is no reason to suppose that the substance of their evidence or their readiness to contribute it will be affected or in any way impaired. Witnesses in an action are credible and reliable or they are not. Our system of trial in which evidence is elicited by examination and cross-examination provides the means of demonstrating the character and quality of a witness.'

Lord Justice Templeman said (page 882):

'In my judgment, the film cannot affect the result of the actions and the court should not be anxious to accept submissions that discussions of a pending action must necessarily be unseemly or harmful to the administration of justice.'

6 The effect of the 1981 Act

The Contempt of Court Act 1981 should be welcomed by investigative journalists. It affirms the Court of Appeal in the *Thalidomide* case – in that it restricts liability to cases where the proceedings are 'active', that is, in the High Court here, from the time that the case is set down for trial. It also supports the decision of the Court of Appeal in the *Primodos* case in that it is only a contempt where there is

1 [1980] 3 WLR 109 at 119.
2 [1981] 2 WLR 848 at 872.

'a substantial risk that the course of justice in the proceedings in question will be seriously impeded or prejudiced'.[1]

I can conceive of no civil cases in the High Court – tried by a judge alone – which could be impeded or prejudiced by a publication of an article in the media. In future, therefore, no newspaper or television company need be worried by the fear of contempt of court. They will be free to discuss the issues in a pending action or make comment on them as they please: provided always that they are innocent of any intent to interfere with the trial; and also that they steer clear of libel or breach of confidence or of privacy.

1 Section 2 (2).

8 Discovery of documents

1 Miss Harman's case

Now I come to the most recent case of all, *Home Office v Harman*.[1] In order to understand it, you should know that, if a person is involved in litigation, the courts can order him to produce all the documents he has which relate to the issues in the case. Even though they are most confidential, they must be produced for the other side to see – and for the court to see. When the courts thus order a party to produce his confidential documents, it is on the understanding that they are not to be used for any other purpose. They are available for the court to see – in order to come to a decision on the merits of the case – but they are not to be used by the other side for any other purpose whatever.

Now Miss Harriet Harman is a solicitor. She acted for a criminal, Michael Williams. He was in prison serving a sentence of fourteen years for armed robbery of a bank. He was put in a special 'control unit'. He complained that, whilst there, he had been subjected to 'cruel and unusual punishments' contrary to the Bill of Rights. He brought an action for damages against the Home Office. Miss Harriet Harman acted for him in the action. She got legal aid for the purpose.

Now Miss Harman was also the solicitor of a society called 'The National Council for Civil Liberties'. It is no reflection on them to say that they were a pressure group. One of their objectives was to see that prisoners were treated fairly – and not cruelly – in prison.

Miss Harman got an order for discovery against the Home Office. The documents relating to the 'control unit' were very

1 [1981] 2 WLR 310.

259

confidential. The Home Office were content that they should be used in the action brought by Michael Williams against the Home Office, but they were not willing that they should be used for the purpose of the pressure group, NCCL. These letters passed (page 324):

From the Home Office to Miss Harman:

'The Home Office would not wish the documents to be used for the general purposes of the NCCL outside your function as solicitor for the plaintiff.'

To which Miss Harman replied:

'As far as "the general purposes of NCCL" is concerned you may rest assured that, as a solicitor, I am well aware of the rule that requires that documents obtained on discovery should not be used for any other purpose except for the case in hand.'

2 A feature article

At the trial the documents were very properly used for the case in hand. Bundles were made of the most material documents. These were put before the judge and were – I would now assume – read out in open court to the judge.

Afterwards, a journalist wished to write a feature article about the case. Miss Harman passed the bundles to the journalist. He wrote an article for *The Guardian* newspaper which was very critical of the Home Office and the 'control unit' which had been set up. It was headed (page 326):

'HOW MINISTRY HARDLINERS HAD THEIR WAY OVER PRISON UNITS

A major Whitehall blunder, involving internal bureaucratic intrigue and ministerial attempts to prevent disclosure, has been revealed in rare detail by documents released to the National Council for Civil Liberties by a court order.'

3 Was she guilty of contempt?

The Home Office took proceedings against Miss Harman for contempt of court. Mr Justice Park held that she had been guilty

of contempt. The Court of Appeal upheld his ruling. I said
(page 328):

> 'The defence of Miss Harman is simple: These documents were
> read out in open court by counsel whom she instructed for the
> plaintiff. Once read out in court, they became in the public
> domain. If the shorthand-writer had taken down the words and
> reproduced them in a transcript, they would have been avail-
> able for all the world to use. So why should they not be available
> from the documents themselves in her office?'

I then gave the basis of the argument:

> 'This contention is said to be derived from the principle stated
> by Lord Halsbury in *Scott v Scott*:[1] "... every court of justice is
> open to every subject of the King". So it is said that every
> document read out aloud in a court of justice is available to
> every subject of the Queen in the court at the time, or outside it
> anywhere at any time thereafter: or if not to everyone, at any
> rate to every reporter or journalist. The document, however
> confidential beforehand, loses all confidentiality once it is read
> aloud in court. The owner of it retains his copyright: and any
> person defamed retains his action for libel. But the owner of
> the confidentiality loses all claim for breach of confidence.'

4 My view

Then I expressed my view:

> 'I cannot accept this argument for one moment. It is one of our
> fundamental human rights that everyone has a right to privacy:
> included in which is a right to respect for his confidential
> documents. This can be overridden in the interests of justice. It
> was so overridden in our present case when the court ordered
> the Home Office to disclose these thousands of documents to
> Michael Williams – so that justice might be done in the action
> he had brought. This overriding meant that the documents
> could be read in open court to the judge who had to try the
> case. It meant that those present could listen: that the reporters
> could take down what was said: and could make from their
> notes a fair and accurate report of the proceedings. But nothing

1 [1913] AC 417 at 440.

more. It did *not* mean that there could be any further use of the confidential documents or any further dissemination of their contents without the consent of the owner. It is of no use to plead the freedom of the press. That freedom is itself subject to restriction. The press is not free to publish confidential documents without the consent of the owner. Save when the interest of the owner in keeping them confidential is outweighed by the public interest in having the matter made public: see the *Primodos* case.[1] I can see no public interest whatever in having these highly confidential documents made public. Quite the other way. It was in the public interest that these documents should be kept confidential. They should not be exposed to the ravages of outsiders. I regard the use by the journalist in this case of these documents to be highly detrimental to the good ordering of our society. They were used so as to launch a wholly unjustified attack on Ministers of State and high level servants – who were only doing their very best to deal with a wicked criminal who had harassed society and was serving a long sentence for armed robbery. For this use I think Miss Harman was herself responsible. It was a gross breach of the undertaking which she impliedly gave to the court and affirmed in writing to the Treasury Solicitor. That undertaking was to use the documents solely for the purposes of the action of Michael Williams against the Home Office. Instead, she used them for the purposes of this organisation called the National Council for Civil Liberties: and that organisation made them available for use by a journalist – and he, whilst the case was still sub judice, wrote an article prejudging the outcome most unfairly. It makes me regret that the court ever ordered disclosure of the documents. The "legal milestone" will have to be taken up and set back a bit.'

I should add that at no time did the Home Office or Treasury Counsel impugn Miss Harman's professional integrity and good faith.

5 How will the balance come down?

In this case there was again a balancing exercise. On the one side there was the importance of preserving the rule that confidential

1 [1981] 2 WLR 848.

documents should not be used for any other than the permitted purpose. On the other hand there was the importance of the freedom of the press – to deal with matters of public interest and concern, especially when they have been ventilated in a court of law. The Court of Appeal held in that case that the balance came down in favour of preserving confidence. Which way will the House of Lords decide? We await the result with interest. If it should be in Miss Harman's favour, she will be vindicated and we shall have been wrong: and I shall be the first to apologise to her.

6 We are upheld

But as I am revising the proofs, the result has come to hand. The House of Lords have affirmed our decision. By a majority of three to two. *The Times*[1] comes out with deep headlines as if in mourning: 'Contempt ruling "a black day for press freedom" . . . MPs will challenge ruling on contempt.' It adds that an appeal will be lodged with the European Commission on Human Rights. In reply I would say with Shakespeare: 'The lady doth protest too much, methinks.'[2] The decision does not restrict the freedom of the press. It only restrains the abuse of it.

1 12 February 1982.
2 *Hamlet* Act III, sc. 2.

9 Remedies for breach of privacy or of confidence

1 Damages to be awarded

If a breach of privacy or confidence is threatened – or if it has actually taken place – what should be the remedy? There has been no discussion as far as I know. It is not at present a crime, nor should it be regarded as such. Criminal proceedings are inappropriate. Breach of privacy or breach of confidence should be regarded as a tort – a wrong – for which, in a proper case, damages should be recoverable against the person who was guilty of the breach – and against the one who knowingly takes advantage of it. Sometimes the breach may result in actual damage, such as in industrial espionage. At other times it may result in injured feelings – as in libel cases – for which damages should be recoverable. I would go further. Sometimes the breach of privacy may be so gross – so wicked an intrusion on a person's private affairs – that there should be exemplary damages – as I have suggested in regard to libel.

But there remains the question of injunction. No doubt if a breach of confidence is threatened, the courts will interfere to stop it. But what about the press? If the press propose to publish matter which is confidential – but which deals with points of much public interest and concern – ought an injunction to be granted? Here I come to a topic which has been much discussed in the United States, but has received little notice here.

2 Prior restraint

Blackstone was against any injunction being granted against the press: so as to stop it publishing what it liked. He realised that the press might do wrong things – it might publish libels – it might write articles prejudicing the fair trial of an accused man – but still no injunction should be granted beforehand. The remedy of an aggrieved person was to take action afterwards for damages or such other remedy as the law might afford. This is how he put it with his accustomed elegance:[1]

'The liberty of the press is indeed essential to the nature of a free state; but this consists in laying no *previous* restraints upon publications, and not in freedom from censure for criminal matter when published. Every freeman has an undoubted right to lay what sentiments he pleases before the public: to forbid this, is to destroy the freedom of the press: but if he publishes what is improper, mischievous, or illegal, he must take the consequences of his own temerity.'

In that passage Blackstone went somewhat too far. It is now settled that, in exceptional cases, where the intended publication is plainly unlawful and would inflict grave injustice on innocent people, then an injunction may be granted.

In the *Thalidomide* case the European Court of Human Rights said that to justify a prior restraint there must be

'a social need sufficiently pressing to outweigh the public interest in freedom of expression'.[2]

This was well summed up by Lord Scarman in the *Exclusive Brethren* case:[3]

'. . . the prior restraint of publication, though occasionally necessary in serious cases, is a drastic interference with freedom of speech and should only be ordered where there is a substantial risk of grave injustice. I understand the test of "pressing social need" as being exactly that.'

1 *Commentaries* IV (17th edn, 1830) 151.
2 *Sunday Times v United Kingdom* [1979] 2 EHRR 245 at 282.
3 [1980] 3 WLR 109 at 138.

10 The future

1 The Law Commission drafts a Bill

This whole subject has been covered by the Law Commission in a Report presented in October 1981 (Cmnd 8388). It contains the best review of the case-law to be found anywhere. It states the basic question to be: Should the law of confidence and privacy be left to be worked out by the courts? or should it be embodied in a statute? It comes down in favour of a statute and gives the draft of a bill for the purpose.

I would give a different answer. This is a subject which should be worked out from case to case. It is being done now – as I have shown in the preceding pages. The Report itself says (page 100) that

> '. . . the Senate of the Inns of Court and the Bar feared that legislation might introduce an element of rigidity into the law and would have preferred the law to be left to the courts to mould to any set of circumstances which may arise in the future'.

But the Report can, and should, play a most important role. Whenever a new point arises, every practitioner should reach for the Report. He should use it as a basis for his argument. The judge should treat it as of much persuasive value, though not of binding force. Then he should decide the instant case according to what good sense – and justice – demand. His decision will be the precedent to be followed. It will be reported in the Law Reports. We shall then have a flexible body of law – which can be changed by the judges themselves if need be – without all the toils and turmoils inflicted by statutory interpretation.

266

2 Observe the Convention

It seems to me that the general principles which should govern the subject are sufficiently stated in articles 8 and 10 of the European Convention on Human Rights which I set out at the beginning of this Part. As to these I agree with Lord Scarman who said in the *Exclusive Brethren* case (page 130):

'If the issue should ultimately be, as I think in this case it is, a question of legal policy, we must have regard to the country's international obligation to observe the Convention as interpreted by the Court of Human Rights.'

But those articles are like an empty house with bare walls and without any furniture. No one can live in it as it is. You must get it furnished. You must have a kitchen to work in, chairs to sit on, beds to sleep in, and so forth. So with these articles. You must have judges to interpret them. You must have examples to illustrate them. You have to know what things are 'necessary in a democratic society' and so forth. This can be shown by decided cases. These will act as precedents for others to follow.

3 Find a new tort

There is no obstacle in the way of the judges. It is open to them to find – as the courts of the United States have found – a new tort. English law should recognise a right of privacy. Any infringement of it should give a cause of action for damages or an injunction as the case may require. It should also recognise a right of confidence for all correspondence and communications which expressly or impliedly are given in confidence. With likewise a cause of action.

None of these rights is absolute. Each is subject to exceptions. These exceptions are to be allowed whenever the public interest in openness outweighs the public interest in privacy or confidentiality. In every instance it is a balancing exercise for the courts. As each case is decided, it will form a precedent for others. So a body of case-law will be established. That is why I have in this Part told you of case after case – showing how the case-law is developing – and will, I hope, develop in the future.

267

One particular topic is investigative journalism. It seems to me that when the newspaper or television company have investigated a matter of general public interest or concern – such that it ought to be made known to the people – the publication of an article or film upon it is so much in the public interest that it ought not to be restrained solely on the ground that the information in it originated in a breach of confidence – or, let us say, in a 'leak' – whether intentional or unintentional. Nor should the newspaper or television company be compelled to disclose the source of the information.

4 Leave it to the judges

I know that there are difficulties in leaving it to the courts. It depends on whether the facts give rise to a point for discussion. It depends on whether the client or the lawyer will take it up. It depends on whether the judges have the wisdom or the courage to develop the law: or whether they will simply say: 'It is not for us. It is for Parliament.'

But my answer is this: Even if you do get Parliament to pass a statute, you will still have many of the same problems. I hope that the judges of the future will do as the judges used to do in times past: they should develop the law according to the needs of the times. They should be among the bold spirits. They should not be timorous souls feebly saying: 'It is for Parliament, not for us': see *Candler v Crane, Christmas.*[1]

1 [1951] 2 KB 164.

Part seven

A Bill of Rights

1 Ever since Magna Carta

1 Always a demand

There has been much discussion on whether we should have a Bill of Rights. Time after time – year after year – Lord Wade has promoted a Bill in the House of Lords for that purpose. He has a Bill of Rights 'Club' of which Lord Scarman is a founder member. He had a notable success in 1981. The Bill passed through all its stages in the House of Lords. But it got no further in the Commons.

The demand for a Bill of Rights arises from like causes as those in the past. There is a feeling among ordinary people that rights and freedoms of the individual have been eroded beyond measure: and that the law, as at present administered, is no longer able to protect the citizen against the pressures of the government, the trade unions, and other all-powerful bodies. So they cry: 'Let us have a Bill of Rights'.

As usual, I go back in time. Our history tells us how our fore-fathers secured their liberties.

2 Magna Carta 1215

I will not pause long over the Great Charter of 1215. I have set it out already in *The Family Story*. King John oppressed the people. The barons rose against him. The City of London turned the scale. The King assented to the Charter. He did it with his tongue in his cheek. Two months later a papal bull declared it void. But after the death of King John, the Charter was re-issued by the young King Henry III. It is that re-issue which is the first in the statutes at large. I only set out here the clauses protecting the freedom of the individual:

'39. No freeman shall be taken, imprisoned, disseized, outlawed, banished, or in any way destroyed, nor will we proceed against or prosecute him, except by the lawful judgment of his peers and by the law of the land.

40. To no one will we sell, to no one will we deny or delay right or justice.'

3 The Petition of Right 1628

King Charles I imposed taxes by royal command without the assent of Parliament. Five Knights refused to pay. The judges were servile. They held that if a man was committed by command of the King, he was not to be released by the court: see *Five Knights'* case.[1] Sir Edward Coke was then a Member of Parliament. As we have seen, he had been dismissed as a judge in 1616 because he would not do as the King asked. At the age of seventy-six in the year 1628 he moved the Petition of Right in Parliament. He said:

'The state is inclining to a consumption yet not incurable. For this disease I will propound remedies. I will seek nothing out of mine own head, but from my heart and out of Acts of Parliament.'

Sir Benjamin Rudyerd put it very picturesquely:

'For mine own part, I shall be very glad to see that old decrepit Law Magna Carta, which hath been kept so long, and lien bed-rid, as it were, I shall be glad to see it walk abroad again with new vigour and lustre: questionless it will be a great heartning to all the People.'

The Petition of Right embodied Coke's concept of 'due process of law'. It contained eleven clauses of which I will quote a sentence from clause 10:

'They do therefore humbly pray your most excellent Majesty,

1 (1627) 3 State Trials 1.

That no man hereafter be compelled to make or yield any gift, loan, benevolence, tax, or such-like charge, without common consent by act of Parliament: . . . and that no freeman, in any such manner as is before-mentioned, be imprisoned or detained. . . .'

The King at first did not assent. He prevaricated. He gave an ambiguous answer. After many to-ings and fro-ings he gave way. At last, on 7 June 1628, the King himself came to the House and assented. The petition was read. The Clerk read aloud in Norman-French the words of approval: '*Soit droit fait comme est désiré*' (Let right be done as is desired).

As the words were pronounced, a great shout rang out and was repeated again and again. News spread to the street – 'broke out', wrote a Privy Councillor, 'into ringing of bells and bonfires miraculously'.

4 The Bill of Rights 1689

King James II was a bad King. It was he who favoured the Roman Catholics and was bitterly opposed to the Protestants. It was he who dismissed the judges. It was he who sent Judge Jeffreys on that Bloody Assize. It was he who directed that the Seven Bishops should be prosecuted for seditious libel – when all they had done was to present a petition to the King himself. It was the acquittal of the Seven Bishops that forced the King to flee the realm. On his way he threw the Great Seal into the river Thames.

It was a young barrister called John Somers who drew up a Declaration of Rights. Although very junior at the Bar, he had made a short speech of five minutes which led to the acquittal of the Seven Bishops. Immediately after that trial, he was entrusted with the task of preparing a Declaration of Rights – to which the new King William assented. This Declaration became the Bill of Rights 1689. It is not easy to lay your hand on any book which contains the full text of this great document. I will set out here a few of the principal clauses:

'The Lords and Commons . . .
I. . . . (as their ancestors in like case have usually done) for the

vindicating and asserting their ancient rights and liberties, declare:

1. That the pretended power of suspending of laws, or the execution of laws, by regal authority, without consent of parliament, is illegal.

2. That the pretended power of dispensing with laws, or the execution of laws, by regal authority, as it hath been assumed and exercised of late, is illegal.

8. That election of members of parliament ought to be free.

9. That the freedom of speech, and debates or proceedings in parliament, ought not to be impeached or questioned in any court or place out of parliament.

10. That excessive bail ought not to be required, nor excessive fines imposed; nor cruel and unusual punishments inflicted.

11. That jurors ought to be duly impanelled and returned, and jurors which pass upon men in trials for high treason ought to be freeholders.

II. . . . That William and Mary prince and princess of Orange be, and be declared, King and Queen of England, France and Ireland. . . .'

Macaulay describes the importance of the Bill of Rights in these words:[1]

'The Declaration of Right, though it made nothing law which had not been law before, contained the germ of the law which gave religious freedom to the Dissenter, of the law which secured the independence of the Judges, of the law which limited the duration of Parliaments, of the law which placed the liberty of the press under the protection of juries, of the law which prohibited the slave trade, of the law which abolished the sacramental test, of the law which relieved the Roman Catholics from civil disabilities, of the law which reformed the representative system, of every good law which has been passed during more than a century and a half, of every good law which may hereafter, in the course of ages, be found necessary to promote the public weal, and to satisfy the demands of public opinion.'

1 *History of England* vol III, p. 1311.

If we are to have a new Bill of Rights, will it too be the germ of the law which, in the complexities of modern society, maintains the rights and freedoms of the individual against the all-powerful bodies that stride about the place?

5 The United States of America follow it in 1791

I would digress here to remind you that our forefathers who went to America took with them the 'rights of Englishmen'. They took with them, too, our Bill of Rights of 1689 and Blackstone's *Commentaries*. After they obtained their independence in 1776 they established on 17 September 1787 the Constitution of the United States. This set out the structure with a President, a Senate and a House of Representatives, and so forth. But one James Madison took the lead in pressing for a Bill of Rights after the English pattern. He said:

> 'I believe that the great mass of the people who opposed it (the Constitution), disliked it because it did not contain effectual provisions against the encroachments on particular rights, and those safeguards which they have been long accustomed to have interposed between them and the magistrate who exercises the sovereign power.'

James Madison got his amendments accepted by the Senate and approved by the House of Representatives. They were ratified by the states. I will set out some of these amendments so that you can see that the framers of them had before them our own Bill of Rights of 1689 and used some of the very words.

> '*Art*. I. Congress shall make no law . . . abridging the freedom of speech, or of the press; or the right of the people peaceably to assemble . . .
>
> *Art*. V. . . . nor shall any person . . . be deprived of life, liberty, or property, without due process of law; nor shall private property be taken for public use without just compensation.
>
> *Art*. VI. In all criminal prosecutions the accused shall enjoy the right to a speedy and public trial, by an impartial jury . . .

Art. VII. In suits at common law, where the value in controversy shall exceed twenty dollars, the right of trial by jury shall be preserved . . .

Art. VIII. Excessive bail shall not be required, nor excessive fines imposed, nor cruel and unusual punishments inflicted.'

Every word of those amendments has been the subject of close consideration by the Supreme Court of the United States. You could fill a whole library with decisions on the meaning of 'due process of law'. The cost in time and money has been enormous. Our own Bill of Rights has not. I do not suppose it has been invoked more than a dozen times in the last 300 years. If we are to have a new Bill of Rights, will there be thousands of cases upon it? Will our courts be cluttered up with frivolous or vexatious actions and complaints?

2 We come to our times

1 The Universal Declaration of Human Rights 1948

In 1940 Mr Winston Churchill and Mr Franklin Roosevelt met on board a battleship in the Atlantic. They formulated a statement of principles which were shared by England (fighting alone against great odds) and the United States (sympathetic but not yet in the war). It was called the Atlantic Charter. These principles were stated eloquently in a speech by Mr Roosevelt on 6 January 1941:

'In the future days, which we seek to make secure, we look forward to a world founded upon four essential human freedoms.

The first is freedom of speech and expression – everywhere in the world.

The second is freedom of every person to worship God in his own way – everywhere in the world.

The third is freedom from want . . .

The fourth is freedom from fear.'

On 7 December 1941 the Japanese attacked Pearl Harbour. The United States came into the war. In 1945 we won. Civilisation was saved. On 24 October 1945 the United Nations Organisation was formed. On 10 December 1948 the General Assembly approved the Universal Declaration of Human Rights. This set out in thirty articles a 'Bill of Rights' for the inhabitants of all the nations of the world. They sound very impressive. Such as:

'17. Everyone has the right to own property alone as well as in association with others. . . .

277

18. Everyone has the right to freedom of thought, conscience and religion. . . .

19. Everyone has the right to freedom of opinion and expression. . . .

20. Everyone has the right to freedom of peaceful assembly and association. . . .

23. Everyone has the right to work, to free choice of employment, to just and favourable conditions of work and to protection against unemployment. . . .

24. Everyone has the right to rest and leisure. . . .

26. Everyone has the right to education. . . .'

That Universal Declaration was absolutely useless for one decisive reason. There was no means of enforcing it. There was no court to give orders. There were no litigants to appear before it. There were no police to arrest offenders. Any one of the nations who signed it could cock a snook at it. And many did so. It can be expunged from any list of Bills of Rights. It was a declaration of pious aspirations – not of enforceable rights.

2 The European Convention on Human Rights 1950

Nevertheless, the Universal Declaration did have an important effect for the continent of Europe. It led to the Council of Europe founded in 1949. The Council produced the Convention for the Protection of Human Rights and Fundamental Freedoms which in 1950 was signed on behalf of the United Kingdom and ratified by the Government. But it has never been made part of our law. It remains an international treaty conferring obligations between the signatory countries on an international level, but without any legal force within the United Kingdom.

Whenever anyone speaks of a Bill of Rights nowadays, most people think that the practical way of doing it would be for Parliament to pass a statute making the European Convention part of our law. The latest Bill (which, as I have said, passed all its stages in the House of Lords) says simply:

'The Convention . . . shall without any reservation immediately upon the passing of this Act have the force of law, and shall be enforceable by action in the courts of the United Kingdom.'

Is this desirable or not? I will first consider the way in which the courts approach the Convention nowadays. Next, I will consider what the effect would be if the Convention were made expressly part of our law.

3 The present approach of the English courts

If one or other party wishes to rely on an article of the Convention, we do not shut him up. We do not say: 'It is not part of our law. We will not look at it.' We do look at it – as if we were doing an exercise in comparative law – to see how other countries have tackled the problem. We do not go into the details of it or into masses of cases upon it. We take the article that is relied upon. We look to see if the line of approach is one which appeals to us as being correct. If so, we use it as a support for our decision. If it does not appeal to us – or if the article is too hedged about with exceptions – we put it on one side. We go about our business – of finding out the English law on the topic – without regard to the Convention. The best way to explain what we do is to take some actual cases that have come up for decision. In doing so, I will set out the articles under discussion so that you will see the way in which the Convention is framed.

3 We turn to the cases

1 The right to marry

In *R v Home Secretary, ex parte Bhajan Singh*,[1] Mr Bhajan Singh came into this country quite illegally. He probably came from India, crossed in a little boat and made his way to the Midlands. Later, he was arrested and detained with a view to his removal and deportation. Then suddenly he said he wanted to marry Miss Paramjit Kaur. He was twenty-six. She was sixteen. Both of them said that they had not thought of marriage prior to his arrest. He asked to be allowed to marry her before he was deported. He relied on article 12 of the Convention which says:

'Men and women of marriageable age have the right to marry and to found a family, according to the national laws governing the exercise of this right.'

But he was met with an exception in article 5(1)(f) which expressly authorises

'the lawful arrest or detention of a person to prevent his effecting an unauthorised entry into the country or of a person against whom action is being taken with a view to deportation or extradition'.

I said (pages 207 and 208):

'What is the position of the Convention in our English law? The court can and should take the Convention into account. They should take it into account whenever interpreting a statute which affects the rights and liberties of the individual. . . .

1 [1976] QB 198.

Article 12 is subject to Article 5(1)(f). A man who is detained as an illegal entrant with a view to his removal has no right to be released in order to get married. The Home Secretary in his discretion is entitled to have him removed. I think there is no ground for mandamus here.'

2 The right to respect for family life

Next came the lady from Pakistan, Salamat Bibi. The case is *R v Chief Immigration Officer, ex parte Bibi*.[1] She arrived at Heathrow with two small children. On the way from Pakistan she had stayed six days at Mecca and three days at Medina, and she arrived at Heathrow at 9.30 a.m. She had not got an entry certificate. She could not speak English, but through an interpreter she said she was coming as a visitor to be with her husband for a couple of weeks. She had about $700 in cash on her, and an open-dated return ticket to take her back to Karachi. She also produced what purported to be an affidavit made by herself declaring that she had been married to one Barkat Ali in 1952 in Pakistan. She produced what purported to be copies of birth certificates showing that the elder child – a girl – was born on 19 April 1967; and the younger one – a boy – was born on 12 October 1971. The certificates were not in English, but translated that is the information which they gave.

A Mr Barkat Ali was at the airport to meet her, together with an articled clerk of a firm of solicitors. Mr Barkat Ali said that the lady was his wife and he wanted her to come in with the children and stay with him permanently, if the Home Office would grant permission. He said that he had been here since 1967. He had come from Pakistan and had settled here. He had gone home for holidays. He said that he had married the lady in 1955 and was the father of the children. He was in business in England earning £2,000 a year and had been claiming tax relief for his wife and children since 1974.

She was represented by Mr Louis Blom-Cooper QC who is an expert in this and other fields. He said (page 984) that the immigration officer

1 [1976] 1 WLR 979.

281

'ought to have admitted the lady because of the European Convention on Human Rights. Article 8 (1) says: "Everyone has the right to respect for his private and family life, his home and his correspondence". In sub-paragraph (2), there is a set of exceptions in the interests of national security, public safety, and the like. We have again been invited to consider how far this Convention is part of the law of this country.'

I then stated the principle in these words:

'The position as I understand it is that if there is any ambiguity in our statutes, or uncertainty in our law, then these courts can look to the Convention as an aid to clear up the ambiguity and uncertainty, seeking always to bring them into harmony with it. Furthermore, when Parliament is enacting a statute, or the Secretary of State is framing rules, the courts will assume that they had regard to the provisions of the Convention, and intended to make the enactment accord with the Convention: and will interpret them accordingly. But I would dispute altogether that the Convention is part of our law. Treaties and declarations do not become part of our law until they are made law by Parliament.'

I added this comment:

'The Convention is drafted in a style very different from the way which we are used to in legislation. It contains wide general statements of principle. They are apt to lead to much difficulty in application: because they give rise to much uncertainty. They are not the sort of thing which we can easily digest. Article 8 is an example. It is so wide as to be incapable of practical application. So it is much better for us to stick to our own statutes and principles, and only look to the Convention for guidance in case of doubt.'

At last we came to a decision. We put aside the Convention altogether as being of no use. I said:

'Coming back to this case, it seems to me that the immigration officer was right to go by the rules: and by the rules, beyond all question, the immigration officer was entirely right to refuse entry to this lady and her children. She had no visa. She had no current entry clearance. She said she was coming as a visitor and he was not satisfied that she was staying for a short period. That is a complete answer to the case.'

3 The right to freedom of religion

Another leading case is on religious freedom. It is *Ahmad v Inner London Education Authority*.[1] Mr Ahmad was a schoolteacher. He was employed by the Inner London Education Authority (ILEA) as a full-time teacher. This meant that he had to attend the school and teach the children on the five days, Monday to Friday inclusive each week, with a break each day for luncheon from 12.30 p.m. to 1.30 p.m.

But Mr Ahmad was not only a schoolteacher. He was a devout Muslim. By his religion it was his duty every Friday to attend prayers at the nearest mosque. The time for these prayers was 1 p.m. to 2 p.m. and the mosque was about 15 to 20 minutes away. So when he went to the prayers he did not get back at 1.30 p.m. in time to teach his class. He only got back at 2.15 p.m. or 2.20 p.m. This meant that he missed about three-quarters of an hour of his teaching duty every Friday. One of the headmasters – at the school for maladjusted children – did his best to help and made arrangements to cope with his absence. But other head-masters in ordinary schools could not do so. His absence disrupted the classes too much. They could not fit it in with the rest of his work. But still he went to his Friday prayers. He said that he was entitled to do so and that, notwithstanding his absences, he was entitled to full pay, just the same as if he had worked for the full five days. Various compromises were suggested to him but he would not accept them. He resigned in protest. He gave as his reason: 'I was exploited and humiliated by the ILEA.' He put in a claim for unfair dismissal, saying that his employers' conduct 'forced me to resign'.

During the argument attention was drawn to article 9 of the Convention which says:

1 [1978] 1 QB 36.

'Everyone has the right to freedom of thought, conscience and religion; this right includes freedom . . . to manifest his religion or belief in worship, teaching, practice and observance.'

There are some exceptions.

To this I said (page 41):

'The Convention is not part of our English law, but, as I have often said, we will always have regard to it. We will do our best to see that our decisions are in conformity with it. But it is drawn in such vague terms that it can be used for all sorts of unreasonable claims and provoke all sorts of litigation. As so often happens with high-sounding principles, they have to be brought down to earth. They have to be applied in a work-a-day world. I venture to suggest that it would do the Muslim community no good – or any other minority group no good – if they were to be given preferential treatment over the great majority of the people. If it should happen that, in the name of religious freedom, they were given special privileges or advantages, it would provoke discontent, and even resentment among those with whom they work. As, indeed, it has done in this very case. And so the cause of racial integration would suffer. So, whilst upholding religious freedom to the full, I would suggest that it should be applied with caution, especially having regard to the setting in which it is sought. Applied to our educational system, I think that Mr Ahmad's right to "manifest his religion in practice and observance" must be subject to the rights of the education authorities under the contract and to the interests of the children whom he is paid to teach. I see nothing in the European Convention to give Mr Ahmad any right to manifest his religion on Friday afternoons in derogation of his contract of employment: and certainly not on full pay.'

I may say that Lord Justice Scarman (then in our court) dissented. It shows what problems we get.

4 The right to join a union

Even on the vexed question of the right to join a union, we have been referred to the Convention. The case is *UKAPE v ACAS*.[1] Some professional engineers wanted to have a small trade union of their own. They did not want to join a big trade union of manual workers. They feared that if they did join the big trade union, they might be called out on strike or be ordered to 'black' goods or services much against their will: and would be liable to disciplinary action, even expulsion, if they refused.

I referred (page 582) to the Convention:

'It says in Article 11 (1):

"Everyone has the right to freedom of peaceful assembly and to freedom of association with others, including the right to form and to join trade unions for the protection of his interests."

That Article only states a basic principle of English law. The common law has always recognised that everyone has the right to freedom of association: provided always that the association does not pursue any unlawful end nor use any unlawful means and is motivated – not by a desire to injure others – but by a desire to protect the interests of its members. As a corollary the common law recognises that everyone has the right to form and to join trade unions for the protection of his interests.

The European Convention has not yet been formally introduced into our statute law. But the proposition in Article 11 accurately states the common law: and for myself, I think that when Parliament enacts legislation on trade unions, it must be taken not to intend to contravene that basic right.

Applying this proposition, it seems to me that these professional engineers have a right to form and join their own trade union. In this case they have exercised that right. . . .

I would hold that this right of free association is part of English law. When the great majority of workers in a particular group wish to be represented by a union of their choice – and

1 [1979] 1 WLR 570.

not to be represented by a rival union – ACAS should normally give effect to their wishes.'

Those four leading cases show the way in which the courts consider the Convention. We look at it for help. Sometimes we find it helpful. Sometimes not. Sometimes we think the articles are too general. Sometimes the exceptions do much to wipe out the principle. So we do not spend too much time upon it.

4 The Court at Strasbourg

1 Its jurisdiction concerns us

Even at present, although the European Convention is not part of our law, nevertheless there is a means by which pressure can be brought upon us to change our law – so as to conform to it. It is because of the European Court of Human Rights which sits at Strasbourg.

Although the decisions of that Court are not binding on us, the United Kingdom has recognised its jurisdiction to the extent that cases from the United Kingdom can be referred to it. This recognition has recently been extended for another five years. So we get cases in which the Court at Strasbourg has held that the United Kingdom has violated the Convention. That ruling cannot change our law. But it means that pressure can be brought on Parliament to change it.

2 It influences our Parliament

In the *Thalidomide* case (*Sunday Times v United Kingdom*),[1] the European Court at Strasbourg, you will remember, held that the English courts had done wrong to issue an injunction against *Times Newspapers*. England had infringed the fundamental human right of freedom of expression. There had been a breach by England of article 10 of the Convention.

The sequel is this: *Times Newspapers* then asked for their costs. The United Kingdom Government opposed. They submitted that it was only by a small majority of eleven to nine that they were held to be at fault.

1 [1979] 2 EHRR 245.

The European Court overruled that objection of the United Kingdom Government. By a majority of thirteen to three they ordered the UK Government to pay to *Times Newspapers* £22,626.78 costs.

Now here is the follow-up. Parliament has now passed the Contempt of Court Act 1981. I have no doubt that it was influenced by the decision of the European Court at Strasbourg. But they also had recourse to the Report of a Committee presided over by Lord Justice Phillimore. Parliament has overthrown the decision of the House of Lords in the *Thalidomide* case. The test about 'prejudging the issue' has gone. The test is simply whether there is interference with the course of justice.

3 The three railwaymen

Very recently three railwaymen succeeded in an important case before the European Court at Strasbourg. They had been employed for very many years by British Rail. Then, *after* they had been long employed, British Rail agreed with the trade union that the railways would be a 'closed shop'. They would only employ members of the trade union. These three men refused to join it. On their refusal British Rail dismissed them. They had no remedy in England – because in English law their dismissal was not unfair. They appealed to the European Commission who referred the matter to the European Court. The men relied on article 11(1) which, as we saw in the last chapter, says:

'Everyone has the right . . . to freedom of association with others, including the right to form and to join trade unions for the protection of his interests.'

The three men argued that the *positive* right to join – carried with it the *negative* right *not* to join. But the Court unfortunately did not rule upon that point. They held in favour of the men on the narrower ground that, being already employed, it was unfair to dismiss them for not joining afterwards. The Court directed that the United Kingdom Government should pay compensation to the three men.

What will the Government do now? At present the 'closed

shop' is not unlawful. Will the Government introduce legislation to make it unlawful?

The decision of the European Court has had its effect. Since I wrote this, there is a bill now, in February 1982, before Parliament. It does not make the 'closed shop' unlawful. It is still open to a trade union to insist that only its members are employed in the shop. But if a man is dismissed because he is not a member, or otherwise suffers, he will get ample compensation.

4 The proposed approach

The proposal is that the European Convention should be made part of our law and be enforceable in our courts – with ultimately an appeal to the European Court of Human Rights sitting at Strasbourg.

I would emphasise here that the European Convention would become completely part of our law – just as much as Community law is now. This follows from two important articles in the Convention:

'1. The High Contracting Parties shall secure to everyone within their jurisdiction the rights and freedoms defined in Section 1 of this Convention.'

Mark that article. It would mean that our courts would have to take the very words of the European Convention – and apply them in our courts as part of our law.

'13. Everyone whose rights and freedoms as set forth in this Convention are violated shall have an effective remedy before a national authority. . . .'

Mark that article too. It would mean that whenever a person alleged a violation of the Convention, he could bring a claim before our courts. It might be far-fetched. It might be unreasonable. But the courts would have to examine it and give effect to it.

Article 45 deals with the jurisdiction of the European Court of Human Rights at Strasbourg:

289

'The jurisdiction of the Court shall extend to all cases concerning the interpretation and application of the present Convention which the High Contracting Parties or the Commission shall refer to it.'

Mark that article too. It would mean that the Court at Strasbourg would have not only jurisdiction over the *interpretation* of the Convention – but also the *application* of it. That is, it would actually decide cases which were referred to it.

Thus you see that if the European Convention should become part of our law, it would go much further than we do in regard to the Treaty of Rome to which I am coming shortly. It would make the Court at Strasbourg the supreme judicial tribunal over us – superior to the House of Lords – in the actual decision of cases.

5 Do not incorporate the Convention

When looking at the position against this background, I hope that we shall not incorporate the Convention into our law as part of it. One principal reason is that it is framed in a style which is quite contrary to anything to which we are accustomed. There are broad statements of principle and broad statements of exceptions – which are so broad that they are capable of giving rise to an infinity of argument. They remind me of the broad statements in the Amendments to the American Constitution. They are so general that they will give rise to a multitude of cases.

The articles were written, too, in 1950 when society was very differently organised from what it is today. They will not stand forever. They will need a great deal of amendment to make them fit our society of the present time. The European Court at Strasbourg will become a policy-making body like the Supreme Court of the United States.

To my mind it would be very unfortunate for our English judges – who will have interpreted the Convention in one way – to be overruled by the European Court of Human Rights at Strasbourg. The English judges would have the 'feel' of the case. They will see how it should be decided in the light of the circumstances prevailing in England. They should not be overruled by judges who have no knowledge of the circumstances in England.

Rather than incorporate the Convention, it seems to me that the present approach is just about right. Let the English courts have regard to the principles and exceptions set out in the Convention, but not so as to be bound by them. Let the judges accept or reject – or qualify them – as they think fit, so as to suit our circumstances here. Let Parliament have regard to the decisions of the European Court at Strasbourg, but not so as to be subservient to it. Let it be for our Parliament to decide whether or not to apply its decisions and make them part of our law. Do not let us be bound by decisions of judges who do not know our way of life – nor anything of our common law.

If the European Convention on Human Rights were made part of our law, we would become subject to it in the same way as we are now subject to Community law. I turn therefore to tell you how we have fared under it.

6 Community law

1 It is part of our law

There is this great difference. By an Act of our Parliament (the European Communities Act 1972), the Treaty of Rome is part of our law. Our courts have to give effect to it just as if it had been passed by our Parliament. It is, however, drafted in the European fashion. There are wide general principles capable of many different interpretations – according to the eye of the beholder. There is one supreme authority to decide what is the right interpretation: it is the European Court of Justice sitting in Luxembourg. But its jurisdiction is confined to the interpretation of the Treaty. It cannot decide cases. It does not decide them. It does not apply its interpretation to the facts. It leaves that – the application of them – to the national courts of each country.

In interpreting the Treaty, the European Court at Luxembourg has done things which an English court would never have done. It has disregarded the actual words of the Treaty. It has filled in gaps. It has altered the meaning of words. It has done what it thinks is best to be done. It has acted more as a legislator than as an interpreter. All of it completely shocking – to the old-fashioned English.

It is well illustrated by the cases about sex discrimination. The modern slogan is 'Equal pay for equal work'. The Treaty of Rome thought that this should be effective throughout the Common Market. But the signatories knew it would take a long time to implement. So they left it to each country to enact its own legislation on the matter. Article 119 of the Treaty says:

'Each Member State shall . . . ensure . . . that men and women should receive equal pay for equal work.'

Some countries passed legislation on the lines of 'Equal pay for equal work'. Others did not. For instance, England had the Equal Pay Act 1970. Belgium had nothing.

If you were to read article 119 with the eyes of an English lawyer, you would think that that article – and the Directives following upon it – imposed on the *member states* an obligation to pass legislation so as to ensure equal pay for equal work, but that it had no direct application of its own force in England. You would think that the English courts could wait and do nothing until they saw an Act on the statute book to give effect to the 'principle of equal pay' or the 'principle of equal value' or the 'principle of equal treatment'. But, if you should think that, you would be wrong.

2 The air hostess seeks equal pay

It was Gabrielle Defrenne, a Belgian air hostess, who made the leading case. It is *Defrenne v Sabena*. She was employed by Sabena, the Belgian air-line. She was doing like work as a cabin steward. She said that she was entitled to equal pay for equal work. She applied to the industrial tribunal at Brussels. They turned her claim down, because there was no legislation in Belgium which provided for equal pay. So she had the case referred to the European Court at Luxembourg – asking what was the true interpretation of article 119.

Now to English eyes article 119 imposed an obligation on the 'member state', that is, Belgium, to pass legislation to that effect. But Belgium had not passed any such legislation. The remedy was to take the Belgian Government to the European Court and make Belgium pass the necessary legislation.

But to European eyes that was much too narrow a view. The European Court would have none of it. They declared that Gabrielle Defrenne could sue herself in the national courts of Belgium – for compensation. Article 119, they said, was 'directly applicable' in Belgium. Even though the Belgian Government had passed no legislation on the point (to give effect to equal pay) nevertheless the Belgian courts had to give effect to the Treaty. So Gabrielle Defrenne went to the Belgian courts and got compensation on the basis of equal pay for equal work.

To my mind the European Court went beyond its terms of reference. It was not interpreting the Treaty. It was legislating on an internal Belgian matter – much as if it was the Belgian legislature. It was telling the Belgian courts what they were to do. And its decision was binding on the Belgian legislature and on the Belgian courts.

That decision concerned Belgium. We have since had several cases concerning the United Kingdom. I have told you already about Miss Van Duyn in *The Due Process of Law* (pages 165–166). The case was *Van Duyn v Home Office*.[1] It was held there that article 48 of the Treaty:

'Freedom of movement for workers shall be secured within the Community . . .'

was directly applicable in the English courts even though we had no legislation upon the point. She failed in her application because of the provision as to personal conduct. It was again a case where the European Court was taking policy considerations into account.

3 Direct applicability

That case established – for the whole of the Community – the principle of direct applicability. It means that all the articles of the Treaty and many of its Regulations and Directives are to be enforced directly by the English courts – even though we have no legislation upon the point passed by our own Parliament – and even though our own courts know nothing of it – except what they know by reading the Treaty or the Regulations or Directives.

That is one great principle. The other is the principle of the supremacy of Community law. The Treaty, its Regulations and

1 [1975] Ch 358.

Directives, take priority over any of our English law. If there is any conflict or any inconsistency between Community law and English law, then Community law is to prevail.

4 Supremacy of Community law

Now I would turn to cases in our courts where the United Kingdom has passed legislation to give effect to the Treaty of Rome. Take this point of 'equal pay for equal work'. The Government thinks it has done all that it is required to do. It has passed the Equal Pay Act 1970 and brought it into force by the Sex Discrimination Act 1975. What then is an English court to do? Is it to go by those English statutes? or by the Treaty of Rome? Again the European Court at Luxembourg has adopted an authoritarian attitude. It has held as matter of policy that Community law is supreme. It has laid down the principle of 'the supremacy of Community law'. I described it in these words in *Shields v E Coomes Holdings Ltd*:[1]

> 'It arises whenever there is a conflict or inconsistency between the law contained in an Article of the Treaty and the law contained in the internal law of one of the member states, whether passed before or after joining the Community. It says that in any such event the law of the Community shall prevail over that of the internal law of the member state.'

5 The woman in the betting shop

The English courts applied the principle in that case. A company had 90 betting shops. Nine of them were in rough areas where there was fear of violence. The man counterhand was paid more than the woman counterhand – because he was thought to be better able to deal with trouble-makers. She claimed equal pay. She put her claim under the English statute (the Equal Pay Act 1970), but this was very obscure upon the point so the court made reference to article 119 of the Treaty and, being influenced by it, decided in favour of the lady.

1 [1978] 1 WLR 1408 at 1415.

There was a significant difference between what they did. The man filled a protective role. He was a watchdog ready to bark and scare off intruders, but otherwise they worked alongside one another hour after hour doing precisely the same work. It was rather like the difference between a barman and a barmaid. They did the same work as one another in serving drinks. Each had his or her own way of dealing with awkward customers. Each was subject to the same risk of abuse or unpleasantness. But, whichever way each adopted in dealing with awkward customers, the job of each, as a job, was of equivalent rating.

I felt great diffidence in coming to a decision on the case, particularly as the industrial tribunal had found that the differences, especially the protective role of the man, were 'real and existing and of practical importance'. This is how I came to my decision (page 1419):

'I thought for some time that this protective role should be rewarded by some additional bonus or premium. But my difficulties on this score have been resolved by giving supremacy to Community law. Under that law it is imperative that "pay for work at time rates shall be the same for the same job . . ." (Article 119); and that all discrimination on the grounds of sex shall be eliminated with regard to all aspects and conditions of remuneration: see Council Directive 75/117/EEC, Article 1. The differences found by the majority of the industrial tribunal are all based on sex. They are because he is a man. He only gets the higher hourly rate because he is a man. In order to eliminate all discrimination, there should be an equality clause written into the woman's contract.'

6 The woman wears the manager's trousers

Another leading case is *Macarthys Ltd v Smith*.[1] In a warehouse the company employed a man as manager. They paid him £60 a week. Five months later they took on a woman as manager. She did the like work as he. But they only paid her £50 a week. She applied for equal pay under the English statute. But the majority

1 [1979] ICR 785.

297

of the court thought that it only applied when the man and woman were employed on like work *at the same period of time* – not when they were employed at *different* periods of time. In this case there was four months' difference. The woman then turned to article 119 of the Treaty. She said that took precedence over the English statute. It came before the Court of Appeal. I first told how the European Commission could take the United Kingdom to the European Court (page 788):

'What then is the position? Suppose that England passes legislation which contravenes the principle contained in the Treaty, or which is inconsistent with it, or fails properly to implement it. There is no doubt that the European Commission can report the United Kingdom to the European Court of Justice: and that court can require the United Kingdom to take the necessary measures to implement Article 119. That is shown by Articles 169 and 171 of the Treaty. That is indeed what is happening now. We have been shown a background report of the European Communities Commission dated 20 April 1979 which says:

"The European Commission recently reported on how the nine member countries of the Community were implementing the Community equal pay policy for men and women. It found that in all countries practice fell short of principle. . . .

Where national legislation does not comply: The Commission has written letters to the following governments outlining why it considers that their legislation does not conform. . . .

United Kingdom: The concept of work of equivalent value seems to be given a restrictive interpretation on the basis of the Equal Pay Act. . . .

The British position: The government has maintained that the Equal Pay Act 1970 and the Sex Discrimination Act 1975 fully comply with Community legislation against sex discrimination. . . ." '

I pointed out, however, that it was unnecessary for the woman manager to wait. She could come straight to the English courts (page 789):

'It is unnecessary, however, for these courts to wait until all that procedure has been gone through. Under section 2(1) and (4) of the European Communities Act 1972 the principles laid down in the Treaty are "without further enactment" to be given legal effect in the United Kingdom: and have priority over "any enactment passed or to be passed" by our Parliament. So we are entitled – and I think bound – to look at Article 119 of the Treaty because it is directly applicable here. We should, I think, look to see what those provisions require about equal pay for men and women. Then we should look at our own legislation on the point – giving it, of course, full faith and credit – assuming that it does fully comply with the obligations under the Treaty. In construing our statute, we are entitled to look to the Treaty as an aid to its construction: and even more, not only as an aid but as an overriding force. If on close investigation it should appear that our legislation is deficient – or is inconsistent with Community law – by some oversight of our draftsmen – then it is our bounden duty to give priority to Community law. Such is the result of section 2(1) and (4) of the European Communities Act 1972.'

The court referred the case to the European Court at Luxembourg. They adopted my view. The case came back to us – when we held that the woman manager was entitled to equal pay with her predecessor. I said:[1]

'The majority of this court felt that Article 119 was uncertain. So this court referred the problem to the European Court at Luxembourg. We have now been provided with the decision of that court. It is important now to declare – and it must be made plain – that the provisions of Article 119 of the EEC Treaty take priority over anything in our English statute on equal pay which is inconsistent with Article 119. That priority is given by our own law. It is given by the European Communities Act 1972 itself. Community law is now part of our law: and, whenever there is any inconsistency, Community law has priority. It is not supplanting English law. It is part of our law which overrides any other part which is inconsistent with

1 [1980] ICR 672 at 692.

it. I turn therefore to the decision given by the European Court. The answer they gave was that the man and the woman need not be employed at the same time. The woman is entitled to equal pay for equal work, even when the woman is employed after the man has left. That interpretation must now be given by all the courts in England. It will apply in this case and in any such case hereafter.'

7 Can we withdraw from the Common Market?

It has sometimes been questioned whether the United Kingdom can withdraw from the Common Market. To that question I gave this answer in *Macarthys Ltd v Smith*:[1]

'If the time should come when our Parliament deliberately passes an Act – with the intention of repudiating the Treaty or any provision in it – or intentionally of acting inconsistently with it – and says so in express terms – then I should have thought that it would be the duty of our courts to follow the statute of our Parliament. I do not, however, envisage any such situation. As I said in *Blackburn v Attorney-General*:[2] "But, if Parliament should do so, then I say we will consider that event when it happens". Unless there is such an intentional and express repudiation of the Treaty, it is our duty to give priority to the Treaty.'

8 The women in the Bank

The supremacy of Community law was well shown in a case where Lloyds Bank had two pension schemes, one for women, and the other for men. The women thought that their scheme was not as favourable as the men's scheme. Under the English statute (the Equal Pay Act 1970) Parliament had expressly excluded pension schemes by section 6(1A)(b) from the equal pay provisions. But the European Court at Luxembourg held that article

1 [1979] ICR 785 at 789.
2 [1971] 1 WLR 1037 at 1040.

119 did cover pension schemes and that the women could enforce their rights under article 119 in the English courts – thus overriding the English statute altogether. The case is *Worringham v Lloyds Bank*.[1] This put the Bank in the greatest possible difficulty. It meant scrapping the old schemes and starting afresh. I must say that I sympathised with the Bank. Its pension schemes were excellent. When made, they were perfectly lawful under the English statute but they were made unlawful by Community law. So the Bank has no option. It must work out new schemes.

9 The Court at Luxembourg

I would pay tribute to the work of the European Court at Luxembourg. I have been there. I have met the judges. They are of the highest quality. If I were to look at their work with the eyes of an English lawyer, I would be critical. But when I look at their work with the eyes of a good European, I think they have done – and are doing – great things for Europe. As I look to the future, I hope we shall support all that the Court has done – and is doing. We should cease to look at its work with English eyes. We should look at it with European eyes. We should strive to wipe out the discord of the past and do all we can to build the new Federation of Europe based on a comprehensive Community law.

As I have said before:

'The Treaty is like an incoming tide. It flows into the estuaries and up the rivers. It cannot be held back.'

1 [1981] 1 WLR 950.

7 What should we do?

This experience of Community law leads me to this reflection: If we are to have a Bill of Rights, it should not be an instrument which is a replica of the Convention on Human Rights.

The articles of that Convention – like those of the Universal Declaration – are too general in their wording to be of much use as they stand. They would need a great deal of interpretation by the Court at Strasbourg. Many would be reluctant to leave so much to that Court – with questions of vital importance decided by narrow margins of eleven to nine – as in the *Thalidomide* case and overruling our own House of Lords. If my analysis of the present position is correct, on any issue of human rights the House of Lords will have regard to the terms of that Convention. They will consider whether it is a proper case or not in which to apply the Convention. That is just about as much weight as we should give it. We should not disregard it altogether. To do so would be wrong seeing that the United Kingdom is a signatory to it. But to swallow it altogether, hook, line and sinker – would be too much of a mouthful.

Should then we have a new Bill of Rights altogether – one which is not a replica of the Convention? It would be an immense task to draft it. It might give rise to similar objections to those I have raised about the European Convention. I would quote some wise words from the Report of the Select Committee of the House of Lords on a Bill of Rights (May 1978):

'In any country, whatever its constitution, the existence or absence of legislation in the nature of a Bill of Rights can in practice play only a relatively minor part in the protection of human rights. What is important, above all, is a country's political climate and traditions. This is, the Committee think, common ground among both those who favour and those who oppose a Bill of Rights, and they received no evidence that human rights are in practice better protected in countries which have a code of fundamental human rights embodied in their law than they are in the United Kingdom.'

There it is: 'What is important, above all, is a country's political climate and traditions'. In England the importance is enshrined in the independence of the judges. They have managed very well in the past to form and maintain human rights and fundamental freedoms. They created most of them by their decisions. You can trust them to continue to do so.

I am therefore against a new Bill of Rights.

Part eight

Misuse of power

Introduction

On 20 November 1980 I gave the Richard Dimbleby Lecture. It was broadcast. Some of you will have seen and heard it on television. Others will not. It contained many suggestions for the future. So, even though it did include one or two matters which I have already mentioned in this book, I have ventured to repeat it here – for those who missed it at the time.

1 A hierarchy of power

1 'Power tends to corrupt'

You will all know the famous aphorism of that great historian, Lord Acton: 'Power tends to corrupt, and absolute power corrupts absolutely.'

In all societies there is a hierarchy of power. At the top there may sometimes be a king or a dictator, at other times a president or a prime minister, or yet again a totalitarian party. Below the top there are hundreds of subordinates who wield power of one kind or another. Throughout history you will find instances of power being misused or abused. On occasion the abuse is so great that the only remedy is by rebellion – as of the barons in 1215 or Parliament in 1642. Yet such a remedy is much to be deplored. The rebels are judges in their own cause. In modern times, as often as not they are terrorists – seeking to change the Constitution by violence. The only admissible remedy for any abuse of power – in a civilised society – is by recourse to law.

2 Recourse to law

In order to ensure this recourse, it is important that the law itself should provide adequate and efficient remedies for abuse or misuse of power from whatever quarter it may come. No matter who it is – who is guilty of the abuse or misuse. Be it government, national or local. Be it trade unions. Be it the press. Be it management. Be it labour. Whoever it be, no matter how powerful, the law should provide a remedy for the abuse or misuse of power, else the oppressed will get to the point when they will

309

stand it no longer. They will find their own remedy. There will be anarchy.

3 The judges must be independent

If I be right thus far – that recourse must be had to law – it follows as a necessary corollary that the judges must be independent. They must be free from any influence by those who wield power. Otherwise they cannot be trusted to decide whether or not the power is being abused or misused. This independence, I am proud to say, has been achieved in England. The judges for nearly 300 years now have been absolutely independent – not only of government and of ministers, but also of trade unions, of the press, and of the media. They will not be diverted from their duty by any extraneous influences; not by hope of reward nor by the fear of penalties; not by flattering praise nor by indignant reproach. It is the sure knowledge of this that gives the people their confidence in the judges.

To prove my point I will take instances, old and new, of the abuse or misuse of power and how they have been dealt with.

2 Of rulers

1 A King

In the days of King James I there was a great judge called Lord
Coke who boldly asserted the independence of the judges. On
one occasion the King summoned all the judges before him and
told them that he proposed to take any cases he pleased away from
the judges for decision and to try them himself. He called in aid
the authority of Archbishop Bancroft, who declared that it was
clear in divinity. Such power, said the Archbishop, doubtless
belongs to the King by the word of God in the Scriptures. But
the Chief Justice told the King that he had no power to do so, and
that all cases ought to be determined in a court of justice. King
James replied:

'I always thought and I have often heard the boast that your
English law is founded upon reason. If that be so, why have
not I and others reason as well as you the judges?'

The Chief Justice replied:

'True it is, please your Majesty, that God has endowed your
Majesty with excellent science as well as great gifts of nature;
but your Majesty will allow me to say so, with all reverence,
that you are not learned in the laws of this your realm of
England . . . which is an art which requires long study and
experience before that a man can attain to the cognizance of it.
The law is the golden met-wand and measure to try the causes
of your Majesty's subjects, and it is by that law that your
Majesty is protected in safety and peace.'

King James, in a great rage, said:

'Then I am to be under the law – which it is treason to affirm.'

The Chief Justice replied:

'Thus wrote Bracton, "The King is under no man, but under God and the law." '

That saying reverberated down the centuries. It was the watchword used by lawyers and Parliamentarians to overthrow the pretensions of King Charles I.

James is said, nevertheless, to have tried his hand as a judge, but to have been so much perplexed, when he heard both sides, that he abandoned the attempt in despair. He said:

'I could get on very well hearing one side only, but when both sides have been heard upon my word I know not which is right.'

2 A President

It is acknowledged now that President Nixon was implicated in the Watergate affair and the cover-up. He did it so as to further his ambition for a second term. Furthermore, it was the President himself who desired that all his conversations – swear-words and all – should be recorded on tape, and preserved for posterity. It was he who claimed a prerogative of silence so as to keep them secret. Yet, the law overtook him. The Supreme Court of the United States held that he had no such prerogative. He was required by law to disclose the tapes: and this led to his downfall. The Supreme Court applied the same principle to the President as the common law applied to the King when he was our ruler.

3 The Prime Minister

Our ruler now – or, at any rate, the man with the greatest power – is the Prime Minister. He (or now it is she) is appointed in theory by the Queen but in practice because he is the leader of the political party which gains the greatest number of seats at a general election. His power has not been conferred on him by any statute. It is given by unwritten conventions. It is the Prime Minister who nominates all the other ministers, and dismisses them. In theory the appointments are made by the Sovereign: but, as our books on constitutional law tell us, 'As against the Queen, the Prime Minister has the final word'.[1] We have seen it happen in recent times. A Prime Minister, Mr Harold Macmillan no less, dismissed several ministers at a moment's notice. Even the Lord Chancellor was dismissed. He was asked to resign, and was bound, by convention, to comply. It was called the 'night of the long knives'.

Was this a misuse of power? I would not suggest that it was. No one questioned its validity. No one brought an action for unfair dismissal. Its acceptance shows the strong force of the conventions – which have virtually the force of the law.

1 Jennings *Cabinet Government* p. 61.

3 Of honours

1 The acceptance of bribes

Through all the pages of history, you will find that those in possession of influence or power have accepted bribes. The most conspicuous case among Lord Chancellors was Lord Bacon: though Lord Macclesfield runs him a close second. They accepted 'presents' in return for favours granted by them. Of all abuses of power this is the most difficult to discover or to suppress: because both briber and bribed are concerned to keep it secret. It takes place on an enormous scale, as has been shown in the last few years. It led to the notorious *Poulson* case. That was only brought to light by the diligence and persistence of the lawyers.

Mr Poulson was an architect. He could not pay his taxes. He was made bankrupt. In examining his affairs, the lawyers became suspicious. They probed and probed. Eventually, they discovered that he had paid money or given rewards to persons in influential posts, so as to get the contracts directed his way. He was convicted and sentenced to seven years. But for his bankruptcy, his wrongdoing would never have been discovered.

Such bribery has been discovered in the case of architects, engineers, planning officers, and even police officers. When discovered, they are prosecuted. But still the evil remains. Every country knows it. Lord Salmon has headed a Royal Commission on Standards of Conduct in Public Life. They sought for a remedy, but with no great success so far. The only way is to educate the people so that they know the wrongness of it. This is possible. In the days when England ruled the Indian Empire, the men of the Indian Civil Service without exception were of the highest integrity. It was a point of honour never to accept any gift in return for any favour. Perhaps they had read of the trial of Warren Hastings. So let us make it part of our code of practice. Shakespeare put it in the scene in Brutus's tent:

> 'Let me tell you, Cassius, you yourself
> Are much condemn'd to have an itching palm;
> To sell and mart your offices for gold
> To undeservers. . . . Shall we now
> Contaminate our fingers with base bribes,
> And sell the mighty space of our large honours
> For so much trash as may be grasped thus?
> I had rather be a dog, and bay the moon,
> Than such a Roman.'

2 Bought for money

The grant of honours is a source of power – a source which can be misused. In the time of David Lloyd George it is said that titles and rank were bought for money – for contributions to the party funds – a plain abuse which was much condemned.

Likewise with patronage. It is capable of misuse. Many instances show it. In the early eighteenth century, when Lord Macclesfield was about to appoint a new Master in Chancery, an applicant offered £5,000. The reply was, 'Guineas are handsomer'. So he paid the 5,000 guineas and got the job. And Lord Macclesfield got the sack.

When I was young, there was a notorious case. Colonel Parkinson made a substantial donation to a respectable charity called the College of Ambulance. He received a most grateful letter from its royal President, Princess Christian. Unbeknown to her, the secretary of the college had promised Colonel Parkinson a knighthood. When he did not get it, he sued the college to get his money back. He failed. The court held that the promise to grant an honour or title – in return for money – was contrary to public policy and could not be enforced. Shortly afterwards an Act was passed to prevent abuse in connection with the grant of honours. It was made a criminal offence.

So that particular form of abuse was ended. Nevertheless, the power to grant honours – or to appoint offices – may be misused.

It is incumbent on all those who exercise it to be most careful about it. If the recipient should prove to be unworthy – if he should disgrace the title or rank which he is given – it tends to bring the whole system into discredit – and the person who grants it.

4 Conventions of the Constitution

1 Are they binding?

Now by a convention of our Constitution, it is the Prime Minister who has the right to advise the Sovereign on the grant of honours, save for a few exceptions. There is a committee of three Privy Councillors who report to him when honours are proposed to be granted on account of political services:[1] but he is not bound to follow their advice. Many honours are granted on other accounts.

One particular power which needs mention is the honour of a peerage, because it carries with it a seat in the legislature, and thus an important voice and vote on matters of state. Some suggest that the Sovereign can refuse to accept a nomination. But this is more than doubtful. It would bring the Sovereign into the political arena. That must be avoided at all costs.

There is another convention, too, by which a Prime Minister who resigns, may nominate persons whom he desires to honour. He does it through his successor as Prime Minister. A question may arise here whether his nominations can be refused. So far as I know, there is no convention by which his successor is bound to put them forward.

All these powers of the Prime Minister are not contained in any statute. These are said to be so strong that they are part of our Constitution. But, I would ask the question: Suppose a future Prime Minister should misuse or abuse the power? Suppose he should assume to create one thousand new peers – with the avowed intention (as his next step) of abolishing the peerage? Would it be lawful? Would it not be contrary to the Constitution? Would not the courts interfere to stop it?

1 Jennings *Cabinet Government* pp. 470–471.

2 The judges are the guardians

To my mind the judges are the guardians of our Constitution here, just as they are in the United States. The only difference is that our Constitution is unwritten. Theirs is written. The judges can – or, at any rate, should be able to – pronounce on the validity of these conventions. They should be able to interfere if they are misused or abused.

The rule in the United States is not contained in their Constitution itself. It is a judge-made rule. It was stated by Chief Justice Marshall in 1803 in the *Marbury* case. Later on Charles Evans Hughes, the tenth Chief Justice, in 1908 firmly declared:

> 'We are under a Constitution, *but the Constitution is what the judges say it is* and the judiciary is the safeguard of our liberty and our property under the Constitution.'

Their Constitution nowhere provides that it shall be what the judges say it is. Yet it has become the most fundamental and far-reaching principle of American constitutional law. I confess that I would like to see us here develop a like doctrine, so as to be able to keep the conventions from being misused or abused.

When I see our rulers – or those who aspire to be rulers – claiming to exercise such great power, I recall the occasion when Henry VIII commanded Cardinal Wolsey to give up the Great Seal. Shakespeare attributed these words to Wolsey, speaking to Thomas Cromwell, sometime Master of the Rolls:

> 'Mark but my fall, and that that ruin'd me.
> Cromwell, I charge thee, fling away ambition;
> By that sin fell the angels; . . .
> Be just, and fear not.
> Let all the ends thou aim'st at be thy country's,
> Thy God's and truth's. . . .'

Then, after his fall:

> 'O Cromwell, Cromwell!
> Had I but serv'd my God with half the zeal
> I serv'd my king, he would not in mine age
> Have left me naked to mine enemies.'

5 Parliament itself

1 Is Parliament supreme?

In our constitutional theory, Parliament is supreme. Every law enacted by Parliament must be obeyed to the letter. No matter how unreasonable or unjust it may be, nevertheless, if it is clear on the point, the judges have no option. They must apply the statute as it stands. Is it not possible that Parliament may misuse its power? A little while ago there was a case[1] where the British Railways Board got a private Act vesting a man's land in the Board without payment. He alleged that Parliament had been misled by fraud. In the Court of Appeal we held that the judges could inquire into it. But the House of Lords overruled us. They held that no inquiry by the judges could be permitted.

You must remember that the party which has obtained the greatest number of seats at an election can enact any legislation it likes. Is there a remedy? Nearly 400 years ago Lord Coke said that:

'When an Act of Parliament is against right and reason, or repugnant, or impossible to be performed, the common law will control it and adjudge that Act to be void.'[2]

This sapling planted by Lord Coke failed to grow in England. It withered and died. But it grew into a strong tree in the United States of America. Under the guidance of the great Chief Justice Marshall, the judges there constantly review legislation: and as constantly set it aside if it is against right and reason or repugnant to the Constitution.

1 *Pickin v British Railways Board* [1974] AC 765.
2 *Dr Bonham's case* (1608) 8 Co Rep 113b, 118a.

2 The judges should have power

The longer I am in the law – and the more statutes I have to interpret – the more I think the judges here ought to have a power of judicial review of legislation similar to that in the United States: whereby the judges can set aside statutes which are contrary to our unwritten Constitution – in that they are repugnant to reason or to fundamentals. Professor Wade has given a good illustration in his lecture on *Constitutional Fundamentals*. He says:

'There can be abuse of legislative power, not indeed in the legal sense, but in a distinct constitutional sense, for example if Parliament were to legislate to establish one-party government, or a dictatorship, or in some other way to attack the fundamentals of democracy.'

To which I might add – as a matter for debate – if Parliament were to legislate so as to abolish the two-chamber system and have one chamber only. In short, if it were to legislate to abolish the House of Lords, as distinct from reforming it. Would that be an abuse of legislative power? If it were done without a referendum on the very point? I do not doubt that Parliament would have power to reform the House of Lords. The Parliament Act of 1911 contained a recital that

'. . . it is intended to substitute for the House of Lords as it at present exists a Second Chamber constituted on a popular instead of a hereditary basis, but such substitution cannot be immediately brought into operation'.

No doubt such a reform would be legitimate; but I doubt whether Parliament could lawfully abolish the Second Chamber altogether. I would expect any such legislation to be challenged in the courts of law; and for the judges to give a ruling on it.

6 Trade unions

1 Their immunities

I wish, too, that we had had some doctrine – authorising judicial review of statutes – when we had the recent spate of cases on the Trade Union Acts of 1974 and 1976. Those Acts gave the trade unions and their members the right to strike and to picket and to 'black' to their hearts' content – so long as they did it 'in contemplation or furtherance of a trade dispute'. The Court of Appeal endeavoured to place some limitation on this right; so as to restrict it to acts which had a close connection with the dispute. But the House of Lords reversed the Court of Appeal. They held that, so long as the trade union leaders believed – in their own minds – that it would further the dispute, they could not be stopped. Nor could they be sued. 'Secondary picketing' was lawful – even though it struck at innocent parties utterly remote from the dispute – so long as the trade union leaders thought it would help their cause in some way or other. It made the trade union leaders judges in their own cause. In the House of Lords Lord Diplock acknowledged that, on his interpretation, trade union leaders could use their power so as to inflict much injury on employers and others quite remote from the dispute, but he felt that the simple words of the statutes compelled him to reach this result.

2 The new statute

The decision of the House of Lords provoked much comment. It showed that the statutes gave the trade unions such considerable immunity that they could damage great industries – and destroy the nation itself – on the plea that they intended to further a trade dispute. In consequence, Parliament passed a statute, the Employment Protection Act 1980, to limit the immunities given to the trade unions. This went some way but not very far.

3 We are reversed again

Since I gave the Dimbleby Lecture, we have had the first case on the 1980 Act. It was *Hadmor Productions Ltd v Hamilton*.[1] I said (at page 151) that

'the legislation intended to protect commercial contracts – made with commercial firms not parties to the dispute – from unwarranted interference by picketing or by blacking.'

But the House of Lords reversed us again.[2] They criticised me roundly for making use of *Hansard*. All I had done was to refer to a speech by a distinguished lawyer, Lord Wedderburn. If he had said the same things in an article in the *Modern Law Review*, they could have made no complaint.

Now there is another bill before Parliament designed to put fetters on unfair actions by trade unions. Will it be passed into law? If it is, will it succeed? Time will show.

1 [1981] 3 WLR 139.
2 [1982] 2 WLR 322.

7 Ministers of the Crown

1 Their discretion

In our time it is the ministers who initiate legislation. They do it through their departments: and are apt often to give themselves great discretionary powers. This may be necessary in the interests of good administration. Time and time again a minister has said to the courts:

> 'The statute gives me an unfettered discretion. It cannot be challenged in the courts of law. If I should exercise it wrongly, I can be questioned in the House. But the courts cannot restrain me.'

This argument held good forty years ago. In many cases during the war – and some after it – if a statute gave the minister power to do a thing 'if it appeared to him' or 'if he thought fit' – the courts held that his decision could not be questioned in the courts. But those rulings are no longer valid. When a minister claimed that he could revoke a television licence – so as to make the holder pay more for a new one – the courts held that he had misused his power. When a minister claimed that he could force comprehensive schools on a local education authority – the courts held that he could not override them. When a minister claimed that he could stop Freddie Laker from flying his Skytrain across the Atlantic – the courts declared that the Skytrain should fly, despite the minister's objection. And it did fly.

2 Save for the Attorney-General

There is one field, however, where a minister's discretion is still absolute. It arose when the Attorney-General claimed that he alone could enforce the criminal law against a trade union – and that the courts could not interfere with his discretion. I ventured to say 'No'. I quoted Thomas Fuller: 'Be you never so high, the law is above you'.[1] But the House of Lords declared that I was wrong. It was held that the Attorney-General had an unfettered discretion to say whether or not the criminal law should be enforced – either against a trade union or anyone else. So that is one respect in which the courts cannot restrain the abuse of power by a minister.

But, save for this exception, I would repeat here what I said in *Laker's* case:[2]

'. . . These courts have the authority – and I would add the duty – in a proper case, when called upon, to inquire into the exercising of a discretionary power by a minister or his department. If it is found that this power has been exercised improperly or mistakenly so as to infringe unjustly on the legitimate rights and interests of the subject, then these courts must so declare. They stand, as ever, between the executive and the subject, as Lord Atkin said in a famous passage, alert to see that any coercive action is justified in law. To which I would add: alert to see that a discretionary power is not exceeded or misused.'

1 *Gouriet v Union of Post Office Workers* [1977] 2 WLR 310 at 331.
2 [1977] 2 All ER 182 at 194–195.

8 Members of Parliament

Members of Parliament, too, have great powers – which they should not misuse. Whatever they say in the course of a parliamentary debate or proceeding is absolutely privileged. They cannot be sued for defamation in respect of it. This was enacted in the Bill of Rights in 1689:

'That the freedom of speech, and debates or proceedings in Parliament ought not to be impeached or questioned in any court or place out of Parliament.'

This, however, is a power that can be misused. Take recently, when a Member of Parliament accused a servant of Rolls-Royce of improper dealings. He did not repeat it outside Parliament, so the injured person could not vindicate his reputation in the courts. I would not suggest that the absolute privilege should be taken away; but it shows that Members of Parliament are expected to – and should – act with a due sense of responsibility. You may be sure that if any Member should act irresponsibly, his colleagues in the House would bring such pressure on him to withdraw that the misuse of power would be rectified.

9 The media

1 Unfair pressure

Nowadays the media are the most powerful bodies in the land. They can make public opinion. And once made, public opinion is irresistible. Witness the story of Thalidomide. In 1962, Distillers marketed the drug. It was prescribed by doctors for pregnant women – to relieve tension. Hundreds of babies were born deformed. Many parents and babies brought actions against Distillers for damages. Some were settled, but after ten years many claims remained outstanding. *The Sunday Times* proposed to publish an article condemning Distillers for negligence. In the Court of Appeal we held that this article was perfectly lawful: because it was fair comment on a matter of public concern. But the House of Lords held that it was a contempt of court. They regarded it as an abuse of power. It prejudiced the issues in the case – and brought unfair pressure on Distillers, to pay up more in settlement than they otherwise would. Lord Reid said in the *Thalidomide* case:[1]

> 'What I think is regarded as most objectionable is that a newspaper or television programme should seek to persuade the public, by discussing the issues and evidence in a case before the court, whether civil or criminal, that one side is right and the other is wrong.'

Now we know that the newspaper articles did influence public opinion against Distillers. Campaigns were launched to make them pay more and more compensation. Their shareholders protested against them. Their customers refused to buy their products. In

1 [1974] AC 273 at 300.

the end Distillers had to pay £20,000,000 as against the £3,000,000 they had offered before the campaigns.

I remain unrepentant. It still seems to me to be fair comment. And our view in the Court of Appeal was upheld by the European Court of Human Rights. But the case remains an example of the great power of the press – in making public opinion – and thus influencing events.

2 Unfair presentation

I would give illustrations of the misuse of power by the BBC about the Irish problem. In one programme they carried an interview with a man who claimed that his group had murdered Mr Airey Neave; and for the other they had filmed a road-block set up by the IRA, following a tip-off from the Provisionals. In fact this second film was not shown, and was rightly rejected by the BBC, but the taking of them was condemned by the Attorney-General, Sir Michael Havers. He wrote to the BBC that these two incidents

'constituted little more than propaganda exercises by terrorist organisations to which your staff have willingly given their support. In both cases, they went to considerable effort to contact persons whom they believed to be connected with known criminal offences and had every reason to believe would be connected with further offences. . . . Indeed in the first incident they went so far as to make a totally false statement implying that they were co-operating with the police at a time when this was not so.'

Sir Michael Swann, then Chairman of the BBC, answered the Attorney-General's criticism. He rejected absolutely the suggestion that the staff of the BBC willingly gave their support to any propaganda exercise by terrorist organisations. He said that the BBC

'attach, as clearly as you do, the greatest importance to reporting as accurately and clearly as we can the happenings in Northern Ireland, and the background underlying them. This is a difficult and thankless task, but in a democratic society it must be undertaken by the free media, and we shall continue to play our part within, inevitably, the constraints of the law.'

3 'Denning is an ass'

The next case is the most illustrative of all. It is the *Granada* case. You will all have read of it. In the British Steel Corporation there was a man supposed to be high up. He took documents of the highest confidentiality out of their safe keeping and handed them secretly to Granada. He has been called a 'mole'. He does his work underground and never comes out lest he be caught. Granada used the information for a television programme. British Steel sought to get the name of the 'mole': but Granada would not give it. The Court of Appeal ordered Granada to give it. I said:

'In order to be deserving of freedom, the press must show itself worthy of it. A free press must be a responsible press. The power of the press is great. It must not abuse its power. If a newspaper should act irresponsibly, then it forfeits its claim to protect its sources of information.'

I still think that was a sensible statement of principle. But the media were outraged by it – and by the decision. They formed up in a united band against the judges, supported by some politicians, Mr Michael Foot said, 'Denning is an ass'. *The Observer* came out with a headline, 'Why Denning is an ass'. *The Times*, more sedately, said, 'Lord Denning, this time, is on the wrong side. . . . The Court of Appeal has done a disservice to the cause of press freedom.' When the House of Lords upheld the Court of Appeal. *The Times* denounced their decision, describing it as 'A Charter for wrongdoing', and added: 'The decision of the House of Lords in the Granada Television case is restrictive, reactionary, and clearly against the public interest'.[1]

1 See now pages 250–251 of this book.

4 Outspoken comment

To my mind these attacks by the newspapers on the judges are an
abuse of their power. At one time the judges might have launched
a counter-attack. They were impatient of criticism and would
have accused the media of contempt of court. But this is out of
date. We stated the modern principle in a case[1] where we were
criticised by Mr Quintin Hogg QC (as he then was):

> 'It is the right of every man, in Parliament or out of it, in the
> press or over the broadcast, to make fair comment, even
> outspoken comment, on matters of public interest. Those who
> comment can deal faithfully with all that is done in a court of
> justice. They can say that we are mistaken, and our decisions
> erroneous, whether they are subject to appeal or not. All we
> would ask is that those who criticise us will remember that,
> from the nature of our office, we cannot reply to their criti-
> cisms. We cannot enter into public controversy. Still less into
> political controversy. We must rely on our conduct itself to be
> its own vindication.'

These illustrations in this very year, of misuse of power by the
media, call for a strict self-examination by them – and by their
staffs – to see that they have always in mind their duty to act
responsibly. If they should repeat their irresponsible conduct,
they will find that curbs will be put on their freedom. I have
throughout my career upheld the freedom of the press, and of the
media, and it is only out of regard for it that I would urge that it
be not misused.

1 *R v Metropolitan Police Commissioner, ex parte Blackburn (No.* 2) [1968] 2 QB 150 at 154.

10 The judges themselves

There remains the most touchy question of all. May not the judges themselves sometimes abuse or misuse their power? It is their duty to administer and apply the law of the land. If they should divert it or depart from it – and do so knowingly – they themselves would be guilty of a misuse of power. So we come up against Juvenal's question, '*Sed quis custodiet ipsos custodes?*' (But who is to guard the guards themselves?) That question was asked in the United States at the time of President Roosevelt's New Deal in 1935. It may be asked here again before long. In theory the judges of the higher echelon are appointed by Her Majesty the Queen: but in practice by the Prime Minister, who in turn looks to the Lord Chancellor. Suppose a future Prime Minister should seek to pack the Bench with judges of his own extreme political colour. Would they be tools in his hand? To that I answer 'No'. Every judge on his appointment discards all politics and all prejudices. You need have no fear. The judges of England have always in the past – and always will – be vigilant in guarding our freedoms. Someone must be trusted. Let it be the judges.

Conclusion

To return to whence I started: 'Power tends to corrupt'. This I have shown you. That is why in civilised society there should be a system of checks and balances – to restrain the abuse of power. It is why in times past we stood firm against the oppression of King John, and set store by our Magna Carta. It is why we rebelled against the divine right of kings and enacted our Bill of Rights. It is why we resist today the conferring of absolute power on any person or body, or any section of the community. There is, as far as I know, only one restraint on which we can rely. It is the restraint afforded by the law. We have to respect all that Parliament has done, and may do, in the granting of powers – and of rights and immunities – but let us build up a body of law to see that these powers are not misused or abused, combined with upright judges to enforce the law. It is a task which I commend to all. If we achieve it, we shall be able to say with Milton:

> 'Oh how comely it is and how reviving,
> To the spirits of just men long oppressed!
> When God into the hands of their deliverer
> Puts invincible might. . . .'

The might of the law itself.

Epilogue

This last year has sped along all too quickly. From time to time I have been upbraided by the House of Lords. The newspapers have been keeping count of the number of times I have been reversed. They say, 'Lord Denning has been overruled ten times in succession'. They forget that it is not only *me*. It is the Court of Appeal. On all these occasions the three of us were unanimous. That restores my morale. My brethren in the Court of Appeal are at least equal to the members of the House of Lords. Most of them will get there themselves before long. So I think to myself, 'We were right after all'. On a number of occasions Parliament has passed legislation to restore our decisions.

What troubles me more is the attack by some quarters on the judiciary. They fasten on me. They accuse me of being politically motivated. I deny the charge. Some decisions are fraught with political consequences – such as decisions about trade unions or local authorities or ministers. Whichever way the case goes, one side or the other will say it is a 'political' decision. That is their way of saying that it is a policy decision with which they disagree. In some quarters our decisions are so unwelcome to them that they issue threats to sweep away the judiciary. *The Times* on 26 November 1981 reported a left-wing Labour bulletin as saying:

> 'Let them be warned. When courts and judges, with all their magisterial splendour, render themselves illegal in the eyes of the people, then they invite us – the moment we are strong enough – to sweep them away.'

I am quite sure that our people will be able to deal with those threats. But to do so we must maintain the high quality of our judges. I would make so bold as to say that their quality is as high as ever it has been. They are not, as some suggest, drawn from the upper classes of society. They are – in their birth and upbringing – as mixed a group as you could find. They are representative of all that is best in our people.

The Opening of Parliament

We have been this year through all our great occasions as usual. There is the Opening of Parliament when the judges sit on the Woolsack immediately before the Queen. (The Woolsack on this occasion is composed of four large upholstered settees on which eighteen judges sit. There sit the Lord Chief Justice, the Master of the Rolls, the Vice-Chancellor and the President of the Family Division.) The Chamber is full of peers and peeresses, ambassadors and bishops. The Lord Chancellor comes in with the ornate pouch containing the Queen's Speech. At precisely 11.30 a.m. the Queen comes with the Duke of Edinburgh and sits on the Throne. This year the Prince and Princess of Wales come as well. The young Princess is the cynosure of all beholders. All are seated awaiting the Commons. Black Rod calls them. They take three minutes to walk the distance. It seems a very long time while everyone stays silent. Lord Hailsham, the Lord Chancellor – despite his arthritic ankles – goes up the three steps to the Throne, kneels before the Queen and hands her the Speech to read. He steps backward the three steps down from the Throne. All wait anxiously to see if he will manage it. We, the judges, are so close that we lean forward to catch him if he falls. He does not. All breathe with relief. The Queen reads the Speech slowly and clearly – not her own words but the words of the Government. Lord Hailsham goes up the steps to receive back the Speech. Again we wait anxiously as he steps backward. Again he manages it. Again all is well. The Queen departs, followed by the Royal Family. Afterwards we all depart.

'Lions under the throne!'

It was Francis Bacon in his Essay, *Of Judicature*, who said:

> 'Let judges also remember that Solomon's throne was supported by lions on both sides: let them be lions, but yet lions under the throne; being circumspect that they do not check or oppose any points of sovereignty.'

True enough if the Throne is occupied by a constitutional monarch as ours is. But the judges are not to be lions under the Government of the day – or of any Government. They are and must be independent of the executive government – ready to check or oppose it if it should in any way misuse or abuse its power.

Francis Bacon ends his Essay with a less controversial precept:

> 'Let not judges also be so ignorant of their own right, as to think there is not left to them, as a principal part of their office, a wise use and application of laws. For they may remember what the Apostle saith of a greater law than theirs: *Nos scimus quia lex bona est, modo quis eâ utatur legitime*'

which is translated in the Authorised Version, I *Timothy* 1:8:

> 'But we know that the law is good, if a man use it lawfully'.

Are robes out of date?

As usual, there is the procession of the judges to Westminster Abbey – on 1 October, the first day of the legal year – watched by the populace with respectful awe. In November the Lord Mayor of the City of London comes to the Law Courts in his splendid coach drawn by six shire horses – and is welcomed by us in our court. Then, a day or so later, the Guildhall Banquet. In the summer there is the Judges' Dinner at the Mansion House (in future to be only in alternate years – to save expense). There are the Grand Nights of the Inns of Court. There are the Dinners and Speeches in the evenings. And withal day-by-day work in the courts. So we spend our time.

We still wear our robes and our wigs. On state occasions our gold robes and full-bottomed wigs. In court our black gowns and small wigs. Some say all this is out of date. Maybe it is. But it gives dignity to the occasions. It conceals the personality and the bald heads. It portrays the judge as the impartial administrator of the law. It is a mark of his authority and a source of respect. So it is good to keep it.

The right way up

My wife and I are in our flat in Lincoln's Inn all the week. We are at home in the country for weekends and holidays. I cannot walk fast or run nowadays. I go slowly, limping along with a stick. The surgeon advised against a plastic hip-joint. But my brain is, I hope, as active as ever. I parody against myself Lewis Carroll's words:

'You are old, Master of the Rolls', the young man said,
'And your hair is getting very white,
But yet you continually stand on your head,
Do you think at your age it is right?'
'In my youth', the Master replied to his son,
'I feared it might injure the brain,
But now I am perfectly sure I have none,
Why – I do it again and again!'

So there it is. In this book I have stood the law on its head – in the hope that you may help to get it the right way up.

Index